Jewish Themes in the New Testament

Jewish Themes in the New Testament

Am Yisrael Chai!

Paul Morris

Copyright © 2013 Paul Morris

First published 2013 by Paternoster
Paternoster is an imprint of Authentic Media Limited
52 Presley Way, Crownhill, Milton Keynes, MK8 0ES.
www.authenticmedia.co.uk
Authentic Publishers, PO Box 185, West Ryde, Sydney, Australia

The right of Paul Morris to be
identified as the Author of this Work has been asserted by him in
accordance with the Copyright, Designs and
Patents Act 1988.

All rights reserved. No part of this publication may be reproduced, stored in a retrieval system, or transmitted in any form or by any means, electronic, mechanical, photocopying, recording or otherwise, without the prior permission of the publisher or a licence permitting restricted copying. In the UK such licences are issued by the Copyright Licensing Agency,
Saffron House, 6–10 Kirby Street, London, EC1N 8TS.

British Library Cataloguing in Publication Data

A catalogue record for this book is available from the British Library

ISBN 978-1-84227-821-5
978-1-78078-309-3 (e-book)

Unless otherwise stated, Scripture quotations are taken from the
New King James Version Bible, copyright © 1982 by Thomas Nelson,
Inc. Used by permission. All rights reserved.

Cover Design by Paul Airy (www.designleft.co.uk)

Contents

Introduction	vii
Part 1	**1**
Privileges and Promises	
1. Yahweh, the God of Israel	3
2. His People	5
3. For the Jew First	11
4. The Olive Tree	21
5. Debtors	28
Part 2	**37**
Hard Truths	
6. Israel's Unbelief	39
7. Kingdom: Then and Now	46
8. Wrath to the Uttermost	53
9. Talkers and Mutilators	76
10. Jewish Opposition to the Gospel	83
Part 3	**99**
Not Cast Away	
11. The Compassion of Jesus for Israel	101
12. Paul's Heart's Desire and Prayer to God	106
13. Sin and Satan Defeated	115
14. I am of Peter: the Apostleship to the Circumcision	127
15. Provoking to Jealousy	133
16. One New Man from the Two	140
17. The Israel of God	163

Contents

18. Pay Attention!	171
19. Culturally Jewish	186
20. The Return to the Land	197
Part 4	221
The Triumph of Grace	
21. And so All Israel Shall Be Saved	223
Subject Index	241
Scripture Index	244
Endnotes	249

Introduction

This book aims to look at what the New Testament says about the Jewish people in the era of the new covenant, the time since the coming of Jesus the Messiah. It has not been written from a remote vantage point but by one who has spent many years as a witness to Jesus among his people, Israel. I am not Jewish but I have endeavoured to sit where Israel sits, and to become as a Jew to the Jews.

Am Yisrael Chai! (The people Israel lives!)

The core of the New Testament teaching on the Jewish people is an affirmation of their continued existence, and God's continued faithfulness to them, despite all that might appear to the contrary. This is what *Am Yisrael Chai!* declares. The Hebrew expression *Am Yisrael Chai!* is best put into English as 'the people Israel lives!'. To English ears that sounds a bit clumsy, so would it not be better to use something more familiar like 'the people of Israel live'? That translation however is misleading because it puts the focus on the individuals in Israel, whereas the first expression puts the emphasis on the people as a body, both now and throughout history. Does it make any difference? It certainly does.

Jewish mentality stresses their corporate identity to a degree rarely equalled in any other nation. Jews think much more collectively than most peoples. Jewish history and experience (by which I mean God's covenant with them, the commands to be separate, the experience of persecution) have led to a sense of togetherness and solidarity, both today and with all Jews who have ever

Introduction

lived, which finds the expression 'the people Israel lives' quite natural. More than that it is an affirmation of faith and a shout of joy. The history of persecution makes the other way of translating *Am Yisrael Chai!*, 'the people of Israel live', a difficult one to use, because if Jews think of themselves as a mass of individuals now and through history, they know it cannot be joyfully asserted that they live, for they are acutely conscious that so many have perished.

Am Yisrael Chai! is actually the title of a modern Jewish song which rejoices in their continued existence, particularly in the light of the Holocaust[1] and because of the establishment of the State of Israel. That song should come as no surprise to someone familiar with the New Testament. That is what this book is about. As a people they live – *Am Yisrael Chai!*

Jewish Themes in the New Testament

The continued existence of the Jewish people is what the New Testament expects, and the word 'themes' in the title is plural because there are many aspects of it to be considered. The writers of the New Testament never imagined that, due to the rejection of Jesus by so many of them, the Jews would simply fade out of history. They wrote in order to help Christians to share the gospel with them, to encourage those who come to faith, to understand the difference between Jews, Gentiles and Christians, and to grasp something of the purposes of God for the Jews as a people. All too often Christian people think only of history or prophecy when the Jews are mentioned, and so the whole matter becomes impersonal and theoretical. This book will consider both history and prophecy, but it is concerned for much more; it is about Jewish people and the Jews as a people.

It may be that the title *Jewish Themes in the New Testament* caused surprise and perhaps confusion. Is this an over-ambitious production which attempts to cover absolutely every major theme in the New Testament? Are not all the themes of the New Testament 'Jewish' in the sense that the New Testament is the fulfilment of all that is promised to the Jewish people in the Old? The aim of this book is not so comprehensive.

Introduction

Our focus is, what of the Jewish people now that Messiah[2] has come? Is it conceivable that they will just drop out of the picture now? That is not the fate we would expect for those who have received God's promises. The New Testament agrees, and as we read it we find that Jesus and his apostles had much to say which has ongoing relevance for the Jewish people, and for the relationship between them and believers in Jesus.

Is this just another book by someone bitten by the 'Jewish bug'? Among Christians today there are those who seem to view the church as a phenomenon which has reached its 'sell by date'; their whole vision has become filled with the Jews, and it seems that they can speak of little else. Such people can be very off-putting to Christians who see the church as the glorious body of Christ but who want to consider these Jewish themes in the New Testament. I hope this book will not put you off but only thrill you, humble you and lead you to praise and prayer.

PART 1

Privileges and Promises

1.

Yahweh, the God of Israel

The gospel is the gospel of God and it is for his glory. That is where our consideration of Jewish themes should start. The people of Israel lives, and that demonstrates something about God himself.

God has a name. He is not an abstract idea but a person, and to the Jewish people he revealed that name and all it means. His name is Yahweh.[1] I am aware that there are different ideas about how the divine name should be pronounced but in this book 'Yahweh' will be used. It is not my intention to use 'Yahweh' everywhere that 'Lord' would be the norm, as it may be too unusual for most readers but I will use it where it first occurs in a chapter to underline the point that God has a name. There is no doubt that the name is most certainly connected to the verb 'to be'. The God of Israel declares by his name that *he is, he lives*. Because he lives we can exclaim *Am Yisrael Chai!* The people Israel lives.

When in Romans 11 the apostle Paul comes to examine more closely the purposes of God for the Jewish people he begins by raising the question of their rejection, and whether, because of it, they are excluded from God's future plans. His response is emphatic – 'God forbid!' or 'By no means!'[2] What is underlined here is that Yahweh is *a faithful God*. Once he enters into a covenant relationship with a people he will never renege on them but will fulfil all his promises to them.

Elsewhere in that same chapter Paul writes that Israel is 'beloved for the sake of the fathers',[3] by whom he means Abraham, Isaac and Jacob. Because of his faithfulness to those men God loves the Jewish people today. He does so freely and unconditionally. The God of Israel is *a God of love*. As one hymn writer put it, the love of God is broader than the measure of man's mind.

The unbelief of many Jewish people and the sorrowful events in their history have to be faced. Paul explains their hardness of heart in terms of God having given them a spirit of stupor due to unbelief, and the Lord Jesus taught that the destruction of Jerusalem and the suffering of exile from the land were 'days of vengeance'.[4] Such things show Yahweh to be a *God of judgement*. It is a warning to us. As Paul wrote to Christians prone to boasting over the Jews, 'Do not be haughty, but fear. For if God did not spare the natural branches, He may not spare you either.'[5]

In Romans 9 – 11 the apostle Paul enters upon the whole question of God's dealings with his people, the Jews, in the days of the Messiah, and his initial focus is the problem of their unbelief. Has God failed? Have all his promises to them come to nothing? Are the Jews particularly wicked? Paul's response begins with God, and his basic explanation is that God makes choices based on his will alone. The point is that *Yahweh is sovereign*. If people believe the gospel it is not because they are somehow more prone to it than others, but because he has chosen them to salvation and given them the grace to believe. This is what is indicated of Jewish believers in Jesus by the words 'a remnant according to the election of grace'.[6] Some Jews believe because of God's sovereign choice. Such truths humble us to the dust and underline to us our utter dependence on God's grace.

At the end of Romans 11 Paul reflects on God's salvation purposes for the Gentiles and the Jews, particularly their disobedience. His response is to marvel at *the wisdom and knowledge of Yahweh*.[7] God's way of working is not something we could have ever guessed at, nor have we contributed a single idea. We utterly depend on him for revelation.

At the end of the same passage of Romans Paul cannot but exult in God and declare, 'to whom be glory forever. Amen.'[8] God is to be glorified by all his creatures for all that he does, but he is especially glorified by the work of mission – the spreading of his kingdom in the hearts of men and women throughout his world. Satan has challenged God, he has tried to mar his glory, but God has the last word through his Son, Jesus the Messiah. The Jews are included in this struggle. The sight of a people in covenant with Almighty God, but marked almost totally by unbelief, is surely a sight pleasing to Satan if ever there was one. Paul assures us that God will have the last word, and he will be glorified.

2.

His People

'I will be your God, and you shall be my people' is the expression which best sums up what it is for a people to be in a covenant relationship withYahweh. It is used in the Old Testament to describe Israel's relationship to God,[1] and in the New Testament similar words are used by Peter when describing the church.[2] What is indicated is that God has placed himself in a position of commitment, and placed people in a position of blessing and obligation. At the beginning of Romans 11, in describing the relationship of the Jews to the Lord in the era of the New Testament, the apostle Paul calls them 'His people'.[3] God is still committed to them, ready to bless them, and they are still under obligation to him.

It may seem strange to us, and especially those who have tidy minds, but this means that there are two groups in the world today who are called God's people: the Jews and the church. Of course, the nature of their covenant relationships is different but that they are both in a relationship of one sort or another is clear. This means that, as far as their relationship with God is concerned, humanity is divided into three groups, as Paul writes elsewhere in the context of food offered to idols, 'Give no offense, either to the Jews or to the Greeks or to the church of God.'[4] To see the world in two main categories, the church and the world, as many Christians often do, is an oversimplification as far as Paul is concerned.

But what is the covenant relationship between God and Israel now? If the Mosaic covenant is abolished then what remains?[5] In Romans 11 Paul writes, 'They are beloved for the sake of the fathers.'[6] He not only tells us the bottom-line attitude of the Lord to Israel is one of love, but he also answers our question. Because of his dealings with Abraham, Isaac and Jacob, because of his promises to them, and despite their unbelief, the Lord is still committed to the Jewish people. They are not on the scrapheap of history. He remains faithful. There are few fathers and mothers who will refuse to visit a son who has been sent to jail for serious crime, despite the shame and grief for them. How much more will the Lord remain faithful to the Jewish people?

Now I am aware that to refer back to the Abrahamic covenant raises difficult questions. It appears to ignore all that has developed out of that covenant. Am I trying to set the clock back and say that all continues as it was when the Lord first made that covenant with Abraham? Of course not. But the fact that Paul makes this connection with Abraham in Romans 11:28 indicates that there is the place we are to look for an understanding of how the Lord deals with the Jews today. The Lord made seven promises to Abraham when he first spoke to him.[7] How we are to understand his faithfulness to those promises today is really the subject of this book.

A Wrong Conclusion

Many conclude that, because the Jews remain a people of God, then, *ipso facto*, they will one day receive back all that was lost through unbelief. They expect the Mosaic order of things to be restored, including the temple, priesthood and kingdom, in a way that ignores the development of God's purposes through the new covenant. The book of Hebrews was written to wean Jewish believers away from such hopes, and it ought to have the same effect on Gentile believers. The institutions of the Mosaic covenant are described in Hebrews 10:1 as 'having a shadow of the good things to come', followed in verse 9 of the chapter by the statement, 'He takes away the first that He may establish the second.' The whole thrust of Hebrews is to underline that we are in the last days of God's dealings with humanity,[8] which are via his Son in the new covenant, and we should expect no further developments before the Son's return, and certainly not anything that savours of a return to the old status quo of the Mosaic covenant.

It seems to me that this expectation of a return to some form of the Mosaic has led to a reaction from others, and they conclude that the unbelief of the Jewish people means that, as a nation, they have lost everything they once had. God has no further dealings with the Jews as a people. They are simply out of the picture. This is a serious overreaction. It will come as no surprise to note that few Jewish believers overreact in this way, it is a Gentile Christian phenomenon which seems to me to have all the hallmarks of that Gentile boasting over the natural branches which Paul rebukes in Romans 11:18,19.

The Jews Are Not the Jews, Christians Are

Some go so far as to say that the people we call the Jews are not really Jews at all. They usually point to Romans 2:25–9 where Paul writes 'he is not a Jew who is one outwardly, nor is circumcision that which is outward in the flesh', and then they conclude that Christians are the only true Jews and that unbelieving Jews are not Jews at all. This is a total misuse of the passage. It is certainly true that Paul argues that Gentiles who have the heart of the matter can be seen as (true) Jews but his purpose in doing this is to awaken unsaved and spiritually complacent Jews; he is not addressing saved Gentiles. Viewed from an eternal perspective, if unbelieving Jews continue in such a state, they will lose everything, all the privileges of being Jewish; that is the warning. Paul is being provocative to achieve his purpose. His purpose is not to de-Jew unbelieving Jews because in the very next verse (3:1) he uses the term 'Jew' to refer to Jewish people as a whole throughout history, believers and unbelievers. And we find the same use of language later in Romans: 'What then? Israel has not obtained what it seeks; but the elect have obtained it, and the rest were blinded.'[9] Here Paul uses Israel to refer to both believers and unbelievers; he does not de-Israel unbelievers. I have even encountered the assertion, on the basis of Romans 2:25–9, that Jews who were not inward Jews in the Old Testament period were not Jews at all. I suppose it is the logical outcome of such a misunderstanding of Paul. If it were true, then the prophets were wrong to accuse them of failing to meet their covenant obligations, and God was horribly unjust for punishing them for that failure when, in fact, they were never in the covenant, not being Jews at all.

It needs to be underlined that it is not Paul's aim to focus on the new status of believing Gentiles in Romans 2:25–9. He does that in Galatians 3:7 and 3:29, where he describes them in terms of their relationship to Abraham. When Paul's purpose is to focus on the new, spiritual status of believing Gentiles, he does not use the term 'Jew'. That would cause confusion. His preference is for terms like 'sons of Abraham', 'heirs of the promise', 'fellow citizens'. Certainly if a Gentile witnesses to a Jewish person and calls themselves a Jew it will cause confusion and offence, but a term like 'child of Abraham by faith' will not. Jewish people are all too familiar with being treated as non-persons, and for a Christian to claim to be a Jew smacks of that.

I find it interesting that, in all I have read by those who say unbelieving Jews are no longer Jews, I have never read of a new name they have coined for them. The impression is that such Christians care very little for the Jewish people as a people; they are just not on their radar. At that point they fail to bear the image of the God they profess to serve.

Some develop this line of thought further by asserting that those calling themselves Jews today cannot really lay claim to descent from the biblical Jews. They claim that because of so much intermarriage, and because of one well-known case of mass conversion to Judaism,[10] the people descended from the patriarchs have simply disappeared from history. Hence, those who call themselves 'Jews' today can lay no claim to those promises being theirs. Paul's whole argument in Romans 11 assumes the continued existence of the Jewish people as a people of the promises, underlined by one of the closing statements of the chapter, 'The gifts and the calling of God are irrevocable.'[11] They still have a calling from God and their unbelief does not negate that, any more than our failures negate our calling.

'Replacement Theology'

If you are not aware of the term 'replacement theology' then this is probably a good place to introduce it. It is a term which has been coined to label the view in the above paragraph – that the Jews today are no longer a people of promise or covenant – by those who do not hold that view. The trouble is that it is a catch-all term which usually lumps together others who love the Jews and recognize them as God's people with those who do not give them that recognition. It is most frequently used by those who expect that there will be a return of the Mosaic institutions for the Jewish people when they are restored to their land and Messiah's earthly, millennial kingdom is inaugurated. Some who have that hope also believe the church was never a part of God's original plan so, to teach as I have done above, that the church is the final stage of God's purpose before the new heavens and the new earth, is viewed as replacing Israel with the church, because Israel will be the final stage in their view. To such people I hold a replacement theology. And yet, in a similar vein, I might stigmatize people holding the view that there is no further place for Israel in God's purposes as 'replacement theologians'. Because it can mean different things to different people I think it is an unfortunate and unhelpful term.

So, is there a better term to use if there is a need to describe the view of opponents of the teaching that Israel continues in covenant with the Lord? I would suggest two possibilities – *exclusion* theology or *boasting* theology. Exclusion is not ideal because it suggests Jews are excluded from salvation, which no one in this debate is asserting, even though some are certainly excluding them from covenant status. It is a better term than replacement because all who hold to the continuing covenant status of the Jewish people can use it and not be stigmatizing each other. However, I prefer the term *boasting theology* because it picks up on Paul's terminology in opposing such erroneous thinking,[12] and it addresses a person's heart as well as their mind.

But all the above is about words used to describe a view which is opposed. What about a term to describe what is believed? More on this later when we consider the olive tree metaphor in Romans 11, where *engrafting* will be emphasized, but surely the New Testament's term is *fulfilment*. The creation of the new covenant church of Jew and Gentile is the fulfilment of God's promises to Israel under the old covenant. The New Testament writers simply could not have used Old Testament terminology to describe New Testament realities if this were not so.[13] Or, better still, the similar term *fulfilling*, which emphasizes that this is an ongoing, present-day work of God. It is a term which cannot allow any trace of a thought of the Jews losing their people of promise status because it underlines that the promises to Israel are still being fulfilled in the work of the gospel today, in particular by the salvation of Jews who believe. It is a term which also keeps the door open to greater future possibilities by a new measure of the work of God's Spirit among Israel.

3.

For the Jew First

Paul's words, 'For the Jew first', are words which produce a variety of responses. For some they are a battle cry in the fight to create an interest in the Jews, but for others they are words to be uttered with a great deal of qualification in case super-race ideas sprout and spread. I want to begin by stepping back a bit to see things in context.

The plan of the Lord Jesus for the spread of the gospel was clearly outlined to his apostles as he was leaving this earth – 'you shall be witnesses to Me in Jerusalem, and in all Judea and Samaria, and to the end of the earth'.[1] His words have been the guide and inspiration for strategies of mission ever since, producing statements like: 'It is unrealistic to be looking far afield if we are not faithful and active where we are.' In other words: start where you are, in your own Jerusalem.

Now that is fair enough as long as it does not lose sight of the larger view of the Lord Jesus' words. There was more to his instruction to the apostles to start at Jerusalem than the simple fact that that is where they were there at the time. After all, they were mostly Galileans, and would certainly have felt more comfortable starting on their home territory, away from Jerusalem, the place where Jesus had been crucified. If common sense were the criteria, then they would have preferred Galilee. However, there was something about the position of Jerusalem in the purposes of God that made it essential to begin there. And the same could be said about the Jewish people themselves. There was something about their place in God's purposes which meant that their nation was to hear the gospel first. That truth was also to affect the first preaching of the gospel beyond the confines of the land of Israel, and it is by looking at that story that we begin to understand why Paul wrote that the Gospel is *for the Jew first and also for the Greek.*[2]

Paul's Practice

Paul was the apostle to the Gentiles but you could be forgiven for thinking he regularly lost sight of that, because wherever he went he always went to the Jews first. Here are some examples. His first missionary journey began in Cyprus – 'And when they arrived in Salamis, they preached the word of God in the synagogues of the Jews.'[3] In Berea on his second journey we read, 'When they arrived, they went into the synagogue of the Jews.'[4] Paul continued in this way in his later ministry in Ephesus: 'And he came to Ephesus, and left them there; but he himself entered the synagogue and reasoned with the Jews.'[5] Finally, when he arrived in Rome under arrest his first priority was to address his people – 'And it came to pass after three days that Paul called the leaders of the Jews together.'[6] The book of Acts closes on the note of the apostle to the Gentiles making a specific attempt to reach the Jews. Luke sums it all up when describing Paul's visit to the synagogue in Thessalonica: 'Paul, *as his custom was*, went in to them, and for three Sabbaths reasoned with them from the Scriptures.'[7] Speaking in the synagogue at Antioch Paul said, 'It was *necessary* that the word of God should be spoken to you first.'[8] It was not simply Paul's bright idea as a clever strategist, but it was an obligation laid upon him.

The Promises of God

When Paul preached to Jews he announced a promise fulfilled, 'And we declare to you glad tidings – that promise which was made to the fathers. God has fulfilled this for us their children, in that He has raised up Jesus.'[9] He never used such language with Gentiles. For them, the gospel was a straightforward call to repentance, God having graciously overlooked their sins of ignorance;[10] he makes no mention of promises to them. In fact, in Ephesians, Paul states that Gentiles are, by definition, 'strangers from the covenants of promise'.[11]

The promises which Paul had in mind were obviously those made by Yahweh to Abraham, and which he repeated and elaborated many times through the prophets: promises concerning their national fortunes, and promises of a Saviour to deliver from the curse of sin – promises which had in view God's compassion for the whole world. In anticipation of their fulfilment one psalmist wrote, 'He has remembered his mercy and his faithfulness to the house of Israel; all the ends of the earth have seen the salvation of our God.'[12] For Paul this meant that, as apostle to the Gentiles, he was under an obligation to tell the Jewish people first.

God is faithful to his promises! He is very careful to make sure that those who have received them do not appear bypassed, for then he would appear unfaithful, and even unloving. As an example we can think of a situation in which identical parcels are being sent to two different people. One person has been promised a gift and told to expect it, but the other is totally unaware of the gift being sent. We would expect the sender to impress upon the carrier that to deliver the promised one first and on time was a priority. The sender's reputation is at stake, and the receiver must be in no doubt about the sender's love and faithfulness in sending the gift. That is God's attitude towards the Jews, and therefore they were the first to hear. But imagine if, in this example, the carrier does not follow instructions, and the person who is expecting and watching sees the gift being delivered elsewhere, and that no effort has been made to get the promised one delivered first and on time. There would be good reason to wonder if the other parcel that the carrier is holding is the promised gift at all. So the Jews would have had cause to wonder whether Jesus was the Messiah if his messengers paid little attention to telling the very people who were waiting for him.

For the Jew First Now

Some might be thinking that this is all very interesting but surely it is no more than history, with little relevance for the work of evangelism and mission today. That might be so if Israel's priority was spoken of only in the gospels and Acts but if we find it underlined in the epistles we should pause for thought. The inclusion of the words 'For the Jew first' in Romans 1:16,17 challenge us to pause. These are Paul's words: 'For I am not ashamed of the gospel of Christ, for it is the power of God to salvation for everyone who believes, for the Jew first and also for the Greek. For in it the righteousness of God is revealed from faith to faith; as it is written, "The just shall live by faith."'

That is Paul's nutshell statement of the gospel, and the rest of Romans is essentially an exposition of it. If you yourself attempted to put the gospel down in two sentences (why not stop and try it now?) I wonder whether you would include the statement 'For the Jew first and also to the Greek'? I think most present-day evangelical Christians would not. But the fact is, Paul did, and for the very good reason that it expressed truth just as fundamental as the other expressions. The mention of Jew and Gentile is a reminder that the gospel is rooted in God's actions in history, and in particular with one people, the Jews. The gospel is not just another set of ideas. The mention of the Jews also declares that the gospel is to do with promises made by God which have been fulfilled. 'For the Jew first' is therefore of the very essence of the gospel.

But for many its significance is forgotten. And yet who would want to overlook the significance of Paul's other terms, such as 'righteousness', 'faith', 'revealed'? All Christians would be horrified at the thought. Yet somehow 'For the Jew first' is seen by many as of only passing relevance. Yet if history and promise dictated that the gospel should be preached to the Jews first in Paul's day, then Paul's inclusion of the statement 'For the Jew first' in his nutshell statement of the gospel, relevant for all time, demands that it affects our preaching of the gospel now. The gospel is still a message rooted in history and it is still the fulfilment of promises to a people, the Jews.

Paul's next use in Romans of the phrase 'For the Jew first' underlines the 'relevant for all time' aspect. He writes of the 'day of wrath and revelation of the righteous judgment of God', and its consequence for the unrepentant: 'tribulation and anguish, on every soul of man who does evil, of the Jew first and also of the Greek'.[13] Whatever that may mean in detail, one thing is clear: Jewish priority because of privileges and promises from God carries on to the very day of judgement, and has consequences on that day.

The end of Acts paradigm

The way Acts closes makes the same point of abiding priority. Luke's account tells the story of how the command of the Lord Jesus to preach the gospel in Jerusalem, Samaria and to the ends of the earth began to be achieved.[14] His account closes in Rome with the story unfinished but on the note of an ongoing witness to all, which included a specific effort by the apostle to the Gentiles to reach the people of promise, the Jews. How the apostle to the Gentiles finishes his course in the record of Scripture is clearly a template for how the church is to continue to the nations of the world. It is as if the Spirit is saying, 'This is how you are to keep on with this task.' It is a task which involves the church in reaching the nations, and always making a special effort to reach the Jews.

Things Are Not Exactly the Same Today

The relevance of 'For the Jew first' remains, but we cannot ignore the developments in the situation since Paul's time. The initial obligation to literally go to the Jews before the Gentiles has been fulfilled and the Jewish community has had, in a general sense, the opportunity to consider the claims of Jesus the Messiah. The Jews today are not a people who are ignorant of his claims. The attitude of the synagogue today has been determined by the Jewish leadership, which has heard of and has rejected Jesus as Messiah. Hence it is not possible to walk into a synagogue, as Paul did, and declare the message of Jesus as if it is news hot off the press.

But if we move away from the broad picture we have to ask ourselves: what of the new generations of Jews which have arisen, many of whom have never heard the gospel for themselves but only a garbled and prejudiced version of it? Obviously, we cannot say that the mandate to take the gospel to all the world is perpetually on hold until we have searched out every Jewish person and told him or her first. Paul did not operate in such a way. In fact, when Paul returned to places he had previously evangelized he did not literally go first to the synagogue, as he had done on his initial visit. Nevertheless we cannot assert that the words 'For the Jew first' have no more relevance for our strategy of mission when the people of promise still live, still need forgiveness of sin and are in ignorance of how it is to be obtained. So what does it all mean for our church's evangelism and our strategy of mission?

'For the Jew First' and the Witness of a Local Church

First of all it is a matter of perspective, of viewing Jewish people as the children of promise. We cannot approach them as just another ethnic group, with their own human culture. They are unique because they are the people to whom God made the promises of the Messiah. For them the gospel of a promised Saviour is peculiarly appropriate. The core of their culture is one which points to a hope of salvation; their whole *raison d'être* is to wait for that salvation. No other nation has been so created and moulded by God. This is why Paul describes them as the natural branches in Romans 11:24, of which more in a later chapter. Jesus must therefore be presented to them as the fulfilment of those promises.

A church near a Jewish community should be prepared and sensitive in its outreach to the Jews in its neighbourhood. Effort should be made to equip the church to reach out to them as the people of promise, and if this is to be taken seriously then someone in leadership in the church should undergo some form of training for outreach to Jewish people, and have responsibility for the church's witness to Jewish neighbours. To have the people of promise in our church neighbourhood should be seen as a privilege from God, not as a nuisance factor. I would be the first to recognize that making a special effort to reach them will probably invite trouble but it does not seem that Paul allowed that to alter his strategy.

Such churches should see the unique opportunity they have to demonstrate the 'one new man' in Christ.[15] God in his wisdom has scattered the Jewish people all over the world, and mostly in lands where they will hear the gospel. Can we not see this as part of God's plan to save some, and bring about his purpose of creating one new man in Christ, composed of Jews and Gentiles?

Such churches should see it as an opportunity for something glorious, not a difficulty to be avoided.

I sometimes wonder if this tendency to overlook the Jewish people is because some Christians think that Jewish people today must already know the gospel since they have the Old Testament. We rejoice to see Messiah Jesus and his salvation in its pages, so surely they can see it too? Nothing could be further from the truth. For example, when I tell Jewish friends of the death of Jesus as fulfilling the great need for the blood of atonement taught in their Hebrew Scriptures, they usually look blank. They are not taught to see any saving importance in those sacrifices, and they make no connection with the blood of Jesus. I also think that some Christians, and even church leaders, are afraid of the Jewish community. They have heard about the opposition that the Jewish community can mount to attempts to evangelize them, and they back off. None of us enjoys such strife but both our Saviour and his apostles trod that pathway; we can hardly expect exemption.

'For the Jew First' and Mission from a Local Church

The church as a whole is still under the obligation to take the gospel to the Jew first and also to the Gentile. If we can be hypothetical for a moment, let us imagine the leaders of a newly planted church sitting down to discuss how they should reach out in mission beyond their own neighbourhood. Their mission programme is a blank sheet. They are aware of their responsibility to reach out to a needy world, but the main questions are about where to go or what to support. But to go back a step, what makes them aware of their responsibility? It is the command of Messiah Jesus to go into all the world.[16] Equally it is the teaching of Paul that as they go, they go to the Jew first. This means that they recognize that they have an obligation to support work among Jews as they also seek God's mind on what to do in the Gentile world. The strategy must always be two-pronged, just as Paul's was right up to the end of Acts. The conclusion is that church denominations or independent local churches have a responsibility, as they consider their work of mission, to be involved in Jewish evangelism. I thank God that many do, but I am also grieved that many fail to see this responsibility. What about you and your church?

Prayer for the Jewish People in the Life of a Church

All that I am saying about going to the Jew first would have come as no surprise to some great men of God in earlier generations. For example, in *The Directory for Public Worship in the Westminster Confession of Faith* of 1646 there is a direction that, when the coming of Christ's kingdom is prayed for, then the conversion of the Jews should be specifically mentioned. In the list of things to be prayed for it is placed first. Those who wrote that directory comprised one of the finest and best-taught bodies of preachers and theologians ever to gather to formulate the teachings of the Scriptures. It is no small thing that they came to this conclusion. It does not take much imagination to grasp how greatly the concern of Christians for the salvation Jews would be stimulated if every preacher prayed for their salvation every Lord's Day! And it is not just for preachers; regular public and private prayer for the Jews by every Christian is obedience to this instruction, 'For the Jew first and also for the Greek'.

Dangers to Avoid

The word 'first' in 'For the Jew first' has often been misunderstood. It does not mean that Jews have an intrinsic spirituality which separates them from others. As one Jewish wit put it, 'We Jews are the same as everyone else, only more so.' A single reading of the Old Testament should be enough to dispel any idea of the Jewish people being a nation of spiritual supermen, yet the idea persists.

However, some persist with the idea that Jewish people do not need Messiah Jesus to get to heaven. They teach that Jews have their own covenant with God and that is sufficient. These statements of Paul and Peter should be enough to refute such an idea: 'All have sinned and fall short of the glory of God';[17] 'There is no other name under heaven given among men by which we must be saved.'[18]

This myth of the intrinsic spirituality of the Jews causes some Christians to view Jewish believers in Jesus as possessors of a special aura. It has often been said to me in rather gushy tones, 'They are so wonderful when they get converted, aren't they.' There is great value in having national and family traditions which are rooted in God's revelation. Everyone has a natural leaning towards their roots, and for Jews theirs are in the Bible. But none of this makes them intrinsically better followers of Messiah Jesus. There is no easy route to being spiritually minded and a spiritual blessing to others; it comes from that slow but sure growth in grace which is the product of submission to God's truth. I do not doubt the importance and value of the presence of Jewish believers in a church, but there is nothing automatic about receiving blessing by it.

Another danger that results from stressing the significance of the Jewish people is that of belittling the church. The new covenant community of Messiah, made up of Jews and Gentiles, has been called the glorious body of Christ, and that is what she is. Any tendency to underplay her scriptural position as the fulfilment and apex of God's salvation purpose must be guarded against when emphasizing God's concern for Israel. I have found in my experience that this tendency in some who have a love for the Jewish people is often the thing which is most off-putting to those who are beginning to consider these truths about the Jews. Some believe that the Lord never planned the church at all, but only brought her in as a sort of Plan B when the Jewish people, as a people, failed to accept Jesus as Messiah. Consequently his plan to establish a worldwide kingdom, centred on Jerusalem, was put on hold, and the 'church-age' was instituted as a stopgap until he comes again to establish his millennial kingdom. Such a view inevitably presents the church as second best and raises serious questions about God's sovereignty.

Difficulties and Objections

I am sure that some readers will have said, 'Yes, but . . .' a few times by now, and I hope I have answered most of the questions which arise out of this issue. However, I can think of two others, which are dealt with below.

The Acts of the Apostles is a period of transition

Acts describes not only the beginnings of the gospel but also a unique period of change from the old covenant to the new. Some things in Acts belong only to that time of transition, e.g. the emphasis of Jewish believers on attending the temple worship. Can the same be said of 'For the Jew first'? The answer is found by asking, is this practice or principle taught in the epistles? If so, it is binding today and not transitional. I have shown above that 'For the Jew first' is clearly taught in the epistles.

Christ breaks down the middle-wall of partition (Eph. 2:13).

He certainly does. But that is done when sinners come to faith in him; it is something which happens in Christ. However, the expression 'For the Jew first' is considering Jews and Gentiles in their unconverted state, whether they have or have not received promises from God. Considered spiritually, the world is not simply divided into believers and unbelievers, but the unbelieving world is further divided into Jew and Gentile in the sight of God, as Paul wrote, 'Give no offense, either to the Jews or to the Greeks or to the church of God.'[19]

4.

The Olive Tree

Do you think of Jews as natural branches or unnatural branches? If the question puzzles you then think of the New Testament church as represented by a tree, one which has its own natural branches, and also some unnatural ones which have been grafted onto it. Do you think of the Jewish people as the former or the latter, the natural ones or the unnatural ones? For Paul, the Jews are the natural branches and all others are the outsiders. That includes me for one. Yet I would suspect that many Christians would not view the Jews as natural branches. The church seems to be the last organization which Jewish people want to be a part of, so how can it be seen as their natural realm? To change the metaphor, the church is the realm where they are more like a fish out of water. What is this all about? To answer that we need to think about the olive tree of Romans 11:16–24.

The Olive Tree image

Paul introduces this illustration as part of his aim in Romans 11 of showing that God has not washed his hands of the Jewish people. His olive tree metaphor is unique in the New Testament because he uses one image to portray God's people from their beginnings in the covenant with Abraham through to their new covenant completion. Other metaphors, like body, bride or temple, may pick up on Old Testament imagery but they do not attempt to portray the transition from Old to New. Through the olive tree Paul presents to us a tree which has a root, sap, and two sorts of branches – natural and grafted ones. Jews are the natural branches and believing Gentiles are the grafted-in branches (see v. 24). In trying to understand his language here it must be remembered that the passage is addressed to Christians from a Gentile background (see 11:17,24) where 'you' – those he addresses – refers to those who do not naturally belong to the tree – Gentiles.

The initial state of the tree is the people of Israel before the time of the coming of Jesus. We may think of the root as the patriarchs, Abraham, Isaac and Jacob, who first received God's promises. The sap would represent the gracious blessing of God flowing to the Jews because they were his people.

There are some who think the tree represents Christ, but that is an idea that emerges more from spiritual logic than the actual wording. Christ is not mentioned in the text, but rather, the focus is upon the people of God. Paul states that the Jews are the natural branches of the tree,[1] therefore the tree, in its initial state, is Israel. Furthermore, the idea that Christ is the tree misses the whole point: Paul's purpose is to keep Gentile Christians from boasting over the Jews by reminding them that they are dependent on what God has done through Israel. To be sure, it is Christ who supplies grace to us, but Paul is not speaking here about the source of supply, rather, about the channel by which Christ's grace is supplied.

However, with the coming of the Messiah a change is introduced. Faith in Jesus becomes the condition for remaining in the tree and receiving God's covenant blessing.[2] Believing Jews remained in – people like Peter, James and John – and received God's new covenant blessings. Jewish people who did not believe – most of the nation as time went on – took a different course. Because they shunned the new churches, and because the temple was destroyed, they were cut off from God's means of grace; for them the sap ceased to flow.

But was not faith just as important and necessary before Messiah came? If it is true that 'without faith it is impossible to please Him',[3] then surely things have not changed that much? Of course that is true, but we also need to remember that under the old covenant an Israelite could lack faith and yet be truly one of God's covenant people, because it was by natural birth. People were cut off only for a limited number of serious sins. As long as an Israelite avoided such, he or she might lack saving faith and yet enjoy some of the temporal covenant blessings of God, such as good harvests, deliverance from enemies and an exalted moral code; things enjoyed by the whole nation. Of course, if they were to experience spiritual blessings and have eternal life then faith in God's way of salvation was essential. If we think back to the reigns of David and Solomon, when the whole nation experienced much of God's blessing, there were surely many from both of these categories. An obvious example would be Nabal and his wife Abigail.[4] It seems that he lacked true faith but clearly she possessed it, yet they both knew God's temporal blessings as part of his covenant grace to the whole nation in the reigns of Saul and David.

In his day, Jesus was the touchstone that demonstrated which of these categories a Jew belonged to. Faith in him was what distinguished the wheat from the chaff. Some, like Nathaniel, moved seamlessly from an Old Testament faith to a New Testament one, without ever going through a cut-off phase; that was a unique generation. But others, by their rejection of Jesus, demonstrated that they never had a living faith, and ended up losing even that which they had.

And then Gentiles began to hear and believe. By faith they became members of God's people and began to receive his blessing. Paul describes this as being grafted in.[5] By birth they had been part of a wild olive tree but now, through new birth, they were grafted into a good one.[6] The wild olive tree represents pagan culture with all its false teachings about God and life, producing lives which bear no fruit to God. God's remedy is not to inject truth into their culture so that their people become the people of God; no, he puts them into what is for them a new people, bound by spiritual ties, with a new spiritual culture, yet it is one which has been growing for many years. This people have a new name, the church – the called-out ones – called out from the nations, and from Israel.

Of course it has to be noted that in saying the Gentile believers are put into a new people and spiritual culture, one which was already in existence, I am not suggesting their new spiritual culture is the law of Moses. Jesus the Messiah has inaugurated a new covenant for God's people, and its conditions and requirements are different from those of the Mosaic, and yet not so that there is a radical disjuncture, as is plain from what Paul taught about God's purpose for his new covenant people: 'that the *righteous requirement* of the law might be fulfilled in us'.[7] The tree into which Gentiles are grafted may look different, but it is essentially the same tree. Gentiles enter into all that Israel had experienced of God through his truth, promises and presence; and more – the fullness of all those things in the blessings of Messiah's kingdom.

To conclude our consideration of the olive tree, the final matter Paul mentions is the grafting back in of believing Jewish people in subsequent generations. Paul wrote, 'God is able to graft them in again.' If we think about the phrase 'graft them in again'[8] it may strike us as odd. Jewish people of later generations were not those who were cut off, so how can they be grafted *back*? Such language indicates how Paul sees the continuity of Israel today with Israel of old. There is a practical reality to that continuity which enables Paul to describe Jewish conversion as being grafted into their *own* olive tree.

Consequences for Israel

All this has consequences for unbelieving Jews, the cut-off branches, and their subsequent history cannot be understood apart from it. They have remained a people with an ethnic identity and a national religion, and they remain 'beloved for the sake of the fathers'.[9] Those born Jewish today are brought up in a religion which outwardly has a resemblance to all God gave to Israel under the old covenant. For example: a belief in the one true God; a reverence for the law and the prophets; the celebration of the Sabbath and festivals such as Passover; times for repentance like the Day of Atonement; and a hope in the promise of the Messiah and life after death. It has its beauties, but it is the beauty of a shell which is empty and a look inside disappoints; there is no salvation.

That should not lead us to dismiss or ignore some valuable effects of Judaism upon the Jewish people, effects that derive from the influence of the Scriptures of the Old Testament as well as from the traditions of the rabbis. Many of the rituals and religious services of Judaism have an ennobling and humbling effect on the human spirit. The Jewish emphasis on justice, morality and charity has benefited Jews and others throughout history. The

Jewish nation may be a cut-off branch but it is not a destroyed one. It has continued to have a cultural life of its own, and a unique religion. They have deviated from Moses but not so far that they can no longer be viewed as the natural branches.

Also obvious is the ongoing rejection of Messiah Jesus by the Jewish leadership. Yet, by God's grace, many do believe. To most fellow-Jews this appears as an alien act, and even some Christians see a Jewish believer as a fish out of water; but Paul did not, for him they have been grafted in again. They have acted naturally, so to speak; they have come home. How is that in experience? This will vary according to the degree of influence of Jewish religion and history on an individual Jewish person, but the following are commonplace. If they had doubts, they now have no doubts that the story of their nation really is God's story. The far-off God of their fathers has come near to them, the promises he made to them have come alive, the atonement spoken of so much is experienced, the law is in the heart and no longer a burden, and the Messiah has come, to them. These are core Jewish things, so it is not surprising to hear a new Jewish believer say, 'Now, I feel really Jewish!' The tree started with their people, and they are back in again.

Someone once put it like this: when God removes the veil from Jewish hearts then the synagogue becomes the church. Now that is not entirely true, because some teachings of Judaism are unbiblical and need repudiating, but it makes the essential point which could not be made of any other people and their religion.

Some Conclusions

One people but different administrations

There is only one tree. Throughout history there has only ever been one people of God. The external differences are because he has ruled over them by different administrations, or covenants. The final administration, before glory itself, is the new covenant of Messiah. The new covenant is not a rejection of all that preceded, a totally new start, so to speak. Nor is it a Gentile entity, as if God has decided to turn his back on Israel. It is a fulfilment of all that preceded it. This is *fulfilment theology*. Or, if we want to take into account the olive tree terminology, it is *engrafting theology*. God does not uproot and relocate.

Two illustrations might help to clarify all this; one emphasizes form, and the other life and splendour. A fairly ordinary detached house in my neighbourhood was purchased with a view to extension into a property about three times the size. However, the extension had to be in keeping with the character of the existing. It did not seem that the two aims were compatible and it was intriguing to see what would emerge. Now it is finished I can imagine that a person new to the neighbourhood might at first sight fail to see the original, but for those who have seen both structures it is clear. The church is like that. It is possible for a newcomer to be unaware of the church's spiritual origins and history, but the better informed can see how her form is determined by what has gone before. Or think of the development of a butterfly from its chrysalis and caterpillar. It is a metamorphosis: the substance is the same but the form changes. It is a perfect illustration of the development of God's people: always one, always living, sometimes changing, and finally arriving at a form which exceeds all expectations. In fact, so much so that we might be forgiven for thinking the finale is something quite different, but it is not. Each stage has a glory, but the glory of the final stage is such that the others appear to have no glory (see Paul's comparison in 2 Cor. 3:7–11.) But they are all of a piece.

For Gentile Christians – do not boast over the Jews!

Paul words in Romans 11:17–22 have a pastoral purpose for Christians from a Gentile background. He must have been aware of an unhealthy attitude to Jewish people developing in some of the Christians in Rome and he aims to correct it. His warning against boasting over the natural branches, because of their fall, indicates that some Christians from a Gentile background had developed feelings of superiority over the Jewish people.[10] They had believed, and the Jews had not.

It seems an attempt was made to give this boasting some measure of justification by appealing to the sovereign purpose of God – 'Branches were broken off that I might be grafted in.'[11] However, they were misusing such a truth to promote themselves as superior. Paul quickly reminds them of two things, firstly that they are a supported people, supported by God's salvation purposes through Israel. Secondly, he reminds them that faith is what leads to being in the tree. Gentiles are not in because they are Gentiles, and Jews are not out because they are Jews.

Paul further aims to puncture Gentile arrogance by pointing out that, for Jewish people to come to faith it is a more straightforward thing than it is for Gentiles. Hence there is something much more so about it for Jewish people.[12] Faith for Gentiles is likened to a wild branch being grafted into a cultivated tree; which is not the norm, or, as Paul puts it, it is against nature. In nature, that will simply produce wild olives. If a farmer wants more good olives then a branch must be grafted from a cultivated tree onto a wild tree. It is tempting to think Paul should have chosen a better illustration, but it is clear that he chose this one precisely because it emphasizes the difficulty for Gentiles coming to faith. They have to move out of their natural habitat, so to speak. Jews do not have to do that; they have to get back into it. Something quite different, prompting Paul to say, 'How much more will these, who are the natural branches, be grafted into their own olive tree.' When God chooses to act in great mercy towards Israel what a homecoming it will be!

It is important to remember that Paul is addressing Christians here, Christians who were speaking about Jews, or to Jews, in this boastful spirit. It is something which is not absent from evangelical churches today, and we all need to check ourselves. It is especially seen today in a particular type of negative attitude to the State of Israel, one which seems unable to countenance the Jews becoming strong again. Paul's warning is included in Romans 11 because the Spirit of God knew it would be a recurring problem. We all stand by faith; and that faith is not in our faith, but in the only one who saves us – Jesus the Lord. We have nothing to boast about. What is your attitude to the Jews?

Surely the desire of every Christian should be for God to so manifest his power that the Jewish people will turn to him, that the veil will be removed and that they will believe. This process is greatly helped when Christians avoid all boastful attitudes, repenting of any they may have, and appreciate that the roots of their faith are the revelation God first gave to the Jewish people.

5.

Debtors

We are all debtors. We are debtors to God; we are debtors to family and friends, to those who may have lent us money, to those who have stood by us when the going got tough – and to those who brought the gospel to us.

Christians from a Gentile background are similarly indebted to the Jewish nation. The olive tree of Romans 11, considered in the previous chapter, makes that plain. Christians from the nations have become partakers of, and are supported by, something described as belonging to the Jewish people. That was so and always will be so. Furthermore we need to remember how the nations first hear about the Saviour. Jews who believed in Jesus went out, at considerable cost to themselves, to tell the world. The Acts was written to tell us how the gospel spread from Jerusalem to Rome, the heart of the Gentile world, but it is easy to lose sight of the fact that the main players were Jews who had believed, who were going out in compassion to a world in spiritual darkness. It was a world against which their upbringing had prejudiced them, and a world which frequently manifested prejudice against them. But they persevered. We should have a sense of gratitude towards those first Jewish evangelists. Think of Peter going to Cornelius with the gospel in Acts 10. That was clearly not easy for Peter but he put to death his reservations, and as for Cornelius, his gratitude seems excessive, 'Cornelius met him [Peter] and fell down at his feet and worshiped him.'[1] When did you last do that for a gospel preacher? Cornelius is a remarkable example to us of an appreciative Gentile.

Western Christians do not find corporate concepts so easy to grasp, as our mentality is excessively individual, so we need to work on it. Africans do not usually have the same difficulty as the following story illustrates. A pastor went from England to visit a few remote mission stations in the Democratic Republic of Congo. He was welcomed with a speech that frequently repeated the expression, 'How grateful we are to you for bringing the gospel to our people.' But he had never preached to them; he had just arrived! What they were saying was, how grateful we are to you because your people (of several generations ago) brought the gospel to our villages. They saw him as part of that same people and so felt gratitude to him. Christians from a Gentile background need to have a similar approach to the Jews.

Let me say a few words to Christians from a Gentile background here. When we go with the gospel to Jewish people this matter of gratitude should be a part of our motivation. We also need to check ourselves for prejudice against Jewish people. Influences in our upbringing may have prejudiced us against them, or we may have become prejudiced as a result of difficult experiences. These things inhibit our ability to witness to Jews and must be put to death. The early Jewish believers had to learn this lesson and we need to learn it too.

There are other ways in which this dependence is expressed. Pre-eminently, and perhaps unnecessary to state, Jesus was a Jew. The humanity essential to his work as mediator was lived out as a Jew, descended from David, in the land of Israel, two thousand years ago. How dependent all believers are on one unique Jewish man! No doubt Jesus had this in mind when he said, 'Salvation is of the Jews.'[2] Yet there is more to his phrase than that. Israel is described as a light to the Gentiles,[3] and this is not just a matter of history. Week by week we hear preachers say, 'Isaiah tells us' or, 'Peter teaches us'. Furthermore, Israel prayed for the nations to be saved. A godly Israelite wrote these words: 'Let the peoples praise You, O God; Let all the peoples praise You. Oh, let the nations be glad and sing for joy!'[4] God heard their prayers.

Paul actually deals with this issue directly in Romans 15:25–8. There he describes Christians from among the Gentiles as their debtors, debtors to the Jewish nation. He is telling the believers in Rome of his plan to visit Jerusalem and to deliver a gift to the believers there from the churches in Macedonia and Achaia. Obviously they gave this gift willingly, but Paul goes out of his way to make the point that there was an element of obligation about it, using similar terms to those he used with the Corinthians, 'For if the Gentiles have been partakers of their spiritual things, their duty is also to minister to them in material things.'[5] Some might think Paul is being churlish – why emphasize obligation when they are giving it willingly anyway? We do not know the answer but he obviously believed he needed to make the point. If it's in Scripture, it's a point that needs to be made today.

Paying the Debt to Jewish Believers in Jesus

Paul had in view the needs of messianic Jews in Jerusalem when he wrote about Gentile indebtedness in Romans 15. There may have been several reasons why those in Jerusalem needed help but surely a significant factor would have been persecution. To be ejected from the synagogue meant reduced employment and trade opportunities, and this would have impoverished many. This is not an unfamiliar experience today for Christians living in anti-Christian cultures.

Such a concern for Jewish believers should mark Gentile Christians today. Rejection and trouble is the norm for Jews who believe in Jesus, and frequently this has material consequences. One of the reasons for the establishing of the International Hebrew Christian Alliance in 1926 (now the Messianic Jewish Alliance) was to channel funds for material assistance to Jewish believers impoverished by rejection and isolation. Not all Jewish people are materially comfortable. In Romania, for example, many elderly Jewish people depend on food parcels from their community, and are afraid to come to hear the gospel in case such a supply is cut off. In Israel today it is not unknown for those who employ messianic Jews to be put under pressure by some from the orthodox community to dismiss them.

Christians from the nations should seek to help such needy messianic Jews with an awareness of fulfilling an obligation. There will always be the danger of charlatans, or schnorrers as they would be called by fellow-Jews, but one way that a Christian can seek to fulfil this obligation with confidence is by giving to experienced missionary organizations, or to umbrella organizations like the Messianic Jewish Alliance, or to churches in Israel, all of which see giving material support to Jewish believers as a part of their ministry.

Paying the Debt to the Jewish Nation as a Whole

Paul's specific instruction in Romans 15 is with regard to believing Jews, but is there any obligation to unbelieving Jewish people? In a sense this has been answered above, but consider again Paul's expression, their 'spiritual things'. Those spiritual things are described in Romans 9:4,5 as 'the adoption, the glory, the covenants', etc. Were these blessings given only to believers in the nation, or to the whole nation descended from Abraham, Isaac and Jacob? The answer is obvious – the covenants were made with the entire nation, and all were expected to obey. This means that Christians from a Gentile background should see themselves as indebted to the people of Israel as a whole for the spiritual things they have received through them.

What does this mean in practice? It goes without saying that the best way for Christians to repay the debt is by sharing with them what is most precious to us, the gospel. Meeting their spiritual need must be our priority. All churches should be praying for them, and taking an interest in those who are called to take the gospel to them. This does not require us to neglect others.

And then there is the matter of meeting their material needs. Jesus and his apostles did not institute any material relief programme even though the world probably needed it more then than now but as they went about preaching the truth they encountered people in need and met those needs. This should be our approach. Our primary ministry to Jewish people is to preach Messiah to them, but where we come across other needs we should be ready to help. If we do this in the spirit of repaying a debt, and tell them so, it will usually kindle an interest to hear more. Among many Jews in the world there is little need of such material help, and they are usually well organized to help themselves. But that is not so everywhere, especially among Jewish people living in the old Eastern Europe bloc. This does not make such help simply a compassionless means to an end –

an accusation we often hear – but part of our love to the whole person.

'Love Israel'

This may well be a suitable place to consider the efforts made by some Christians to 'bless' Jewish people and to help Jewish people return to the land of Israel. This is not just a matter of wishing them well, but involves the creation and running of organizations to achieve these goals. They call on Christians to love Israel because there is hatred and indifference all around her. Hence I put it all under the banner of 'Love Israel'. Why should Christians do this? The answer given is that we are indebted to the Jewish people and this is the way, in our generation, of showing our gratitude. I am reluctant to criticize such groups because I warm to their love for the Jewish people but the good can be the enemy of the best.

A muted witness

My concern is that evangelism is off the programme. An examination of their web sites shows that this is either an emphasis which is absent, or it is specifically repudiated. Some speak of a desire to 'share the message of his love both for Israel and the church', but there is no mention of the gospel. Can we bless Israel, and show them God's love, but with the gospel not clearly on the agenda at all? Years of personal witness to Jewish people, be it ever so low-key, have shown me that Jewish leaders and organizations do not want our love if it comes with the gospel. A leader article in the *Jewish Chronicle*[6] some years ago addressed this issue, and ended on this note: that if Christian love comes with the gospel, 'reluctantly, we will walk separately'. Yet, and this is important, many individual Jewish people do not respond this way. Showing a deep interest in their concerns, while nevertheless being up front with the gospel, is usually much appreciated, even when there is no obvious openness to the message. A well-known example is the life of Corrie Ten Boom.[7]

It seems to me that the lesson is clear, if Christians form organizations to show love to Jewish people, and then attempt to interact with Jewish leaders and institutions, they will come under strong pressure to leave out the gospel. Sadly, many have done this. It seems to me that if they want to go down this path they must be upfront about their conviction that Jews need to believe in Jesus. If that leads to reduced influence, then so be it. They can continue to provide teaching and information regarding the Jewish people for Christians, as well as encouraging and guiding individual Christians how to show love, friendship and support for Jewish people in a way that does not to downplay the gospel.

End-time prophecy influence

One particular justification for this downplaying of gospel witness is a link to end-time prophecy. Most who get involved in Love Israel activities have a particular view of end-time prophecy which appears to allow them to downplay evangelism. When the apostles asked Jesus for information on the timing of God's plans for Israel his reply was pointed, 'It is not for you to know times or seasons which the Father has put in His own authority. But you shall receive power when the Holy Spirit has come upon you; and you shall be witnesses to Me in Jerusalem, and in all Judea and Samaria, and to the end of the earth.'[8] This is starkly informing us that the timing of such things is not, and will not be revealed. We do not know the when, and any who think they do are misled or, worse, false prophets. The other point Jesus makes to the apostles, and to us, is that our preoccupation is to be the preaching of the gospel. The implication is that evangelism is never to be put on hold because of a conviction about the time we are in; such will always be wrong.

Assisting with **Aliyah**[9]

One specific outworking of Love Israel is assisting Jewish people return to the land of Israel. I mention it here because it is strongly connected to end-time prophecy and knowing the time. Our day is viewed as a special moment in the purposes of God, and it is time for all Jewish people to return to the land to be ready for God. Some even assert that most Jewish people will be saved after they are brought back to their own land – not before, justifying their lack of public witness. I can see no justification for this particular activity, and in case any should think that this approach leaves poor Jews abandoned in remote places it should be noted that the *Jewish Agency* is very efficient at getting back to Israel those who desire to go but lack the resources.

It seems to me that there is another error here – the belief that we are to understand end-time prophecy so that we can play a direct part in forwarding God's purposes. This is what, in effect, such groups are doing. They have even sent people into remote parts of places like Russia to 'fish' and 'hunt' Jewish people, so as to encourage them to return to Israel. But what example does the Bible give us for such a course of action? The fact is, God has placed no such charge or responsibility on Christians. The only way in which we specifically forward his kingdom purposes is by the work of evangelism and mission – a task we are commanded to do.

Supporting Israel in the Israel/Palestine conflict

In recent years many Christian groups have been established to show support for Israel's concerns in the Middle East conflict. They mostly come under the banner of Christian Zionism, and all have the certainty of knowing the times when it comes to end-time prophecy and the significance of the return of the Jewish people to their ancient homeland. I mention it in passing here, because the motivation for this is connected to being indebted to the Jews. I will say more on the issue in my chapter on the return to the land but let me make one simple point here. It is not necessary for Christians to have all this prophetic baggage to express their concern. Allow me to repeat that; it is not necessary! For the sake of argument let us set aside prophecy and consider the State of Israel as simply another Jewish community, but one under threat of annihilation. Christians should be concerned. Prophecy does not need to come into it. At the end of the nineteenth century the Jews of Russia suffered systematic persecution in a manner which indicated some connivance by the Russian authorities. Large public meetings of protest were organized in Britain and America by Jewish leaders, church leaders, union leaders and academics, and some changes followed. Prophecy did not enter into the matter. Undoubtedly, our times are different but political and social processes remain similar. Let Christians get involved in such to express their concern for Jews to have a homeland of their own, and to be protected from the deadly threat to their survival. The problem now is that the certainties produced by what I call the 'prophecy baggage' has led to a tendency to overlook Israeli injustices, so there is an understandable Christian response calling for voices to be raised for the plight of Palestinians, especially Christian ones. I look forward to the day when there is a working together under a banner like 'Christians for Justice and Peace in the Israel/Palestine Conflict'.

Christians from a Gentile background are indebted to the Jewish nation for all that they have received through them, but they should be level-headed and biblical about how this is expressed, and not be swept along by sentiment or dubious spiritual reasoning. May God help Christians from a Gentile background to bury pride and crucify self-sufficiency, so as to humbly acknowledge their debt to this often despised people.

PART 2

Hard Truths

6.

Israel's Unbelief

How often have you thought, 'Yes, but . . .' when God's ways are considered? It seems that something about the facts leads to a different conclusion. Or, there appears to be another truth which contradicts what has been said. I anticipate a 'Yes, but . . .' at this point in the book. I can hear someone saying: 'Yes, I see that the Bible has a lot to say about Yahweh's love for the Jewish people, but, why do so few believe? And, why have they suffered so much? Asking such questions is nothing new. What Paul wrote in Romans 9 and 10 indicates he had heard such questions. The triumphant note at the end of his exposition of the gospel in Romans 1 – 8 begs such questions. He exults that nothing 'shall be able to separate us from the love of God which is in Christ Jesus our Lord',[1] but this begs the question: Look at Israel; if God has not succeeded in keeping them, then might not the same happen to Christians today? Paul knew the time had come to face the difficulty.

The Elect

Paul's answer begins with God, and the immutability of his promises. However, he does not launch straight in, but commences by expressing his grief at Israel's loss. It seems to me that he starts by telling us of his deepest feelings because he knew that he had some hard things to say about Israel, and he wanted to make it quite clear that his attitude was not triumphalist. He is not glorying over a vanquished tormenter but grieving at the loss of beloved compatriots.

Paul begins with the sovereign choice of God. In reply to the thought that God's word, containing his covenants and promises, appeared ineffective because so many of Israel were remaining in unbelief, he simply states, 'they are not all Israel who are of Israel, nor are they all children because they are the seed of Abraham; but, "In Isaac your seed shall be called."'[2] Paul's point is that just as God made a choice between the physical descendants, the seed, of Abraham (Isaac was chosen and Ishmael was not), and between Jacob and Esau, so he makes a choice among the physical descendants of Jacob (Israel). We can best paraphrase 'they are not all Israel who are of Israel' as, 'they are not all princes with God that are descended from Jacob'.[3] This understanding of the first Israel in Paul's expression causes us to focus on their spiritual character, which is Paul's point here.

These are the elect. Paul's first use of such terminology in this passage is: 'that the purpose of God according to election might stand, not of works but of Him who calls',[4] and his design is clear, to underline that God's choice is not based on anything in them but his own inscrutable and sovereign will. If there is any doubt that this is what he is teaching we need only to look at the difficulty he anticipates in verse 14, 'Is there unrighteousness with God?' Such a question will be asked only when something appears unfair, and the teaching of unconditional election tends to provoke that response. In Romans 11 Paul teaches the same truth of God's choice among the Jewish nation when he describes the believing Jews of his own day as 'a remnant according to the election of grace'.[5] In grace the Lord had chosen them and therefore they believed, and remained faithful.

Mysterious as it may be to us, that is the explanation as to why many Jewish people remain in unbelief. God has not chosen them all to be saved. It may seem to us that God, having spent so many years preparing a people for the coming Messiah, would ensure that most of them believed in him, and that they would then carry the good news to the world; but we would be wrong, his ways are not our ways. We can only stand in awe and bow before him in humble adoration.

Some dislike such teaching and find it hard to accept, but if we care about Jewish people being saved then it is teaching full of hope, because if God had not chosen some to salvation then

Israel's Unbelief

none would be saved. The words 'I will have mercy on whomever I will have mercy',[6] remind us that we are hopelessly lost in sin, as utterly dependent on the mercy of the Lord as climbers who depend totally upon their rope when they lose their footing. The words of Isaiah put it more forcibly: 'Unless the LORD of Sabaoth had left us a seed, We would have become like Sodom, And we would have been made like Gomorrah.'[7] It is God's purpose of election, his determining that some will believe, and who they are, which ensures that the ruin is not total.

How else can we be sure of a great turning to Messiah among the Jewish people? If such a future hope for Israel depended in the last analysis on their responsiveness, then there could be no guarantee whatever that it would happen.

Responsible

Paul's explanation of Jewish unbelief does not stop with the sovereign choice of God; there is also the matter of human responsibility. What is the responsibility of Jewish people in this matter; have they made a conscious choice which results in guilt? If Jewish people are punished for failure to believe is that because of non-election or unbelief? There can be no punishment without guilt, and no guilt without sin, and Paul makes it plain that Israel's rejection of Jesus makes them 'a disobedient and contrary people'.[8] There was sin in the camp, and it was the sin of 'seeking to establish their own righteousness'.[9] That is not to say that all Jewish people were intensely focused on attaining such a righteousness through their religion, but when the reasons for Jesus' rejection are considered a few stand out as critical, such as Jesus' assertion of his equality with God and this one mentioned by Paul, establishing their own righteousness. Today, whether a Jewish person is diligent in Judaism or not, the effect of Judaism's assertion of the possibility of attaining righteousness has filtered down into the mentality of all Jewish people. I cannot remember meeting a Jewish person who did not see himself or herself as acceptable to God because they were a good person. This does not mean sin is ignored, but rather their righteous acts are overvalued, especially repentance. There is a story told of how a notorious Jewish sinner turned from his ways in a period of intense repentance, and it was observed that 'so intense was his repentance that in a few hours the sins of a lifetime were washed away'.

Messiah Jesus came to do all that was needed for sin to be forgiven and for the provision of a righteousness from God for sinners. This was the whole goal of the law revealed to Israel, but it had been misunderstood. They had made the mistake of thinking that a legalistic obedience to the law, what Paul calls the works of the law, was the way to righteousness before God, whereas it was a gift to be received by faith even while living under the law, as he explains in Romans 9:31,32, 'but Israel, pursuing the law of righteousness, has not attained to the law of righteousness. Why? Because they did not seek it by faith, but as it were, by the works of the law.'[10]

There was a life of obedience to God under the law of Moses which was not legalistic, but lived in humble gratitude for his goodness, trusting in his provision of forgiveness through sacrifice, and aware of the gift of righteousness for those who believed. Paul demonstrates this in principle in Romans 10:5–8 by explaining the words of Moses in Leviticus 18:5 and Deuteronomy 30:12–14, giving them their New Testament application in verse 9. The one who understands the message of the law must end up conscious of hopelessness. Moses anticipated this and assured Israel that it was not beyond them, as they thought. He did not mean by this that they could make it if they tried hard enough; rather he wanted them to see that if the heart was receptive to all the law said about their sinfulness, and all it offered of mercy by the sacrifices, and if they were willing to confess this, then they could be confident of God's mercy and forgiveness. This was dependence on God and not themselves. This was the word of faith. In New Testament times that is expressed by faith in the Lord Jesus, in particular his having been raised by God from the dead.

At the time of Jesus there were Israelites with such an understanding of Moses, people like Zachariah, Anna and Simeon, of whom we read in the early chapters of Luke. Their faith and humility shines out from the page. I cannot doubt that as the message of Jesus became clear to them, they would have accepted it as entirely consistent with the faith they already possessed. For many others, as they heard the gospel message, they understood for the first time about their hopelessness in sin and saw the provision for righteousness in Jesus. They believed and were forgiven. But too many in Israel thought otherwise and continued, in one way or another, in a self-righteous approach to God. In this they were fully responsible for their thoughts and actions. This way of righteousness is still taught by the rabbis, and its consequences for most of Israel have been disastrous.

Some Reflections

Alternative explanations

I am aware that many Christians find the teaching of God's election to salvation a difficult one to accept. They happily acknowledge that God is sovereign over all things but are uneasy with a teaching which seems to imply that humans have no freedom, a sort of fatalism. But I do not find that such Christians have a problem with God's way of choosing Israel. They accept that God chose Abraham, Isaac and Jacob, and in so doing passed by other individuals and other nations in the world, yet have difficulty in accepting that he acts in the same way when a person becomes a Christian. They stand or fall together.

Serious implications

What should be recognized is that to reject this truth of election has serious implications. The first is that the Jews are more wicked than other people; an implication which would delight anti-Semites. What I mean is, if there is no such thing as unconditional election by God then human responsibility is the key factor. That being so, and bearing in mind that the Jews have received more privileges than others but remain more determined in their unbelief, they must somehow be much worse than others. Not a conclusion we should welcome.

The second implication is that missionaries to the Jews must be seriously inept at their work compared to other missionaries because they see so little fruit by comparison. To escape such conclusions some like to stress the effect of 'Christian' anti-Semitism as having made it especially hard for Jews to consider Jesus. I do not doubt that the persecution of Jewish people in the name of Jesus has had disastrous effects, but the rejection of Messiah Jesus and the apostles by the majority of the nation and its leaders began long before any such phenomenon as 'Christian' anti-Semitism.

Encouragement to Witness

God has guaranteed fruitfulness for the gospel among Jewish people! Paul teaches in Romans 11 there will always be some saved because of God's election of grace.[11] I do not know that there is such a promise to any other nation. Witness to Jewish people is strewn with difficulties, but God encourages us to persevere by assuring us the work will be fruitful.

A Restraint on Frustration

Resistance to the gospel by Jewish people is often very persistent. The fact that we start with the same book and come to radically different conclusions can produce irritation and frustration. The fact that someone very precious to us (Jesus) is dismissed or even derided is hurtful. This may go on from year to year in our encounters with Jewish neighbours or work colleagues. It is tempting to dismiss them as hopeless cases. The doctrine of election reminds us that we are in God's hands and if he chooses he can change the situation in a moment.

Election in Apologetics?

There is no doubt that we must present the gospel to Jewish people and warn them of their responsibility to believe it, and sometimes we will need to use apologetics to answer difficulties and objections, but should we ever mention election as the reason for Jewish unbelief? Jesus is our example here, as in John 10:26 when he speaks of his sheep, telling those who were antagonistic, 'You do not believe, because you are not of My sheep.' It seems to me that this was an extreme measure designed to alarm people who were confident in their rejection of him. Later in the same encounter Jesus says to them, 'Though you do not believe me, believe the works', showing that he still held out hope to them. I have often heard it said by Jewish people, 'Jesus could not be the Messiah because most Jews do not believe', as if the key factor is their wisdom. It may be appropriate to point out the factor of God's choice. Hopefully this will dent their self-confidence and cause them to humbly seek God.

Unbelief is Serious

Paul's stress on election did not lead him to tone down his remarks on their responsibility to believe. They were not ignorant; rather he describes them as disobedient and contrary. It is the same today. If a Jewish person fails to turn to Jesus then the day will come when he or she will become aware of their great loss and that they have only themselves to blame. This should impel Christians to face Jewish people with the danger of seeking to establish their own righteousness and rejecting Messiah's, all the while encouraging them with the knowledge that God's arms are open wide.

7.

Kingdom: Then and Now

'Therefore I say to you, the kingdom of God will be taken from you and given to a nation bearing the fruits of it.'[1]

Ominous words! Words spoken by Jesus during his final visit to Jerusalem. He had entered the city riding on a donkey and many of the people had greeted him as Messiah, laying their clothes or palm branches on the ground before him, crying out praises and the messianic greeting, 'Blessed is he who comes in the name of Yahweh'. Excitement and anticipation filled the air. However, there can be little doubt that his first action would have shocked many – he cleansed an area of the temple of its traders, overturning their tables and driving them out. Shocking it may have been but it presaged more of the same. As might be expected, the chief priests and rulers did not take it lying down but questioned him the next day with the words, 'By what authority are You doing these things?'[2] What followed was a set of dire warnings to Israel's leaders that their attitude to him was leading the nation to the edge of a precipice, resulting in the loss of the kingdom.

Warnings to Israel's Leaders

Our Lord's response to their question is in Matthew 21:23–46 and it has several parts but our concern is his ominous declaration – 'The kingdom of God will be taken from you and given to a nation bearing the fruits of it.' The sense of it seems clear – the national entity of Israel, living under the Mosaic covenant, would no longer be the people who would be the exclusive possessors of

God's kingdom in the earth; others were to receive it – but what exactly did he mean? As we look at this matter more carefully we should note that the words were spoken to the legitimate Jewish leadership and, as such, to those whom they represented. This is a prophecy spoken to the whole nation, something that will be underlined when we look at the word 'nation'.

The Kingdom of God

What is the kingdom of God? Literally, the phrase means 'the kingship of God', and points to the people over whom God rules, those who submit to him. As Jesus spoke, the nation of Israel was that people and in Romans 9 Paul lists some of the manifestations of this status: a written revelation from God, the visible manifestation of God's presence, his covenants and promises, a land in which to dwell, and a means of approach to him.[3] Much of this was visible and tangible and it all seemed set to endure, but no Israelite should have expected things to remain exactly as they were, because the kingdom was always understood to have an eschatological dimension – the hope of a more glorious future with a worldwide dimension. One of Jesus' hearers, apparently a man of some significance in the community, called out to him during a meal, 'Blessed is he who shall eat bread in the kingdom of God!'[4] As an Israelite was he not in the kingdom already? Clearly he understood that some better thing was promised for the days of the Messiah.

Jesus' own language of the kingdom expresses the same idea of development. He frequently used the phrase 'kingdom of God' (or kingdom of heaven) as if he was speaking of something entirely new, as if there was no kingdom of God around on the earth before. And yet it was not completely new, for Jesus spoke of it being taken away, teaching that the kingdom of God he announced was in fact a development of what God had already established. Clearly, the degree of change expected under Messiah was so great as to be almost something completely new, despite being a development from what existed.

Jesus also spoke of the kingdom as something yet future. In his description of the final judgement he portrayed himself as saying to his people, 'Come, you blessed of My Father, inherit the kingdom prepared for you from the foundation of the world.'[5] The kingdom has yet to reach its glorious consummation.

In summary we can say that a great change came with the Messiah's appearing. God had come among his people as he had promised. With that glorious incarnation came other changes. The manifestations of God's kingdom were to be less visible and tangible, more spiritual. Jesus says to Pilate, 'My kingdom is not of this world',[6] and the apostle Paul wrote, 'For the kingdom of God is not eating and drinking (referring to the clean/unclean distinction of the law), but righteousness and peace and joy in the Holy Spirit.'[7] Also, the kingdom is entered differently, by regeneration, a spiritual birth from above,[8] whereas before it was by natural birth and circumcision (or by conversion for proselytes). The final change will come with Messiah's second coming, the resurrection of the body to be a spiritual body. Then the kingdom will take on its final form, which Paul tells us 'flesh and blood cannot inherit'.[9]

The Kingdom Nation

To whom was Jesus referring when he said, 'The kingdom of God will be . . . given to a nation bearing the fruits of it'? Who is this nation? A brief word study may help at this point. *Ethnos* and *laos* are the two main words used in the New Testament to refer to a group of people. Although they contain overlapping ideas they emphasize distinct concepts, as can be seen by their both being used in John's full-orbed description of the whole of humanity in a verse like Revelation 5:9, 'Out of every tribe and tongue and people (*laos*) and nation (*ethnos*)'. *Ethnos*, the word from which we derive 'ethnic' in English, is almost always translated 'nation', and refers to what we would call national entities (not necessarily our modern nation states), people bound together by ties of blood, geography, history, culture, etc. It is used by the Lord Jesus of the nations of the world,[10] and the Jewish leaders used it to describe the Jewish people.[11] *Laos* is best-translated 'people' and is a more general term, frequently used to describe a crowd gathered for some purpose, or a group defined by some common experience. It is significant that *ethnos* is used to describe this new group to whom the kingdom was to be given because we might have expected *laos*. We might have expected Jesus to indicate a forthcoming internal transfer of power to another group of leaders within Israel, e.g. the apostles, and for that *laos* would have been appropriate, indicating a continuing, distinctively Jewish entity. But *ethnos* indicates a much more drastic change. It actually sounds as if another ethnic group, say the Greeks or the Egyptians, was to now have the kingdom. An unthinkable thought!

Elsewhere in the New Testament we see God's purpose of world redemption unfolding with Gentiles included among believing Jews in a new entity. Among the terms used to describe this new entity is 'kingdom', using a variety of phrases to express it. For example, 'For the kingdom of God is not eating and drinking, but righteousness and peace and joy in the Holy Spirit. For he who serves Christ in these things is acceptable to God and approved by men.'[12] Believers in Jesus – Jew and Gentile – are the kingdom. They are the ones to whom the kingdom has been given; they are the new *ethnos*, the new nation of which Jesus spoke.

As stated above, we might have expected *laos* to be used because what binds these Jews and Gentiles is belief in Jesus, but when we appreciate that these believers are also bound together by the indwelling of a divine person, the Spirit of the living God, then we are not so surprised that Jesus used *ethnos*. Here is a community dramatically distinct from Israel because of such a privilege, and dramatically distinct from the unbelieving world around them. For such, *laos* is not strong enough and *ethnos* is necessary.

There are places in the New Testament where both words are used of this new kingdom people. The apostle Peter uses both *ethnos* and *laos* together to describe believers in Jesus. They are, 'a chosen generation, a royal priesthood, a holy nation (*ethnos*), His own special people (*laos*)'.[13] They are a *laos*, being bound by belief, trust, spiritual life, etc., but they are so distinct from those around them that they can be described as an *ethnos*, holiness being what distinguishes them. Peter is describing the *ecclesia*, the church, that community which was composed of all believers in Jesus, whether Jew or Gentile; they are a people and a nation.[14]

If any readers still have doubts about the church being the new kingdom nation then it may help to consider that all the characteristics of the kingdom under Moses are seen, in their new covenant form, in the church. Israel was called out to be God's people; they were brought into a covenant with the Lord, receiving promises and possessing a written revelation from God; so too the church. As Israel had a priesthood and knew God's Shekinah presence, so the church approaches the Lord through Messiah's priesthood, and God's presence is among them by his Spirit. This is especially seen by the way the New Testament refers to the church as 'the temple of God'[15] and as 'Jerusalem above'.[16] Such descriptions indicate a clear continuity between the church and the nation of Israel, one being the fulfilment of the other, but also a new phase of God's work of redemption in the world – the kingdom of his Son.

One practical point I would make here is that Christians should be careful with their terminology. Often when Gentile Christians describe this body, the church, they speak as if it is a Gentile entity. It is as if Jesus had said, 'The kingdom will be taken from you (Israel) and given to the Gentiles', but he said no such thing. It is a body composed of Jews and Gentiles who believe. What God began with Israel, he has expanded to include the Gentiles. In so doing he has altered its form, but he has not abandoned the Jewish people.

While all this change was according to the predetermined plan and purpose of God, yet the element of judgement upon Israel cannot be ignored. God's kingdom was taken away because of fruitlessness, a fruitlessness vividly pictured in an incident previous to this encounter between Jesus and the Jewish leaders, his cursing of an unfruitful fig tree.[17] The nation as a whole was not bearing fruit to God, particularly manifested by their negative response to the Messiah among them. Of course, many did believe, and many continue to do so now but the majority did not, either then or now. This fruitlessness drew down God's judgement.

The sad reality of this fact can be illustrated by comparing a true church today with a synagogue. If you want to know the way back to God, how to be forgiven and how to have everlasting life, you will not hear a message within a synagogue explaining these truths to you in a way that is in line with the Scriptures. The synagogue has much that is beautiful about it in its services, even containing many words of Scripture and expressions of biblical truth, but it has Ichabod written all over it – the glory has departed. By contrast, all those things of salvation and a present experience of God are found in a New Testament church. There, salvation can be experienced, God is among his people and there he reigns as king.

The People of Israel Today

So where does all this leave the Jewish people, as a people, today? Does the loss of the kingdom mean the loss of everything, except that God will always save a remnant from among them? In answering such questions Christians tend to polarize. Some believe they have lost everything, others that it will all be given back when Jesus returns. I want to go into more detail on this issue in a subsequent chapter but here I would simply like to draw attention to the distinction between kingdom and covenant, because I believe this helps to avoid polarization.

Kingdom and Covenant

The kingdom has been taken away but Israel's covenant status remains. Romans 11:1 has been alluded to before, and will be again, but it bears repeating that for Paul to describe Israel in unbelief as 'his [God's] people' is to state unequivocally that a covenant relationship remains in force. Later in the same chapter this is underlined by 'the gifts and the calling of God are irrevocable'. If it is asked, which covenant, then it must be the Abrahamic, which is made clear by Paul's words in verse 28, they are 'beloved for the sake of the fathers'. If it is asked what is meant by gifts and calling, then Paul must have in mind the privileges he lists in Romans 9:4,5.

The Abrahamic covenant is God's foundational promise covenant. Both the Mosaic and the new covenants can be viewed as administrative covenants, built upon that promise covenant to Abraham, designed to administer the promise in their two different situations. It is as if an architect designs a foundation for a house with two structures in mind. The first one for a family's initial needs, which will be demolished at some point to make room for a larger and better home when the family has grown. However, there is a problem. Some members of the family have decided they prefer the first house and have built something with a passing resemblance to it on a corner of the foundation. The architect has graciously allowed for this in his plans but has warned them that, although their house will survive, yet it will not last very long and they need to leave it and get into the new house if they want to be safe. The covenant which gave Israel the kingdom (Mosaic) has gone, and the kingdom with it, but the covenant made with Abraham and his offspring remains, full of promises, especially of Messiah and his new covenant, to be entered by faith.

8.

Wrath to the Uttermost

Awesome words! They were written by a Jew who tells us elsewhere that he had continual grief in his heart over the unbelief of his people. Paul's love for his people meant he was not afraid to face and teach hard truths about them, as his words in 1 Thessalonians 2:14–16 make plain.

> For you also suffered the same things from your own countrymen, just as they did from the Judeans, who killed both the Lord Jesus and their own prophets, and have persecuted us; and they do not please God and are contrary to all men, forbidding us to speak to the Gentiles that they may be saved, so as always to fill up the measure of their sins; but wrath has come upon them to the uttermost.

By these words Paul describes the consequences for his people of their wrong religious attitudes. It is a bleak picture, and so we are tempted to avoid it, but the words must be faced and considered carefully. I believe the best way to approach this subject is to state the relevant biblical principles and then to try to understand their relationship to Israel's troubles. In doing so there is a need to acknowledge that the details of God's ways are often hidden from us and beyond our grasp, for God is God and we are but finite creatures.

God Punishes the Disobedience of His People

This is quite explicit in the terms of the Mosaic covenant and a passage like Deuteronomy 28 makes it clear. For example, Moses taught:

But it shall come to pass, if you do not obey the voice of the LORD your God, to observe carefully all his commandments . . . the LORD will change the rain of your land to powder and dust . . . the LORD will strike you with madness and blindness and confusion of heart . . . the LORD will scatter you among all peoples, from one end of the earth to the other . . . you shall fear day and night and have no assurance of life.[1]

Although it is a mistake to portray Old Testament history as all failure yet there were times of disobedience which led to punishment. The most signal one in that history was the deportation of God's people to Babylon after the fall of Jerusalem to the Chaldeans in 605 BC. God had warned it would come because of persistent idolatry and it did come. For many years he had been good to Israel, blessing their obedience and being patient and longsuffering with their sins, but when the time came for punishment he acted. Exile was God's extreme and through it God was saying he wanted them out of his sight, away from the temple where his presence was manifested; their sin had made them unbearable. It happened through the Chaldeans and again in AD 70 when the Romans conquered Jerusalem. Jesus clearly taught that the reason for this second exile was 'because you did not know the time of your visitation'.[2] That is, they had failed as a nation to recognize the Messiah in their midst. There could be no greater failure to listen to God than to resist the words of the great Prophet when he came. The God of Israel will act against sin in his people and in his world.[3]

The Greatest Punishment

In 1 Thessalonians 2:14–16 Paul was writing to the believers to encourage them, informing them that they were not alone in their sufferings; their brothers and sisters in Judea had likewise suffered. He then elaborates regarding the unbelief of the Judeans, their behaviour and its consequence. It is at the end of this passage that he uses the expression 'wrath . . . to the uttermost'.

Paul's primary focus is the sins of the Jews in Judea and particularly their leaders. Later in this chapter we will consider John's use of the term 'the Jews' and see that his focus is the same when it comes to apportioning blame for the death of Jesus. However, Paul's reference to killing their own prophets broadens his consideration to earlier generations and his phrases 'wrath . . . to the uttermost' and 'always to fill up' mean that the effects upon future generations are within his horizon. Hence we have to consider what Paul is saying about the Judeans and also the impact upon subsequent generations of Jewish people.

Wrath to the uttermost

These words tempt us to think of the destruction of Jerusalem by the Romans, or even other events further on in history, but I do not think Paul had such in mind because he writes in the past tense, 'wrath has come upon them'. The destruction of Jerusalem had not taken place when Paul wrote, so he could not be referring to it. It seems to me that Paul was thinking of something we have already considered – the taking away from the Jewish people of their unique status as God's kingdom in the world. There could be no greater punishment than to lose that status; and it had happened; the kingdom had already being given to others. It was the most extreme manifestation of God's anger towards a people – wrath to the uttermost. But what have been the consequences for subsequent generations? Paul's phrase 'always to fill up' takes us into this area of consequences.

Filling up the Measure of Sin Always

The ongoing sufferings and troubles of the Jewish people must be viewed in the light of Paul's expression: 'so as always to fill up *the measure* of their sins' (italics here indicate words supplied by my translation, some use the words 'to the limit'). Paul sees their sinful behaviour as having a filling-up effect. To understand this unusual phrase we can go to two other places where it is used in Scripture. In Genesis 15:16 Yahweh tells Abram something about the future of his descendants, particularly their time in Egypt and subsequent deliverance. The timing is described in this way: 'In the fourth generation they shall return here, for the iniquity of the Amorites is not yet complete [i.e. full].' We know that Israel's return involved judgement upon the people of Canaan (here described as the Amorites), and it is clear from these words that at the time the Lord spoke to Abram their sins had not reached the point which God had fixed as the level for judgement. Further degeneration was necessary for them to reach that point, and then God would punish. The New Testament passage is Matthew 23:32 where Jesus is in the middle of giving his most serious warning to the Jewish leaders, who were refusing to hear him and were plotting his death. He portrays them as following in the footsteps of those before them who had put to death the prophets of Israel, and he concludes by saying, 'Fill up, then, the measure of your fathers' guilt.' Again we have this concept of sin accumulating to a fixed point, to a measure. He is saying that their rejection of him will be the sin which brings to completion, which fills to the brim, this particular guilt of Israel's leaders in rejecting God's spokesmen. Judgement would come upon their generation, with the loss of the kingdom and the destruction of Jerusalem in AD 70.

It is within this framework of thought that we are to understand Paul's expression regarding the sins of his people. The difference being that Paul uses the word 'always' – 'so as always to fill up'. What he is teaching is that this process goes on. Throughout history there will be times when their sins will reach a point when God will act to punish. The picture is of a people who experience much of his goodness, grace and longsuffering for much of the time, and yet are still living in disobedience to God, still rejecting his Son, so that the measure of their sin mounts. Then at some point, known only to God, everything changes, the moment for punishment arrives, and the means he has appointed will appear, and troubles will come upon Jewish people somewhere.

This is not an especially Jewish experience. God deals with all nations on the same principle. His words to Abram about the iniquity of the Amorites not yet being full were referring to a Gentile nation, a nation not in any special covenant with God, as per all the nations of the world today. The only difference lies in the nature of the sins described by Paul in 1 Thessalonians 2:15,16, ones typical of Jewish people. Due to events of history and dearly held philosophies, nations develop their own sinful traits. The Jewish nation is no different and to that extent they are to be viewed like other nations. They are not to be singled out as particularly evil, doomed to a permanent curse under the Mosaic law, never to have hope as a nation of anything other than permanent wandering, servitude and fear.

Other Explanations for Subsequent Jewish Sufferings

Here I want to very briefly present some other thoughts from Jews and Christians.

Jewish thinkers

The Jewish people themselves have a variety of answers, from agnosticism regarding God's ways to blaming their fellow-Jews who are not observant of the Torah. The religious would see Moses' law as still in force and so today's failures to obey have consequences in the here and now. However, the more careful religious thinkers would point out that if they are out of the land it is because of a sin committed by the people while still in the land, and so any troubles today are traceable back to some ancient sin which led God to send them into exile and there to turn his back upon them. When he does that his protection is lost and there will be times of trouble from their enemies. As to why troubles happen in one place and not another, at one time and not another, very few would venture to suggest.

The Mosaic covenant today?

As Christians think about the experiences of the Jewish people they inevitably wrestle with these same questions. The first question concerns the Mosaic covenant; is it still in force? The answer of Scripture is surely, no. Jeremiah spoke of a new covenant which God would make with Israel as a fulfilment of the Mosaic one.[4] Zechariah described God's breaking of his covenant and linked it to their contempt for the Lord's servant.[5] Jesus the Messiah inaugurated this new covenant with Israel at his final Passover meal with his disciples.[6] In Hebrews we read: 'In that He says, "A new covenant", He has made the first obsolete' and, speaking of Jesus,

'He is also Mediator of a better covenant, which was established on better promises.'[7] Finally, the apostle to the Gentiles described himself as a minister of the new covenant.[8] All of which makes it quite plain that the Mosaic covenant is no longer in force, either for Israel or the church of Jesus the Messiah.

However, there is a sense in which the Mosaic covenant still affects the Jewish people. The dispersion of the Jewish people among the nations was a consequence of one major act of disobedience under the Mosaic covenant – the rejection of God's Messiah by the leaders and the majority of the nation.

The fathers and the children

This matter of consequences is what is indicated by the words in the second commandment: 'I, the LORD your God, am a jealous God, visiting the iniquity of the fathers upon the children to the third and fourth generations of those who hate Me.'[9] The 'visiting' refers to the consequences of the sins of the fathers, not that the children are accounted guilty. There is cause and effect in God's moral universe and God has not undertaken to constantly intervene to prevent consequences. However, he has promised a limit.

This raises a question with regard to Israel, how come the consequences have gone on for generations? To answer this I want to look at the sins of the Judeans which Paul mentions, and consider how they are manifested among Jewish people today because it is the continuing wrong attitudes in the same vein that fill up the measure of sin.

Why Is Paul Doing This?

This is a reasonable question. He could have stopped at the end of 1 Thessalonians 2:14 as that would have made his point, that the Thessalonians should not be surprised at these troubles – they had been experienced by believers since the gospel began in Judea.

One answer is that he is making it quite plain that the Judeans of Jesus' day were especially guilty of the particular sins mentioned and, most significantly, of the death of Jesus. Maybe people in his day were already blaming all Jews for the death of Jesus. If so, Paul is firmly knocking such an idea on the head.

A second consideration is the context of the Thessalonians. It seems to me that the opposition from Jewish people in Thessalonica was unusually energetic. We read in Acts 17 of them gathering a mob, causing city-wide uproar and hauling some believers before the rulers, and then, when they heard of how the gospel preachers were having similar success in Berea, they headed off there and stirred up the crowds again.[10] It is not difficult to imagine such hostile Jewish individuals taunting the new believers, especially the Gentiles; boasting that they were the real Jews who understood the law and could not get it wrong about the Messiah; Gentiles were just too ignorant of these matters to get it right. The letters of Jesus in Revelation to the churches in Smyrna and Philadelphia indicate that this was a problem, because there Jesus speaks of 'the blasphemy of those who say they are Jews and are not, but are a synagogue of Satan'.[11] In this context we can see why Paul would elaborate the sins of Israel, especially the long tradition of rejecting God's spokesmen, to demonstrate that their opponents had no automatic claim to wisdom because they were Jewish. This is an ongoing problem for Gentiles speaking with Jewish people, more especially the orthodox. I cannot remember how many times I have been told, or been taunted by religious Jews that, 'We are the people, you need to come to us if you want to understand the Scriptures'. It is a daunting challenge for the unwary and it seems to me that these words of Paul are designed to help Gentile Christians not to be intimidated.

The Particular Sins Paul Mentions (1 Thessalonians 2:15,16)

This is not an easy matter to deal with. Not simply because I have no desire to appear censorious or self-righteous but also because we live in a day and age in which it is still a taboo subject due to the Holocaust. But we have to face up to what Scripture does say. Before Paul launched into Romans 9 – 11, aware that he had some hard things to say about his people, he first of all declared his love for them.[12] Likewise, I can only declare that, as a non-Jew, I have given my life to the wellbeing of Jewish people and continue to aim at the level which Paul reached – a continual grief in the heart at their great loss and a willingness to make any sacrifice that would assist their salvation.

As Paul describes his countrymen's particular sins we must take note of the context so as to keep things in proportion. The whole subject arose because the Thessalonian Christians were being persecuted by their own countrymen, which underlines that persecution of the disciples of Jesus was not unique to the Jews; non-Jews were doing it too. It was a common manifestation of humanity's hatred of the light.

Paul has six particular charges to lay at the door of the Judeans concerning their response to God's truth. When we consider how this has affected other generations I believe the focus must be on those who have the religious mindset of those Judeans, by which I mean deeply religious, orthodox Jews. When we consider the effects on Jewish people today I want to temper what is said regarding the Jewish people by noting how the same undesirable qualities can be seen in people of other religions and how Judaism and Jewish culture produce many beneficial effects. However, the negative cannot be avoided.

'Who killed the Lord Jesus'

It is a stark fact of history that some of the Judean leaders plotted to kill Jesus, arranged for his arrest and trial, condemned him for his claim to be the Messiah, stirred up their compliant countrymen to have him condemned by the Roman governor and approved his execution. This action, in the face of his perfection, truth, grace, power and love was more reprehensible than any other in history. Even Pilate, the Roman governor, detected they were motivated by envy,[13] finding no fault in him.[14] Any reader not disposed to accept the New Testament account may find it helpful to take note of the fact that the prophet Isaiah expected that God's innocent servant–Messiah would be unjustly condemned to death,[15] and King David spoke of Messiah being rejected by the rulers of his day.[16] The New Testament is not charging Jewish people with something the Hebrew Scriptures did not anticipate. God had come among them in the person of his incarnate Son and had been refused and rejected and put to death. Yet it ought to be remembered that, in a spiritual sense, this is what all people do when they refuse to acknowledge God or obey him – they want him dead.

To lessen the impact of this charge it is often pointed out that Jesus was condemned and crucified by the Romans, who alone had the power of capital punishment in Judea at that time. The inference being that they bore the greater guilt and so the Gentiles were more culpable than the Jews. Jesus himself taught the opposite. Speaking to Pilate he said, 'The one who delivered Me to you has the greater sin.'[17] The plotting of the Jewish leadership made their crime more heinous. The laws of most nations make a distinction between premeditated murder (in cold blood) and a killing done in the heat of the moment. The former is rightly seen as worse than the latter, and that was how Jesus was killed. Pilate was not guiltless, for Jesus' words state that his actions were sinful, but they were not as sinful as the actions of others. Pilate had declared Jesus innocent and then proceeded to hand him over to death.

Another way that the charge is lessened is to say that there is a sense in which we all killed Jesus, because the cross was necessary to pay the price of sin, and we are all sinners. I am happy to acknowledge the truth of that thought. What it does is to prevent others from pointing the finger self-righteously at the Jewish people, although it does not really lessen the charge itself.

While Jewish people today are not guilty of the act of crucifying Jesus yet their continuing rejection of him as Messiah, following in the footsteps of those who did condemn him, is a serious sin. Those among them who justify his execution as an apostate are approving what their forefathers did. These attitudes are sins which 'fill up the measure of their sins' and are related to the original sin of the Judeans.

'Killed their own prophets'

This charge links the Judeans who condemned Jesus with the actions of their fathers. Why mention this? It seems to me that, as mentioned above, Paul is helping the new Christians in Thessalonica not to be intimidated by Jewish claims to a long pedigree of wisdom. Paul's point is that they also had a long pedigree of rejection. It is a sad fact that today relatively few Jewish people read the prophets, and the orthodox who do will usually see the prophetic denunciations as directed to Jews other than themselves.

'Have persecuted us'

This pattern of rejection continued in the way Jesus' messengers were treated by the Judeans, as Paul's own experience in Judea demonstrated. Here again was encouragement for the Thessalonian believers who were Gentiles. A Jewish scholar like Paul was receiving the same treatment as they were; being 'ignorant' Gentiles was not the issue.

This persecuting behaviour towards fellow-Jews who believe in Jesus, and towards those who take the gospel to Jewish people, continues to this day. At best such are grimly tolerated, but more often they are despised, reviled, threatened and sometimes abused and disowned. It is a price which they expect to pay but that does not lessen the guilt of the persecutors. This is not a uniquely Jewish phenomenon; many who convert from a traditional religion to Christianity are persecuted by their countrymen.

'Do not please God'

This expression is primarily concerned with their religious attitudes and behaviour, not moral lifestyle. It was one in which they sought to establish their own righteousness and rejected that offered by Messiah Jesus;[18] something deeply displeasing to God. Again, we may detect a note of 'don't be afraid of them', to help the struggling Thessalonian Christians. Among the Jewish people today the majority is in the category of those who do not please God. Their failure to trust the Lord's way of salvation means they displease him. The same goes for multitudes of religious people in the world who reject God's way of salvation, church-attenders included. This is not meant to deny that there are many Jewish people who are good citizens who behave in law-abiding ways and are good neighbours, trying to do things which God's word approves.

Judaism today, for all its good points, is a religion which has rejected Jesus as Messiah. The word 'Judaism' (*Ioudaismos*, Gk) appears only twice in the New Testament,[19] where Paul uses it to describe the religion he held to before his conversion – 'For you have heard of my former conduct in Judaism'. He sees it as a religion which opposes the gospel, and it remains such today. It can be defined today as, 'the religion of the Jews in contrast to that of the Old Testament'.[20] A book written to describe modern Judaism to the outsider has the title, *To Heaven with the Scribes and Pharisees*, and the sub-title, 'The Jewish Path to God'. You can't get much more 'in your face' than that, because the author knew full well that Jesus taught the opposite.

I could write more but I have no great desire to do so. Jewish religious practice does indeed have a beauty which uplifts and enriches in a religious and moral way, but God is looking for a love for his Son.

'Contrary to all men'

This is an astonishing statement in that it seems so comprehensive. Where is the amiable, socially adept Jew of Paul's day who oiled the wheels of commerce, played a significant role in politics, society and the arts, and whose contribution to humankind's wellbeing was the same then as now? We need to remember again that Paul has in mind those deeply religious Judeans of his day, not all Jewish people. It seems to me that he particularly has in view people like himself before his conversion because this is the sort of language he uses to describe himself as he was. In 1 Timothy 1:13 he writes, 'I was formerly a blasphemer, a persecutor, and an insolent man.' It is this latter expression that is akin to the idea of contrariness. He had been there and understood.

What produced this contrariness, and still produces it today among the spiritual descendants of the Judeans? My understanding is as follows. The Judeans were conscious of their calling to stand for God in an idolatrous world but without divine favour or power then the task was beyond them. Rather than being winsome they were contrary. For today's religious Jews, living among the nations constantly brings them into conflict with the views and practices of others and they have not done any better. Non-Jews have often made matters worse by the way they have reacted, setting up a cycle of contrariness. Christians will understand this struggle. They experience the difficulties of the same calling but they are born again of the Spirit and indwelt by him; they have the resources to enter the conflict with grace and truth. Even so, history and experience show how often they have failed. It seems that the way religious Jews have coped is by both defensiveness and aggressiveness, and the outcome has been contrariness. This is not helped today by some teachings in Judaism which promote pride. The traditional story of Judaism, that God offered his law to all the nations at Sinai but none wanted it but the Jews, is hardly designed to produce humility before God or a humble attitude to others. The mystical teaching among some Hasidic Jews that only a Jew has a second soul which is part of God and hence capable of great good, whereas the Gentiles have but one soul which is capable of nothing but evil, is not likely to create a positive attitude to non-Jews either. As a man thinks so he is.

This is relevant to the contemporary situation in the Middle East and I think it is worth pausing to make a brief comment. There are clearly two conflicts going on between Israel and the Palestinians. There is one between the fundamentalists on both sides and one between the remainder on each side. The majority in the 'remainders' not only wants peace but also is prepared to make painful compromises to get it. It is the fundamentalists who are holding things back. Most blame attaches to violent Islamists but those orthodox Jews who exhibit this contrary spirit because of their religious principles, and will not compromise on land but want all which belonged to Israel in Bible days, are not helping, especially when they use illegal methods to obtain it.

'Forbidding us to speak to the Gentiles'

It would seem that this was a greater problem to Paul than it is today. Not only did many Jews disagree with Paul's message about Jesus the Messiah but also they felt threatened by so many Gentiles believing it, and hence some opposed it.

Is this likely to happen today? Certainly Jewish religious leaders might be tempted to lend their voice to the chorus of disapproval which greets Christian claims today, if only to ward off attempts to evangelize them. But beyond that one well-known orthodox rabbi has used arguments which would certainly lead to 'forbidding to speak to Gentiles'. In 1998 Rabbi Shmuel Boteach, in his anger at attempts to convert Jewish people, described evangelism as 'racist'.

His reason for using such a term was that, in his view, all religions are an expression of the genius of the community which created them, hence to oppose that religion *in toto* would be to denigrate that people themselves, a sort of racism. By such reasoning Christianity is racist.

Paul's description of his own people is a sorry one, and one which caused him much heartache. It has not been an easy one to explore here but it has had to be faced, and my hope is that good things will come out of it. The 'filling up of sins' considered here can best be neutralized through Jewish people turning from them and believing the good news. Christians must share that good news with Jewish friends and they must realize that to be involved with ministry to the Jewish people is no easy matter, however, they should not be intimidated.

Four Specific Consequences for Jewish People

Elsewhere in the New Testament there are statements that more precisely describe the consequences of unbelief for Jewish people, and we need to look at these briefly before looking at the matter of the responsibility of those who have brought trouble on the Jewish people.

Hardening

In Romans 11:7–10 Paul quotes from the Old Testament to describe a hardening which will affect Jewish people who do not believe, producing a 'spirit of stupor', along with a blindness and deafness to the truth. The same hardness will affect any who hear about Jesus and firmly reject his claims. Someone may attend a church for years and then turn their back on it all. The effect on them will be the same as described here. Elsewhere Paul describes the effect on Jewish people as 'a veil . . . on their heart' when the law is read, so that they cannot see Messiah in it.[21] It has often been said to me by Christians, 'Why can't they see it? It's so clear!' Yes, it is, but there is a veil on the heart obscuring the truth. That is not to say the Jewish people cannot intellectually grasp that messianic prophecy portrays Jesus. I was a steward at an exhibition of Jewish artefacts where the only presentation of the gospel was the text of Isaiah 53 on a poster on the wall. Having read it an educated Jewish lady came up to me and asked if Isaiah lived before or after Jesus. When I had told her the answer she remarked, 'Makes you think, doesn't it?' Intellectually she had no problem grasping what Isaiah was saying and the connection to Jesus. None of this indicates hopelessness; God removes the veil when a Jewish person's heart turns to the Lord.

Synagogue of Satan

It seems to me that this hardness and blindness, with a consequent preference for error and false doctrine, led to the synagogue being described by Jesus as a 'synagogue of Satan', and Jews as those 'who say they are Jews and are not'.[22] I referred to this briefly above and I want to mention it again to make the point that although such powerful terms can conjure up a picture of all sorts of wicked goings on in a synagogue, akin to satanic worship, and of Jews as somehow in league with the devil, nevertheless such conclusions should be firmly resisted. The words are meant to point only to the fact that those who remained in the synagogue were following a lie, and hence under the control of Satan though unaware of it. The same can be said of churches which have denied the gospel but continue on like a religious theatre.

There is much to admire about the synagogue, the building is often fine and the services beautiful, the people are usually cordial and educated, and the social activities beneficial, but at its spiritual core it is a Messiah-rejecting institution.

Table a snare; backs bent

In that same passage of Romans referred to above (Rom. 11:7–10) Paul quotes from the Psalms, 'Let their table become a snare and a trap, A stumbling block and a recompense to them.' It is possible that the expression 'their table' is referring to the set feasts of Israel. Most Jewish people know about biblical events from these celebrations but the problem is that, although their messianic import is not totally ignored, the stress is on what God did for them in the past and that he is with them today. The danger is to become fixed in a confidence that all is well. The feasts are significant social occasions and Jewish people have an admirable capacity to socialize and enjoy life; it is something I have enjoyed through friendships with Jewish people over many years. It is a blessing for churches when Jewish believers bring this gift to church life.

The expression 'bow down their back always' at the end of Romans 11:10 is a dismal picture of either an oppressed condition or a state of fear, both of which are all too accurate descriptions of the Jewish people at certain phases of their history. It has not been all doom and gloom, far from it, but the gloom has been very gloomy; we can but sigh deeply when we consider such matters.

Bondage to the law

In Galatians 4:25 Paul describes Jerusalem, meaning the Jewish people as a nation, as 'in bondage with her children', bondage to obedience to keep the whole law with all its rituals and statutes, coupled with an inevitable burden of guilt at the failure to do so. Paul's statement is a religious one and refers to the lives of religious Jews. It is a bondage which contributes to a driven mentality, which I have observed in orthodox Jewish people whom I have got to know. There is no peace but only a sense of ceaseless activity leading, for many, to tiredness and depression, with no one willing to go to the core of the problem. It causes us to sigh, especially if they will not turn to the one who said: 'Come to Me, all you who labor and are heavy laden, and I will give you rest.'[23]

Persecutors of Jewish People

Most of the troubles which have come upon Jewish people have been at the hand of those who indulged anti-Jewish attitudes. Those attitudes need to be examined. Some among those who persecute Jewish people have no concern to provide a moral or pious justification for what they do, however, most do, although they are plainly bogus. There is one that stands out.

A notorious, bogus justification for anti-Jewish attitudes – authorized by God

Some excuse their persecution of Jewish people on the basis that they have somehow been charged with forwarding God's judgement. The Bible is indeed clear that God does act in judgement against sinners before the great day of judgement, and that it is Jesus who is the ruler and judge; the book of Revelation makes that plain.[24] But none of this justifies men and women taking things into their own hands because they believe others are under God's judgement. A passage in Jeremiah shows how Israel's enemies indulged this habit of justifying their oppressive behaviour because Israel had sinned: 'All who found them have devoured them [Israel]; And their adversaries said, "We have not offended, because they have sinned against the LORD."'[25] When such a justification is heard today it will often be connected to a misunderstanding of the way the phrase 'the Jews' is used in the New Testament. This needs examining.

'The Jews' in the New Testament

This deserves a book on its own, and for a brief but fuller study than this I suggest *Anti-Semitism and the New Testament* by Steve Motyer.[26] I can only make the main points here. There is no doubt that expressions within the New Testament about the Jewish people, like the ones considered above from 1 Thessalonians, have been misused to justify anti-Jewish behaviour. What is obvious is that they should be read in conjunction with other statements in the New Testament by the same speakers or authors, concerning their personal attitude to the Jewish people. Jesus said some strong things about 'the Jews' but he wept at their coming sufferings.[27]

Very often this accusation is made against the New Testament because readers have forgotten that it was fellow-Jews who made the statements they dislike. They perceive the New Testament as a Christian book, and so these statements are by Christians about Jews. But they were by Jews about Jews; it was an internal argument, so to speak. Critics should simply see the New Testament critique of Jewish behaviour as no different from what is read in the Old Testament. There, Jewish prophets said some strong things against the behaviour of their people, as if all were guilty but, to my knowledge, those prophets have never been accused of anti-Semitism.

John's use of the term 'the Jews'

John's Gospel in particular comes in for strong criticism because of the way he uses the term 'the Jews' and because he uses it much more frequently than the other gospel writers. The concern is that it appears as if the entire Jewish people are presented as hostile to Jesus. It is asserted that when Christians read such texts it encouraged negative attitudes in them towards the Jews as a people and led to anti-Semitism, involving persecution and violence. There is no doubt that happened, but is the New Testament to blame? In fact the New Testament is very philo-Semitic; it teaches that the world owes a debt to the Jews and it rebukes Gentile Christians who boast over the Jewish people. What more could it do? Those who want a good reason to hate those they envy will usually be able to find it, even in a holy book they respect. In fact the Old Testament is open to the same misuse. For example, the destruction of the Canaanites recorded in Joshua could be misused by opponents, such as secular anti-Semites, to accuse the Jews of one of history's worst premeditated genocides; and to make matters worse they justified it by saying God told them to do it. I have no doubt that God commanded it but if people don't believe that then they will draw the conclusion that the Jews are a reprehensible people, willing to go to appalling lengths to secure a homeland for themselves. Religious texts can always be misused.

So why did John use the term 'the Jews' so much, and how was he using it? The answer comes down to one simple fact. John gives us much more detail about Jesus' visits to Jerusalem than the other gospel writers, and 'the Jews' was a term used to describe those who lived in Jerusalem and its surrounding area, Judea. It might have been better translated, 'the Judeans' in those instances. John uses the term sixty-seven times in his gospel, forty-six to describe those whom Jesus encountered in Jerusalem; most of the remaining usages were simply descriptive terms like 'a Passover of the Jews', referring to all Jews. An illustration of this is found in John's account of Jesus' plan to return to Judea. He said to his disciples, who were all Jews, 'Let us go to Judea again', and they replied, 'Rabbi, lately the Jews sought to stone you, and are you going there again?'[28] Clearly the disciples were using the term 'the Jews' to refer to the Judean Jews, seeing they too were Jews. Among the Judean Jews were the leaders of Israel and probably twenty-three of the forty-six references to Judean Jews are actually describing the leaders. An example of this is in John 7:13 where John records people in Jerusalem (Judeans) were discussing among themselves if Jesus was the Messiah; John records, 'However, no one spoke openly of Him for fear of the Jews.' The people engaging in discussion are Judeans, elsewhere called 'the Jews', so John is obviously using the term here to refer only to the leadership.

It seems to me that John's use of the term 'the Jews' is intended to do the exact opposite of what his critics have concluded. Critics see it as a term aimed at tarring all Jews with the same brush – all guilty of the death of Jesus – whereas he is wanting to lay that blame at the door of a particular generation living in Judea, and particularly in Jerusalem, and more particularly the leaders who ruled from there.

This is exactly how it appears if we compare Peter's sermons to Paul's. Peter preached to the Jews in Jerusalem just after Jesus' death and says to them, 'Him [Jesus], being delivered by the determined purpose and foreknowledge of God, you have taken by lawless hands, have crucified, and put to death.'[29] He blames them in particular. When Paul preached to Jewish people more than fifteen years later, in a synagogue in Antioch (Turkey today), he said, 'Those who dwell in Jerusalem, and their rulers, because they did not know Him, nor even the voices of the Prophets which are read every Sabbath, have fulfilled them in condemning Him.'[30] He makes no accusation against his Jewish hearers concerning Jesus' death but only against those who dwelt in Jerusalem and the leaders at that time. Any attempt to accuse all the Jewish people of this crime, at that time or over all time, is utterly misplaced, and provides absolutely no justification for being negative towards them. I have described such justification as bogus, so what has motivated oppressors of Jewish people? A few things are worth examining.

Other Motivations of Persecutors of Jewish People

Power and profit

There were times among the nations of European Christendom when rulers saw the wealth of some Jews and found a religious justification for harassing and fining them, and later banishing them from their realm and confiscating their goods. They even charged them to return if they desired to do so. The expulsion of the Jews from England in 1290 by King Edward I was one instance. Islam has a similar record due to the negative view of Jewish people in the Koran. In AD 627 Mohammed killed all the men of the Qurayza, a Jewish community in Medina, which he mistrusted. The women and children were sold. Ever since then fundamentalist Muslims have taken a similar view of the Jews: they are not to be trusted, and God is against them, so it is a Muslim's duty under God to oppose them.

The ability of Jewish people to do well despite adverse circumstances, especially through their trade links and linguistic ability, gave them an appearance of superiority over their Christian or Muslim neighbours. That might suggest their religion was superior or that God was not against them. This had to be disproved, and so oppressing them and banishing them was one way that others could assure themselves that God was with them and that their faith was superior.

Different from us

Societies which take pride in their cohesiveness due to racial, religious or social uniformity, have often turned against the Jews because their separateness is seen as a weakening influence. An obvious biblical example is Haman's justification to the Persian king for their destruction.[31] An example from more recent times was the attitude of some of the leaders of the Enlightenment of the eighteenth century who were not happy for the Jews to enjoy the new-found liberties of the French Revolution if they wanted to cling on to their distinctives. Similarly, the only way that Jewish citizens of communist states could rise to any position of prominence was by separating themselves from any expression of Jewishness. Totalitarian societies whether religious or atheistic have been the worst offenders. It seems they cannot abide a people whose presence and beliefs challenge theirs, even if no public challenge is mounted. At bottom, they are fighting the one true God.

Racially inferior

The term 'anti-Semitism' was coined in 1873 by Wilhelm Marr on the back of a theory which stated that genetics and race were key factors in the development of nations; the proposers of the idea naturally seeing themselves as highly developed. Evolutionary thinking lay behind it, asserting that purity of race was necessary for survival, progress and development, and that this process best took place in that race's natural homeland. The Jews did not fit. They allowed racial mix by conversion and above all they had no homeland, only living in the lands of others. They were therefore viewed as racially deficient, permanently and unalterably deleterious to those among whom they dwelt; they were parasites. This was anti-Semitism when the term was first coined,[32] and it was what drove the Nazi plan to destroy the Jewish people. Beneath it all we see a hatred of God and fear of Jewish strengths, as well as a greedy desire to lay hands on their goods.

Anti-Zionism

This brings us right up to date. The Jewish State acts as a lightning conductor for people's attitudes to Jewish people today and it has certainly thrown up plenty of hateful ones. The issue is not a theoretical one for armchair historians but has an outworking today which affects us all. Negative attitudes to Jewish people are often expressed by negative attitudes toward the State of Israel but are covered over by the plausible explanation that the person is not against Jews per se, but is opposed to the concept of a Jewish State and all it has involved. In other words people say they are not anti-Semitic, but they are anti-Zionist. Of course, this is theoretically possible, and people's integrity in professing it should not be questioned unless their underlying feelings to the Jews are exposed as negative. However, it is rather prevalent as a justification. A leading editor has admitted to being 'puzzled' by the anti-Israel attitude of so many in the British media: 'It is a massive puzzle because journalists are normally on the side of the little guy, and there can't be a smaller guy in the Middle East than Israel.' He went on to question whether British journalism was basically anti-Semitic.[33] Most Jewish people are cynical about claims to be anti-Zionist but not anti-Semitic. Thousands of years of oppression at the hands of the nations, during which time they have heard many pious justifications for apparently reasonable opposition to them, and which have masked deeply negative feelings toward them, has produced an understandable scepticism.

When such a profession of not being anti-Semitic is accompanied by a failure to use the same yardstick for self-criticism there is strong mistrust. For example, some oppose the right of the Jewish people to be there as if they are just alien conquerors and colonizers, or deny them the right to retain any lands taken when attacked, as a future defence against an implacable enemy, until peace is agreed. But such critics frequently come from nations who have established themselves by conquest and have for years refused to grant concessions to indigenous people who have petitioned for such. Israel is not an alien conqueror, Jews have always lived in the land since Abraham, and she has shown herself willing to return lands when there is a possibility of genuine peace.

Again, many equate Zionism with racism because the State of Israel desires to be a Jewish state, even though all its citizens are not Jews. But what nation does not have a central, guiding philosophy which has emerged from the natural characteristics, religion and common history of its dominant people? It is quite natural among all peoples and happens everywhere. Are the Jews not entitled to this? What is unnatural, and immoral, is to develop a society in a way which fails to recognize the common humanity of all citizens and leads to oppression of those who are an ethnic minority. No doubt Israel has had its failures at this point, but what nation has not? Israel is also criticized as racist for giving favourable status to Jews wanting to return there. But their unique situation ought to be recognized. What other people (and there are some others, Armenians for example), scattered across the globe for centuries, has had the opportunity to resettle its ancient homeland and rebuild a national entity from scratch? Most peoples have established themselves through centuries of development, creating their own unique national culture. Israel is aiming to do it almost instantly. Unusual measures are necessary, which may be modified once their situation is settled and secure. Israel's critics are akin to those who lambaste the weakness of democracy in some emerging nations, forgetting that their own democratic traditions took centuries to develop, even involving much strife and civil war.

It is the hostility of the criticism, not criticism as such, which alarms Jewish people and leads them to suspect anti-Semitism. As one young Israeli once asked me, 'Why do they hate us so much?' Hate he could understand, for he is aware of Israel's failures, but its intensity puzzled him. No doubt it can be accounted for by jealousy and fear of Jewish strengths. It can also be explained by that sinful desire to pull down those who hold to a strong morality. Through the Jewish nation the world has received its greatest moral code and fallen people gain a perverse satisfaction whenever they can drag such down. The fact that many Jewish people have held their privileged position in self-righteousness, and Israel has certainly not always got things right, has unfortunately spurred their antagonists on. Again, beneath it all we see the desire to oppose a people whom God has chosen. Satan, the arch-opposer, is ever ready to stir up such base feelings.

Christians, beware!

Although Christians should not be guilty of the worst forms of the justifications mentioned above, yet such may lurk within because of wrong attitudes, especially if they were indulged before conversion. Christians should allow the Holy Spirit to search their hearts for any tendency to justify a fixed, negative attitude towards the Jewish people because they are seen as under God's judgement, or different, or racially inferior, or because they dislike Zionism and the behaviour of the State of Israel.

Let the reader beware

There will undoubtedly be consequences for those who have negative feelings towards the Jewish people as a people, and indulge them by opposition of one sort or another. I do not believe in making pronouncements against individuals, or this or that nation which has opposed them, but the word of God frequently focuses its judgements upon those who oppose or oppress those with whom the Lord identifies: Christians, the churches, the poor, widows and orphans; and the Jewish people. Let the reader beware.

9.

Talkers and Mutilators

The last letters written by the apostles are full of warnings about false teachers and Paul particularly singles out 'the circumcision' as being prominent among them. Again, not an easy subject to examine but it is there in the pages of the New Testament. If it was a matter of only historical interest we could leave it to one side but it is not, it is a live issue. A typical text is Paul's warning to Titus about the difficulties elders would face as they taught sound doctrine, 'For there are many insubordinate, both idle talkers and deceivers, especially those of the circumcision, whose mouths must be stopped.'[1] Other texts are scattered throughout the New Testament.[2]

The Circumcision

When Paul pays particular attention to those he calls 'the circumcision' he mentions their interest in subjects such as Jewish fables, the law, the commandments of men, genealogies and circumcision.[3] He describes them as idle talkers and deceivers and he sees them as disobedient and interested in dishonest gain, controlling small groups and boasting over those they mislead. Some of them claimed to be apostles and were obviously people of some influence.[4]

'The circumcision' is a term which Paul does not always use in the same way. It may be a general term to describe a Jew or Jews as opposed to a Gentile or Gentiles, or it may be used negatively to describe professing Jewish believers in Jesus who were misleading others; the context makes it clear when this is the case.

One such use is in Titus 1:10–16 and the other is Philippians 3:2. In the former Paul's focus is on idle talkers, in the latter on those who emphasized circumcision. In the Philippians text Paul's term for these people seems to be deliberately contemptuous and to translate it 'circumcision' is inaccurate; words like 'concision' or 'mutilation' are better. These two texts seem to point to three types of Jewish false teachers: those who were not teaching serious error but whose teachings were 'unprofitable and useless',[5] and those whose emphasis on circumcision was either serious error or heretical. Those who taught circumcision and the law as essential additions to faith in Jesus were in the 'heresy' category, as Paul makes plain in Galatians 1:6–10, where he describes it as 'a different gospel, which is not another'. Those who taught circumcision and traditions as having an added spiritual value for Gentiles are not condemned in such strong terms by Paul but in Colossians he makes plain that they are of no value, 'Therefore, if you died with Christ from the basic principles of the world, why, as though living in the world, do you subject yourselves to regulations', and he concludes, 'These things . . . are of no value against the indulgence of the flesh.'[6]

If we ask why these professing Jewish believers were so prominent among false teachers we can point to Jewish believers being the originals. Jews were the first to believe, they had a long tradition of knowledge of the Scriptures, their lives had been moulded by biblical behaviour patterns, and they had a feel for the types and shadows of the Mosaic covenant due to a lifetime of practice. It put them in a position to be pillars in the new churches among the Gentiles. It seems that other Jews who professed to believe were prepared to take advantage of the prestige this gave them and set themselves up as teachers. Some went so far as to dog Paul's steps and introduce error and heresy into the churches he founded, making themselves out to be apostles of a superior ilk.[7]

Then and now

To some readers this phenomenon may seem somewhat remote. However, in a small way, things are getting back to what they used to be. The rise of what has been called the Messianic Movement since the 1960s has produced a new wave of Jewish believers who are much more focused on their Jewish culture in the expression of their faith in Jesus. Some are very well educated and are able teachers. This is a joy to see, and the general growth in numbers, growth in Jewish awareness, concern for their people and concern that they and their children should be identifiably Jewish is something which I warmly welcome. So too is the fact that most have taken their place in local evangelical churches and bring to the life of those churches their unique contribution as Jewish believers in Jesus. However, just as there was a downside in apostolic times so there is today, from some within this movement.

Influence on Gentile Christians Today

The spiritual dangers for Jewish believers themselves will be examined in a later chapter, but Paul's focus in the passages we have referred to is the negative influence upon believing Gentiles.

Gentiles acting Jewish

One place this happens is in a messianic congregation, of which more in a later chapter. Such a congregation could be described as a Jewish ethnic church, which is usually started out of a desire to do things Jewishly, to celebrate the Jewish festivals and incorporate some synagogue customs into church worship. What is unusual about them is that it is quite normal for 50 per cent or more of the congregation to be non-Jewish. It begs the question, why should Gentiles desire to behave as if they are Jewish? We will consider this phenomenon in more detail in Chapter 16 but here I want to focus on the keeping of Jewish traditions. Some Gentile Christians come to value them because they believe they have greater authority than church ones; others say they find them to be spiritually helpful. But the fact is they are just cultural traditions; they have nothing of special religious significance that draws down the Spirit's blessing on them. I believe it is the responsibility of the spiritual leaders of such congregations to disabuse them of that notion. But do they?

Gentiles keeping the law

There are those in this movement who clearly teach that Gentile Christians are free to observe Jewish laws and customs, the underlying assumption being it will be spiritually beneficial for them, so they are effectively encouraging them to do so. David Stern writes in his discussion of the Acts 15 debate about Gentile believers keeping the law, 'However, Acts 15 also teaches that although Gentiles were required to observe only four laws on entering the Messianic Community, they were permitted to learn as much about Judaism as they wished and presumably to observe as many Jewish customs as they wished.'[8] He refers to Acts 15:21 for proof of this statement. However, that text is referring to the pre-gospel situation of Gentiles drawn to Judaism and attending synagogues to learn, which was all before they came to faith in Jesus. How they relate to such customs after conversion is dealt with in letters like Galatians and Colossians. There they are given no encouragement to take on Jewish customs. Galatians warns against adding such things to Christ for salvation,[9] and Colossians warns against thinking such things have a special spirituality.[10]

Talkers

Beyond the confines of messianic congregations, and without necessarily teaching Gentile believers should act like Jews, there are those who like to dispense knowledge about Jewish things as if they have the key to a new level in the Christian life. They touch upon matters of Old Testament background, rabbinic methods of Scripture exegesis, Jewish traditions, Jewish stories, root meanings of Hebrew words and mystical Jewish teachings. Now such things are often very interesting and may well have value, much the same as any extra-biblical information on Israelite culture, archaeology, etc. Therefore, it should not be assumed that someone teaching such things is automatically a 'talker'. What is important to discern is whether the teacher is presenting himself or herself as introducing you to spiritual truths that you could never have known otherwise, even from the Scriptures; with them you go up a gear, so to speak. There is a need to be on the lookout for the sort of qualities Paul condemns: divisive, insubordinate, financially motivated, self-willed, flatterering, controlling and falsely humble. Let me give some examples of the things which may be used to suggest special knowledge. I want to emphasize the word 'may'; there is a valid use of such areas of understanding.

Knowing the root meaning of Hebrew words

This may be used to give a novel understanding of a text. The problem is that to separate a word into its root consonants and a pattern of vowels is only academic. It is not as if Hebrew has many sets of consonants (the root), all of which have a distinct meaning and from which words are formed. The root only has existence insofar as it is part of a word. We can consider four Hebrew words with the consonants ḥrb: *ḥarab* (to dry up), *ḥarab* (to be desolate), *ḥarab* (to attack, smite), *ḥereb* (a sword). Here are four words each of which has a distinct meaning to the user. If there is any basic notion to the sequence of consonants *ḥrb* then it will be derived by working back from the meaning of the four words, not vice versa. Hence to claim as some do that 'the meaning of the Hebrew root gives us a deeper understanding of this word and hence of the text we are considering' makes no sense.

Knowing about the Jewish way to interpret the Old Testament

The rabbis devised rules for this, which are of some interest. However, Christians have the definitive Jewish interpretation of the Old Testament in the New Testament. There the Lord Jesus and his apostles show us the way to interpret the Old Testament. It could not be more Jewish.

Knowing about Bible background information culled from rabbinic sources

The key thing to discern is the value being given to the information, the danger being to detract from the sufficiency of Scripture. All the knowledge we need to understand the Bible's message, to understand details in a particular passage, to deal with its internal problems in the text, etc., can be found in Scripture. Undoubtedly, outside information may bring colour and extra interest but is not essential to understand the text and the message.

Knowing about Hebrew thinking, not Greek

The influence of Greek ways of thinking on the early churches is presented by some as pernicious; we need to be more Hebraic in our thinking. Greek thinking is said to have become dominant because church leaders used the terminology then current in the Greek language to debate doctrine between themselves, and to formulate early doctrinal statements like the Nicene Creed. Obviously there was a danger of absorbing unbiblical thought forms but what were the church leaders supposed to do? Did they have any option? Surely, the key question is whether they ended up with false doctrine due to the influence of Greek thought. Even those on the extreme wing of the Messianic Movement do not criticize the Nicene Creed as unbiblical.[11]

The main point to remember is that all the errors of Greek thinking had begun to influence the churches during the times of the apostles. Their letters confront these errors and keep us on the straight and narrow, along the lines of biblical, Hebraic thought (despite being written in Greek.) For example, Greek thinking is criticized for its dualism, seeing the soul as good and the body as evil. That error is confronted in Colossians and 1 John. We have all the Hebraic thinking we need in the New Testament (and the Old Testament too, of course). In fact, most of the church failures pointed to as due to Greek thinking take little or no account of the Reformation. They focus on errors that crept into the churches in the post-apostolic era as if none of it was corrected at the time of the Reformation onwards.

Mutilators

As I wrote above, those whom Paul calls mutilators fall into two classes, those whose teaching is condemned in Galatians as another gospel and those ideas in Colossians which are seen as of no value. I am glad to say that those who teach the Galatian heresy

– that Gentile believers need to add circumcision and keeping the law to their faith in Jesus for salvation – are few and far between. However, there are those who call their faith 'Messianic Judaism', who believe in Jesus as the only way of salvation from sin but want their faith to be seen as a Judaism, expressing that faith according to Jewish traditional practices, and some among them – and I emphasize some, not all, and certainly a minority – advocate the conversion of Gentile Christians in their midst to being Jews, Jews who believe in Jesus. Richard Nichol argues for this from a variety of perspectives but his main one is identity.[12] In any normal synagogue, visitors are welcome to come and learn but only bona fide Jews can engage in certain practices or have certain roles, e.g. things like wearing of the tallit (prayer shawl) and coming up to the bima to read Torah. Nichol believes that because Messianic Judaism is essentially a Judaism then only Jews should do such things. If Gentile Christians ('messianic Gentiles' is their preferred term) do such things then that is seen as against Jewish law and unacceptable to other Jews. The solution is to put such Gentile believers through a conversion process, which would involve circumcision for men and learning and doing those practices of Judaism agreed upon by their group of messianic rabbis.

We have to ask whether Nichol and those who agree with him are doing these Gentile Christians any favours. Will the wider community accept such converts as Jewish? Most certainly not; for them the issue is Jesus, and you cannot be Jewish and believe in Jesus. Their children will not be accepted as Jewish either, so such families will end up locked into their small group, being unacceptable elsewhere in the Jewish community, and will feel out of place in a normal church. It is all beginning to look very much like a sect or even a cult. Colossians would certainly support the idea that such teachers as Nichol are doing Gentile Christians no favours by teaching them to focus on 'the basic principles of the world', subjecting themselves to regulations.[13] And there is no doubt that such a conversion and religious lifestyle would encourage those Gentiles whose profession of faith is false to trust in circumcision and law.

10.

Jewish Opposition to the Gospel

Ecclesiastes 1:9 tells us 'there is nothing new under the sun', so it should surprise no one that there was opposition to the teachings of the Lord Jesus and his apostles. What began when Israel's prophets proclaimed God's word resurfaced when Israel's Messiah preached the same divine message. Such opposition is still very much alive in the Jewish community today. My purpose in this chapter is not negative. I want to encourage Christians to respond to opposition with understanding and patience, as well as firmness, and to discourage either an adversarial or obsequious response.[1] I want Jewish readers to see that Jewish opposition to Jesus is not because 'Christianity doesn't look Jewish', as some would put it, but is part of a tradition of Jewish communal tension stretching back to Joseph and his brothers.

It goes without saying that opposition to the gospel from Jewish people is caused by the same sinful nature which they have in common with all Adam's children, but that is not what is under examination here, that is taken for granted. What I want to look at is the specific ways in which Jewish people express that sinful opposition due to the influence of their religion, history and culture.

Opposition to Jesus

Anyone who has read the gospels will know that opposition was not the first response of Jesus' hearers; it was something which developed within some as time went on, as they began to grasp the significance of his message. One of its earliest forms was not so much theological as personal. When Jesus spoke against hypocrisy, a merely external religion and particular sins, people were convicted of sin; some repented, but some resisted. Malachi foresaw this with the words, 'Who can endure the day of His coming?'[2] Jesus' exposure of the sins of Israel's leaders brought a fierce response, 'And as he said these things to them, the scribes and the Pharisees began to assail him vehemently, and to cross-examine him about many things.'[3] They could not endure the day of his coming and their opposition grew.

Jesus' miracles were an obvious testimony to his divine authority, so opponents sought for an alternative explanation. It was soon forthcoming after he healed a demon-possessed mute – 'He casts out demons by the ruler of the demons.'[4] There was novelty in Jesus' teaching so his opponents were on the lookout for deviation from God's law. The Sabbath was a touchstone for Jesus' attitude and so he was watched, and when he stepped outside their boundaries he was accused of unlawful behaviour, or of condoning such in others – 'Look, Your disciples are doing what is not lawful to do on the Sabbath!'[5] When Jesus spoke of God as his father and of being one with him an attempt was made to stone him, his opponents' justification being, 'for blasphemy, and because You, being a Man, make Yourself God'.[6] Hidden within all this opposition was an envy of his popularity with the people, an envy that the Roman leader, Pilate, could recognize: 'For He knew that they had handed Him over because of envy.'[7] Orthodox Jewish tradition views Jesus in the same light today. He is seen as a deceiver and blasphemer, one deserving of the lowest hell.

How did the Lord Jesus respond to all this? With infinite patience, and always with the intent of winning over his detractors. For example, when his authority was questioned his response was to asked a question back: 'The baptism of John – where was it from? From heaven or from men?'[8] His purpose was to expose their incompetence to judge him, and his subsequent parables encouraged them to think again and repent.

All the examples I have given are of opposition from Jewish religious leaders. But they did not all oppose, as is shown by the incident of the healing of the man born blind in John 9. There the leaders argued among themselves, some saying Jesus could not be of God because of his disregard for the Sabbath, others disagreeing because it was obvious to them that a sinner could not work such miracles.[9] Similarly, we know that the generality of the people were divided in their opinions and not all opposed Jesus. However, what we find in this encounter is that the opposition group shouted the loudest and won the day. Their conclusion was, 'We know that God spoke to Moses; as for this fellow, we do not know where He is from.'[10] It seems the doubters were reduced to silence. As a spout sets the direction in which water will flow, so this opposition mentality came to dominate the leadership and encouraged the Jewish people in an attitude of opposition. Many would refuse that course and become devout followers of Jesus the Messiah but the stage was being set for an opposition mentality.

The Jewish leaders bore a heavy responsibility for this. Jesus charged them with obstructing those who were seeking to enter the kingdom,[11] and described them as 'blind leaders of the blind',[12] warning his disciples to beware of them and their doctrine. However, they were not alone, many of the people willingly followed them.

Opposition to the Apostles

The Acts of the Apostles paints a similar picture, detailing the further development of opposition. From the earliest days the apostles in Jerusalem were threatened, the aim being that, 'They speak to no man in this name'.[13] Their response was to continue preaching Jesus as Saviour, and many of the people and of the priests believed.[14] Predictably, the opposition increased too: Stephen was martyred, the believers were scattered from Jerusalem and Saul began his campaign of suppression. As Luke continues his account the picture is much the same. Paul meets opposition from all quarters but the most vehement and persistent is from his own people. They argued against him,[15] pursued him from place to place to stir up opposition,[16] plotted against him,[17] and had him arrested and put on trial in Jewish and Gentile courts.[18] Paul's response was the same as that of the Jerusalem apostles. We know from 2 Corinthians that Paul suffered more than is recorded in Acts – 'From the Jews five times I received forty stripes minus one.'[19] This is a testimony to his love for his people, because he did not use his Roman citizenship to evade such a beating. If he had done so it could have undermined the Jewishness of the gospel in their eyes.

Judaism and Jewish Particularities of Opposition

No one rejects the gospel in a vacuum. As an actor in a play is seen against the stage backdrop, so people respond from within the thought framework of their family or culture. When Jewish people choose to reject Jesus it is within a Jewish framework. I would not press this too far, for we all have a common humanity, which is a fallen one, and it determines certain common responses regardless of culture. However, there are particular expressions of opposition due to the influence of Judaism, which Jewish people manifest as a group. The teachings we will examine all crystallized through opposition to Jesus. Other factors have led to an intensification of opposition, e.g. Christian anti-Semitism, but it all began in New Testament times.

The place of the law of Moses and Jewish particularity

This issue was crystallized by Jesus' teaching on the Sabbath and became one of the first points of contention with the Jewish leaders. Very early on Jesus showed a different approach to the Sabbath, and even claimed lordship over it.[20] Of course, he was far from dismissing the law of Moses; rather, he taught that it must all be fulfilled. However, the discerning among the Pharisees must have sensed he was paving the way for radical change, and so it would have caused no surprise that this was a principal charge against him at his trial, where he was accused of saying he would destroy the temple.[21]

Similar bitter hostility erupted against Stephen who, whatever he himself actually said, was accused of teaching an end to the temple and the customs taught by Moses. Such a response can be understood when it is a reaction to a watering-down of the unique revelation given by God through Moses to the Jewish nation, but when it is resistance to a change which Scripture clearly indicated would come, by a new covenant, then it is sinful obtuseness. That resistance was even more reprehensible when we observe that it was motivated by a concern for the preservation of their own unique particularity. This can be seen during that occasion in the temple when a religious mob tried to kill Paul.[22] They happily listened to what he related about Jesus but when they heard that he had gone to Gentiles they erupted in murderous rage, thus demonstrating that their main concern was to preserve their particularity.[23] We might call it the Jonah Syndrome. The book of Jonah stood as a warning to Israel against a particularity which shut out a concern for the lostness of the Gentiles. Likewise Isaiah had prophesied, 'My house shall be called a house of prayer for all nations.'[24] People like Zachariah and Simeon had learnt that lesson; they were Israelites who possessed a concern for the nations. Holding the infant Jesus, Simeon said, 'A light to bring revelation to the Gentiles, And the glory of Your people Israel'.[25]

Today it is no different. Judaism's opposition to the gospel will often focus on the apparent abandonment of the law of Moses as, for example, expressed by Isaac of Troki, a leading Jewish apologist of the sixteenth century: 'The law of Moses is not to be revoked, and . . . no second revelation is to be added to the former.'[26] Hence Judaism sees Christianity much as Christians see Mormonism – a heretical offshoot, possessing an extra written revelation which abandons existing divine norms. While such opposition has an appearance of piety it is undermined by the fact that the Hebrew Scriptures point to a superseding of the temple[27] and the Mosaic covenant;[28] to be expected when the Messiah comes. So the question really boils down to whether he has come.

Justification by faith alone

For a religious Jew, faith is obviously important and the liturgy of the synagogue is full of expressions of dependence on the mercy of the Lord. But this does not mean that, according to Judaism, obedience to the law does not play a part in a righteous standing before God. Jesus' parable of the Pharisee and the tax collector makes it plain that Pharisaic thinking was marked by a sense of spiritual self-sufficiency and that it did not lead to justification.[29] It was not just that some Pharisees were self-righteous but that the whole system of thought was such, and because they were making the religious running in those times it was necessary to expose their error and emphasize the place of faith. This was the significance of Jesus' frequent expression, 'Your faith has saved you . . .' Deliverance was not a reward but a gift received through trusting the giver. Paul was equally aware of the need to spell this out, which is why he emphasized the negative in his Antioch synagogue sermon: 'from which you could not be justified by the law of Moses'.[30] Elsewhere he demonstrated that this should come as no surprise to the people of the book because it was the religion of Abraham, 'For what does the Scripture say? "Abraham believed God, and it was accounted to him for righteousness."'[31] This was offensive to Jewish leaders then and it remains so today.

The new birth

It was to a Pharisee that Jesus first explicitly taught the need for the new birth. Not that Jesus saw this as a new truth. One passage he would have had in mind was from Moses, 'And the LORD your God will circumcise your heart.'[32] Moses made it plain to Israel that any return to God after persistent disobedience required a work of God at the core of their being. Nicodemus eventually believed it but, sad to say, many of his fellows did not and do not to this day.

The whole philosophy of spiritual self-sufficiency within Judaism hangs together and has a sort of 'domino effect' on biblical doctrines. As it opposes one so it inevitably opposes others. If you can justify yourself then you do not need to be born again as you have the capacity to work righteousness. As Rabbi Chaim Pearl expresses it: 'Although a man may be sinful by inclination he has within him the power to rid himself of sin.'[33] The practices of Judaism are seen as the means for achieving that goal; a miraculous change is not viewed as necessary.

Bondage to sin

Jesus' hearers in John 8 took offence at being described as 'slaves to sin', and Judaism opposes any such idea today. Its doctrine of human nature has people caught up in a struggle in which they are pulled one way by an evil inclination (*yetzer ha-ra*) and another by a good inclination (*yetzer ha-tov*). They have the power to choose one or the other and are in no way enslaved by the former, although in a rebellious world there is much against them. To quote Rabbi Pearl again, 'Man is born without sin . . . Judaism repudiates any idea that he is born with an original sin.'[34] It fails to take sin's power seriously enough but King David clearly did when he wrote, 'Behold, I was brought forth in iniquity, and in sin my mother conceived me.'[35]

Pre-existence and divinity of Messiah

The heavenly nature of the Messiah was not one of the first truths our Lord emphasized, as it was too meaty to digest early on, but he gradually brought it to the fore. His words, 'I and My Father are one', brought an accusation of blasphemy: 'You, being a Man, make Yourself God.'[36] Clearly, his words were not misunderstood, nor can we miss the intensity of opposition in the Jewish leaders. And yet the Scriptures clearly present the conundrum of a Messiah who is both human and divine. Jesus' hearers were perplexed and silent when he drew their attention to this by asking whose son is the Messiah, and then by pointing out the difficulty that Messiah is both David's son and his lord, indicating both his humanity and divinity.[37] Although the claim that Jesus is divine is frequently misunderstood by many Jewish people today, i.e. many think it means he was a man who became God, yet their teachers well understand what was claimed and emphatically reject it. Michael Asheri writes of the Jewish belief in Messiah and takes a swipe at Christianity in the process, 'This Jew, and he will be a person, not an incarnation of God, as if such a thing were possible, is called Mashiach, or Messiah.'[38]

Source of all life

It must have been thrilling to be in the temple at the Feast of Tabernacles and hear Jesus' voice ringing out with the words, 'If anyone thirsts let him come to Me and drink.'[39] The chief priests and Pharisees were not thrilled and did not slacken the pace of their attempts to have him arrested. Such a total dependence on the Messiah for all that sustains life, especially the spiritual, is still unacceptable to Judaism today. Messiah is little more than a very special man of God and should not receive the trust due to God alone, as Rabbi Louis Jacobs wrote of Messiah: 'He is not, however, a redeemer. God alone is the redeemer and the Messiah-king is only the leader of the redeemed people.'[40] For Judaism, Messiah is not essential to life or salvation, which can be received without him; he is no more than the icing on the cake. What Jacobs overlooks is that Messiah is also a priest,[41] and a priest in the law not only does what is needed to redeem sinners but also mediates God's spiritual blessings to them.[42] Without him they have nothing.

Death and resurrection of Messiah for atonement and justification

There was no lack of discussion about the Messiah in Jesus' day; people obviously studied the Scriptures and tried to produce a coherent picture. Yet one thing on the canvas is noticeable by its absence: a suffering Messiah who atones for sin. No one expected it; 'suffering' and 'Messiah' were polar opposites. Later when the significance of this event was spelt out by the apostles many of Jesus' own continued to reject, seeing his blood only in terms of accusation, not deliverance. It became the major sticking point for Jewish people – 'Christ crucified, to the Jews a stumbling block'[43] – because it obstructed that comfortable spiritual pathway which the Pharisees and their followers had constructed for themselves. To this day Judaism rejects any suggestion of atonement by blood sacrifice. On the subject of forgiveness of sin, Rabbi David Berger wrote: 'For the Christian mind, this is accomplished by the death of Jesus. How does Judaism deal with the problem? It does so through the idea of repentance ... Any Jew who does so will be forgiven by God ... When sacrifice is not possible [because of no temple], God forgives those who sincerely repent.'[44] What teachers like Rabbi Berger refuse to acknowledge is that sacrifice is no longer possible for the simple reason that the sacrifice God required has now been accomplished, once and for all, by the one who both died and rose again, as Isaiah prophesied: 'When You make His soul an offering for sin, He shall see His seed, He shall prolong His days, And the pleasure of the LORD shall prosper in his hand.'[45]

Some Reflections

It has to be faced, with sorrow but with frankness, that Judaism's opposition to the gospel is more pointedly anti-Christian than it is against any other religion. At every point regarding the doctrine of salvation it is diametrically opposed and actively hostile. While Christians must have a high regard for the Jewish nation because of God's covenant with them, and the blessing of God they themselves have received through them, they must not allow this to cloud their judgement on Judaism.

There is something unique about Jewish opposition because the difference of belief goes to the core of Jewish existence and self-awareness. If Jesus is the Messiah then the very reason for Israel's existence has come to fulfilment, and so not to believe is to be living a lie; to be Jewish yet fail to act Jewish. It is to be only a shell. Jewish people understand this implication, especially their religious leaders, and hence the sense of offence is deep and the opposition is strong. Even non-religious Jews, who set no store on belief in Messiah, are conscious of the implication. The gospel has to be disproved so as to validate their Jewishness without Jesus and the genuineness of their Jewish lifestyle. Of course the pressure to do so would be small if the influence of the Christian faith was of the same order as Zoroastrianism's, but it is not; it is followed by multitudes, many fellow-Jews being among them. There is hardly a culture where significant numbers of Jewish people live which is not dominated by the Christian faith. It is therefore difficult to escape the challenge and the pressure. Jewish people are proud of their established culture wherever they are (much of which is to be admired), but if you assert that the most important thing is missing they will take offence. Thoughtful Jewish people are aware that Christianity's existence says, 'Your Jewishness is askew', and others are aware of it in a more intuitive fashion. When the gospel confronts such a Jewish person it is inevitable that their initial reaction will be opposition of a unique sort. There is a deep personal need to oppose it.

There is also something unique about Jewish opposition because, starting with the same book, a radically different conclusion has been reached. Watching one of those TV programmes where the latest films are discussed is fairly tame if there is but one reviewer, but if there are two or more expressing radically different opinions of the same film then the tension rises in the studio. Such commentators often pride themselves on their intellect and insight, so if one says the film is trashy and the other sees it as deeply insightful and uplifting then someone is likely to be a fool, but which one? So it is between Judaism and Christianity. How is it that with the same book they have come to such very different conclusions? Someone is foolish. Hence, Jewish people feel all but bound to oppose Christian beliefs, for if they are wrong then they are exposed as lacking in all insight because they have missed the very thing they are meant to be looking for. Furthermore, the whole history of their people subsequent to Jesus is also put under the microscope and in danger of being exposed as containing a gargantuan mistake.

Opposition in Today's World

Should we expect any significant change now that much water has flowed under the bridge since those tense, early days? Nowadays many Jews take a positive view of Jesus, and Christendom has recognized that its behaviour has at times been deplorable and too often dishonourable towards the Jewish people, so we might expect less opposition and a more harmonious atmosphere. In one sense that is true, however, Paul indicated we should expect no fundamental change: 'Concerning the gospel they are enemies for your sake.'[46] The relationship between Christians and unbelieving Jewish people is determined by how Paul describes them in Romans 11:28,29: they are enemies of God, beloved of God and ongoing recipients of his gifts and calling. There is nothing that necessitates Christian believers and Jewish people to be enemies, quite the contrary, but rejection of the gospel by Jewish people has led to a situation where they are enemies when the gospel is under consideration. Unless and until there is a radical change in attitude to the gospel among the majority of Jews then this situation will continue. To imagine that today's increase in toleration and the influence of multiculturalism has done anything more than paper over the cracks is a delusion.

Difficulties with generalizations

What has been difficult to avoid in the above is the danger of stereotyping the Jewish people as all rejecters of the gospel. Because of the need to avoid constantly qualifying terms then phrases like 'the Jewish people' have to be used as generalizations when discussing opposition, and it is not an unfair generalization because opposition to the gospel has become the set position of the Jewish community. Paul himself does this in Romans 9:31 when he writes, 'Israel, pursuing the law of righteousness, has not attained to the law of righteousness', even when many Jews like himself were obviously not included. Such generalizations can lead Christians to adopt an adversarial attitude to individual Jewish people, as if at the drop of a hat they are all ready to launch into an attack on Christianity. It is similar to the problem many Christians have with Muslims; they are often tempted to see them all as extremists, and yet a quick chat with a Muslim neighbour shows that to be far from the case. Christians should always bear in mind that the unchangeable thing between God and Israel is that they are beloved because of the covenant relation through Abraham and the patriarchs. Their status as enemies is changeable, by God's grace. Hence the bedrock attitude of the Christian towards Jews is one of 'beloved', and the enemy status is one they prayerfully seek to change by the gospel.

This generalization of terminology can create difficulties for Jewish believers in Jesus because other Christians often draw the erroneous conclusion that, as they no longer oppose Jesus, then they are no longer Jewish either. Which is not only a rather foolish conclusion, it is also deeply hurtful for those who identify with and love their own people, just as other nations do.

Today's Manifestations of Opposition

I want to begin by considering general community opposition and move on to opposition 'on the street'.

General community opposition

Outright attacks on Christianity by Jewish leaders in the public arena are rare. In New Testament days they were in the majority and took advantage of that position, then the situation changed, and things were very much the other way around. However, the playing field is now much more level. The atmosphere today is very much one of all religions have a contribution to make towards the sum of humankind's religious insight. Therefore they are rarely judged against the backdrop of rejecting Jesus but more against the colourful patchwork of humanity's religious thought. They complement rather than contrast; they are valued contributors rather than irritating opposers.

Thus it has been possible for the Jewish leadership to marginalize those who engage in any form of witness to Jewish people. For example, Jewish leaders have long been involved in religious dialogue with Christian denominations, even evangelical ones, but whereas the original point of such was to create better mutual understanding while recognizing differences and the Christian obligation to evangelism, now however proselytizing is frowned upon. For example, the Council of Christians and Jews (CCJ) in the UK issued a code of practice in 1996 containing this clause: 'Aggressive proselytism is always wrong and if this or any unsuitable behaviour is reported to the CCJ, appropriate action will be taken. Concern will not be confined to behaviour within the CCJ.' The concern was ostensibly about missionizing at CCJ events but the final phrase shows they are ready to exclude any who are supportive of normative Jewish evangelism – 'aggressive proselytism'. However, it has to be said that this is not always applied.

All this is a subtle form of opposition to the gospel which aims to slowly chip away at Christian commitment to evangelism of Jews with the goal of isolating those involved in it. Sometimes it bears some very significant fruit, as when a recent Archbishop of Canterbury was prevailed upon by the Jewish leaders not to accept the role of honorary president of a mission to the Jews associated with the Anglican Church. The tradition was that Canterbury's archbishop always accepted such a position ever since that mission first sought ecclesiastical patronage in 1841. To default was to marginalize Jewish evangelism in the Anglican Church, and the Jewish community saw it as a great triumph.

However, it is heartening to know that not all respond to pressure in such a fashion. In the USA the Southern Baptists continued with their plans to set up a department for evangelism among Jewish people despite the reverberations felt among Christian–Jewish dialogue groups which included Southern Baptists. Rabbis who had previously participated threatened to withdraw but the department exists to this day.

The presence of many Jewish academics in institutions of higher learning is obviously to be welcomed but in the current climate it is also quietly changing things. One senses that out of respect for them the teaching of theology, religion and Christianity is much more deferential to Jewish sensitivities. Academically respectable ideas, such as the Two Covenant teaching, became more acceptable through such influence.[47] In such an atmosphere those who support the evangelizing of Jewish people are clearly out of step.

It seems to me that we are moving back into a situation more akin to New Testament times when the church was a minor player in the world, one difference being that she is now seen as a moral dinosaur rather than a new moral force. Some may think I am simply reflecting the situation in the UK and Europe and failing to take account of significant differences elsewhere. Undoubtedly the UK is further down this track than many but Jesus' words, 'When the Son of Man comes, will He really find faith on the earth?'[48] lead us to expect an increasingly marginalized church as time goes on. This will lead to bolder institutional opposition from the Jewish community, as per the Acts of the Apostles. For example, a feature article in a British Jewish newspaper even suggested that they should lend their voice to the call to disestablish the Church of England,[49] not something anyone could have imagined such a paper publishing even twenty years ago.

In Israel the situation is different in that there has never been a nominal Christian majority. Woven into their religion and culture is a level of opposition to the message of Jesus. There are those who want to build on that and have legislation which bans missionizing, and the opponents are not always religious Jews. They have already made several failed attempts to introduce such laws. The government and the courts uphold freedom of speech and liberty of conscience to change religion but it has to be said that most Israelis feel little sympathy towards fellow-Jews who believe in Jesus.

Opposition to witnessing

How does this opposition manifest itself in the workplace or on the streets? For most Jews their opposition is expressed with a polite, 'No' usually coupled with, 'I'm Jewish.' Some, who have probably heard or read arguments against Christianity, will respond with reasons why Jesus cannot be the Messiah.[50] The more determined and committed will ask to be left alone. Then there are the anti-missionaries who are committed to actively opposing the efforts of Christians who specifically evangelize Jews or churches in Jewish neighbourhoods who make a special effort towards Jewish neighbours. Organizations like Jews for Judaism have trained workers who are always on the alert to foil Jewish evangelism. Their passive strategy is to provide seminars and literature to teach their people arguments against the gospel. Their active approach is to interfere with street evangelism, picket special meetings (including getting the latter banned if local authority premises are used), and to contact recent converts to 'de-programme' them. In Israel the methods are similar but of a more threatening nature because believers in Jesus can count on much less sympathy from neighbours and authorities. The very presence of such opposition is a relatively new phenomenon; a response to a steady increase in fruitfulness and to more overt efforts to reach Jewish people with the gospel. In that respect it is a backhanded compliment, although that does not make it any easier to handle.

Christian Response

Whether the opposition is of a more general nature or 'on the streets' the responses we see in the Acts are our guide. We may have to move on from an area of intense opposition. We may choose to endure ridicule, hindrances and violence for the sake of the gospel. We should not be surprised if the authorities are stirred up to oppose the gospel but we can also appeal to them for freedom and vindication. We may be arrested or imprisoned, as Paul was, but hopefully the authorities will learn that the gospel is no enemy to society. What we must not do is listen to people rather than God.

Christians should not therefore be surprised at Jewish opposition to the gospel. It is possible for Christians to feel intimidated. Jewish scholarship can be formidable and in many countries the Jewish community has considerable influence with government and authorities. Such strong opposition can create anxiety in a Christian's mind, and if that is coupled with an unfamiliarity with Jewish arguments, it is tempting, if arguments fail, to respond by putting Jews down – 'We're the king of the castle, you're the dirty rascal' type of attitude. Paul counters such tendencies in Romans 11 when he tells Christians (Gentile ones) not to boast against unbelieving Jews. Paul's own example, despite enduring a level of opposition none of us is ever likely to experience, was to maintain a heart's desire and prayer to God for their salvation.[51]

It is also possible for Christians, in their desire to treat Jewish people as beloved, to forget that 'concerning the gospel they are enemies', and to arrive at a position where there is no tension in the relationship because of the gospel. Jesus warned, 'Woe to you when all men speak well of you.'[52] This is a particular danger for Christians who seek to 'bless Israel' (the State of Israel), and they need to remember there is this 'enemy' aspect which can be changed only by the gospel.

PART 3

Not Cast Away

11.

The Compassion of Jesus for Israel

'Jesus wept' – the words of the shortest verse of the Bible,[1] isolated in one verse to ensure we do not miss their uniqueness. The Son of God weeps! The universe should take note. The gospels tell us of two occasions when Jesus wept, at the tomb of Lazarus and when overlooking Jerusalem just prior to his triumphant final entry to the city. The first shows his compassion for humanity, suffering the consequences of sin; the second his compassion for his own people Israel, in their unbelief.

Jesus' progress towards Jerusalem for his final visit had been steady, described by Luke from 9:51 onwards. Expectation was rising among his disciples and in Luke 19:28–48 we read of his entry to the city as its King. The final stage of that journey led from Bethany to the top of the Mount of Olives, from where the whole city could be seen across the Kidron Valley, with the temple dominating the skyline. Such a view would surely have focused his mind even more intensely on what would soon take place – his own sacrifice. We might have expected some expression of joy from Jesus; he was about to achieve all he came to do to save sinners and around him are hundreds of disciples, excited and exulting; but he weeps. Jesus' focus was the city's coming destruction. How he had longed for its people to benefit from all the Lord had for them, but most of them were refusing and the consequences would be dire.

These are the words Jesus uttered as he wept, and they encapsulated all that moved him to tears:

> If you had known, even you, especially in this your day, the things that make for your peace! But now they are hidden from your eyes. For

days will come upon you when your enemies will build an embankment around you, surround you and close you in on every side, and level you, and your children within you, to the ground; and they will not leave in you one stone upon another, because you did not know the time of your visitation.²

What Jesus Wanted for Israel

The short answer is: peace, peace with God. What he grieved over was their ignorance of 'the things that make for your peace'. Most of them simply had not understood the way of salvation revealed in their Scriptures nor had they responded positively to Jesus as he had expounded them. Some focused on political means to achieve peace, whether by the compromising approach of the Sadducees or the violence of the Zealots. Others, like the Pharisees, at least understood that peace was primarily a spiritual matter but had made the mistake of focusing on their religious activities as the path to peace. They had missed the key point, that our works contribute nothing to our salvation; salvation is a gift of God to be received by faith by those who come to God saying. 'Nothing in my hands I bring.'

It is no different today for those who follow rabbinic Judaism, which teaches 'All Israel has a place in the world to come'; assuring Jewish people that the vast majority of them will know everlasting blessing in the world to come.³ That many lack sincerity, faith, humility and a love of God's truth is an inconvenient reality which is swept under the carpet. The ability to gain merit before God is frequently emphasized by the rabbis, a typical quote being, 'It pleased God to make Israel able to acquire merit. Therefore he multiplied to them Torah and commandments.'⁴ There is no focus on being saved through an act of faith in a saviour.

Jesus' Grief

As he wept, Jesus used four expressions that conveyed his feelings for them in their unbelief. Each one appears to have added to his emotion.

It's too late

The first is 'if', or, as in some versions, 'if only'. The 'only' is added to make sure the sense is not misunderstood. Jesus is not indicating they were just plain ignorant, rather he is expressing an emphatic wish that they had grasped what he had been telling them all along, but he knows it will not now happen. 'If only' is an expression we use to indicate our desire to reverse a situation, but it is too late, and that is the deep feeling Jesus is expressing here. Perhaps you have hesitantly lent something valuable to a friend only to learn it has been damaged. What did you say? 'If only . . .' but it is too late. On reflection this may seem a strange expression from the lips of the Son of God. For him nothing was outside the divine will and purpose, and yet he grieves over this unbelief. It is difficult for us to hold together in our minds that God ordains all things but also grieves over sin and its consequences, and yet it is so. The danger for us, two thousand years after these events, facing the same unbelief in Jewish people and asking ourselves why, is to content ourselves with understanding why it has all happened, but fail to be moved by the loss the Jewish people have suffered.

Privileges

Jesus' grief is compounded by the second expression, 'even you'. The fact is, they should have known better. 'Even you' is the sort of expression we might use when viewing a group of children accused of vandalism and seeing among them one who was not one of the usual suspects, one who is from a good home. What is he doing here? 'You? Even you?' we think to ourselves. Let me be hypothetical for a moment. If Jesus had been standing on Mars Hill in Athens or on one of the seven hills of Rome would it have been fair for him to say to them, 'Even you'? No, because Greeks and Romans were ignorant of the prophecies of the Messiah. However, Israel was not; they knew better. Of all people, they should not have rejected God's Saviour when he came because they had God's blueprint. They were in a position to say, 'Yes, this is the One.' The fact that they were failing to do so weighed Jesus down even further.

Most Jews today are not as privileged as Jesus' hearers but they know more than many in this fallen world. Christians should be careful to make sure that their response to Israel's failure to live up to their privileges is not self-righteous disapproval, but the sorrow of Jesus.

The unrepeatable moment

'In this your day' is Jesus' next expression, one which focuses on the specialness of the moment. Some versions only have 'in this day' because they use a Greek text which lacks the word 'your'. The words 'in this day' point to the specialness of the moment but the presence of 'your' makes it more obvious. We all want the special, unrepeatable moment to go well. We get tense over a wedding because it cannot be done again next week if things do not go as we hope. The coming of the Messiah to Israel, the incarnation of the Son of God, was one such 'tense moment', an unrepeatable event. For this moment Israel had been created, had been undergoing God's preparation for 1,500 years, had been further prepared by Jesus, and it appeared to be going badly wrong – most were not believing. As Jesus looked out over the city it would be only a matter of days before many of its people would cry out for his death, or at least be indifferent to it. He longed for it to be otherwise. Elsewhere he expressed his longing with these words, 'Oh Jerusalem, Jerusalem, the one who kills the prophets and stones those who are sent to her! How often I wanted to gather your children together, as a hen gathers her brood under her wings, but you were not willing!'[5] His longing was as old as the city itself. And now he was among them; the special, unrepeatable moment had come. We can imagine him thinking, 'Yes, things have not gone well in the past but I'm prepared to put that to one side; now is special – get it right!' But most were missing the moment, and Jesus wept. We too should grieve.

Judgement

What remains when the best God can give has been ignored or rejected? Not nothing, nor 'life as normal', but an inevitable judgement on sin. This judgement Jesus proceeds to announce – with tears. The judgement is twofold: Israel will experience spiritual blindness and also the destruction of their beloved Jerusalem. The spiritual blindness meant they would develop a unique inability to perceive 'the things that make for your peace'. They would not be blind to all spiritual realities but to the one which is essential for salvation. This has happened. Israel has been content with a light which is darkness, as Jesus put it, 'If therefore the light that is in you is darkness, how great is that darkness!'[6] Almost every nation on the earth has some admiration for Jesus, but Israel's most famous son is lightly esteemed among his own, and while the State of Israel has built many memorials, it has erected none to Jesus. He foresaw this blindness of mind and heart – and wept. Christians should too, and avoid uttering words like 'Why can't they see it?' as if they have some superior innate ability.

Jesus went on to describe the destruction of Jerusalem, which was brought about by the armies of Rome in AD 70. Often called the city of God, it had now become the place of his Son's rejection and crucifixion; it had failed to recognize its time of visitation. It could not expect to survive such a sin and it did not. The siege and destruction of Jerusalem has gone down in history as one of the most horrific in the annals of warfare. Through internal strife and external force millions of Jewish people died, and the city and temple became a ruin. As Jesus overlooked the city and the temple he alone in the vast crowd saw what was coming, and spoke of it with tears in his eyes.

Jesus' Attitude Today

Does Jewish unbelief still grieve Jesus today? Hebrews tells us, 'Jesus Christ is the same yesterday, today, and forever.'[7] These words indicate he is still grieved by the unbelief of his people Israel and this is proven beyond doubt by the work of the Spirit of Jesus in the life of Paul. In the next chapter we will consider Paul's heart for his people.

12.

Paul's Heart's Desire and Prayer to God

What we have seen in the Lord Jesus we now see in Paul, through his own words in Romans 9:1–5. The obvious difference is that Paul is an imperfect being, a redeemed sinner, and because that is where all Christians stand then Paul challenges us in a different way. What should be the Christian's heart attitude to the Jews? Paul shows us the way.

Paul's Words

The title of this chapter comes from Paul's words in Romans 10:1, which encapsulate the full expression of his feelings in Romans 9:1–5:

> I tell the truth in Christ, I am not lying, my conscience also bearing me witness in the Holy Spirit, that I have great sorrow and continual grief in my heart. For I could wish that I myself were accursed from Christ for my brethren, my countrymen according to the flesh, who are Israelites, to whom pertain the adoption, the glory, the covenants, the giving of the law, the service of God, and the promises; of whom are the fathers and from whom, according to the flesh, Christ came, who is over all, the eternally blessed God. Amen.

This comes as a rather abrupt statement at the start of a new section in his letter. Paul has just reached the heights at the end of Romans 8, where he has declared the certainty of a Christian's salvation in Messiah Jesus, the Son of God. Then, all of a sudden, he is telling us of a deep sorrow within him. He seems to assume we understand it is because of Israel's unbelief, which he plans to explain but because he has some hard things to say he gives us these personal statements to indicate that he has not hardened his heart to his people. Paul is far from indifferent to their fate – and he does not want his readers to be either.

Who Are Israelites

Before we examine more closely the sentiments Paul expresses we need to look at what he tells us about the people he has in view. No one can be in any doubt Paul is writing about the Jews. He describes the people here as 'my brethren' and as, 'my countrymen according to the flesh'. The latter is an expression we all use to describe those of the ethnic group into which we are born, and Paul was born Jewish, and in particular he was of the tribe of Benjamin. His use of the word 'brethren' tells us of his affection for his people. His faith in Jesus, and the rejection of Jesus by most of them, had not led him to keep his distance or become indifferent.

Paul calls the Jewish people 'Israelites' because he wants to draw attention to the privilege of being descended from the one who wrestled with God, prevailed in faith and was subsequently a 'prince with God'. Few Christians have such an illustrious forefather, we mostly have warriors or human idealists of one sort or another, but what a blessing to have that sort of family example to look up to and to follow! By remembering the history and following Jacob's example the Jewish nation was to live a life, not of self-reliance, but of trusting God.

We should not miss Paul's emphatic use of the present tense here – 'who *are* Israelites'. The verb 'to be' is often omitted in Greek, but here it is included for emphasis. Put the other way we can say that he certainly did not write 'were Israelites'. Some of the privileges he is about to mention have become only a memory, but such losses do not take away the nation's status. And he goes on to state, 'to whom [belongs] the adoption'. They are still an adopted people of God. To be part of a nation that God had chosen to be his special people was an immeasurable blessing, especially when we remember the sad lot of the rest of the world left in ignorance and the degraded practices of idolatry.

Israel's Privileges then

Paul lists out the privileges of his nation because his purpose is to underscore the greatness of Israel's blessings and hence the greatness of their loss. To have friends who are poor and live in a tiny, cramped home may make us sorry for them but to have friends who once lived in a ten-bedroom mansion, lost it all, and now live in a tiny, cramped house brings an added note of sorrow to us. Such was Israel.

'The glory' is the visible manifestation of God's presence, and 'the covenants' refers to those commitments of God made to Abraham, to the nation at Sinai, to David and in the new covenant. 'The giving of the law' not only refers to the receiving of it but also encompasses the whole experience of living under God's law, and 'the service of God' describes the worship at the temple. 'The promises' calls to mind those key assurances of God concerning the land and offspring and the coming saviour but also refers to the many particular commitments God gave over the centuries. 'The fathers' refers especially to Abraham, Isaac and Jacob but no doubt includes all who stood as godly heroes of faith.

As Moses surveyed the blessing of possessing all these things he wrote, 'Happy are you, O Israel! Who is like you, a people saved by the LORD.'[1] Too often Christians have a limited, and even condescending view of Israel in the Old Testament period. They read the New Testament condemnation of legalism and imagine that that was Old Testament life. They hear sermons on Israel's failures and forget what the book of Ruth describes of the righteous, joyful lives of the godly even though they lived in times of decline; or they overlook the times of great revival in Israel in the days of David, Asa, Jehoshaphat, Hezekiah, Josiah and Ezra, when thousands repented, turned back to the Lord, lived joyfully under his law and made renewed efforts to ensure the temple and its worship were maintained.

There was the joy of going to Jerusalem to worship the Lord, especially at festival times when there was rest, renewal of family ties and personal friendships, and above all the solemn, pure and joyful worship of Yahweh. In times of trial, enemy attack, adverse agricultural conditions, they could hold on to his commitment to them to be their God and support them. The promises of the Lord could be recalled and the memory of his dealings with their forefathers would inspire. And, then, they had what all people need, a sense of purpose, of destiny – there was a coming one, a person who would bless them.

I can imagine the response, 'Well, not all in the garden was rosy, was it?' I have no wish to deny it but failure should not be allowed to obscure the existence of true spirituality. When people criticize the wider church, true Christians will often respond, 'Yes, but that is just religion, the true, living faith has been lost there', and then they go on to point out where the latter can be found. The Old Testament situation was identical.

This note of the Messiah, the Christ, is the one on which Paul finishes his list of privileges, for it is the pinnacle of Israel's blessings – the Saviour of the world was born among them, born a Jew. To underline the greatness of that honour Paul makes one of his most emphatic statements on the divinity of Jesus, 'who is over all, the eternally blessed God'.[2] God himself took a human nature, one with Jewish characteristics, and lived among the Jews, living their cultural life, walking along their roads and over their fields. Who would not like to read that in the history books of their nation? As Moses wrote, 'Happy are you, O Israel! Who is like you?'

Paul's Experience: Hope and Disappointment

Paul was a man immersed in all these good things that Israel possessed from his earliest years. Before his conversion the truths of God's dealings with his people were his daily bread and he devoted himself to obedience to God's law. After his conversion he saw Israel's privileges in a new, spiritual light, but it was not one that led him to belittle them, as he wrote in Romans, 'What advantage then has the Jew, or what is the profit of circumcision? Much in every way!'[3] Jesus had had mercy on him, the chief of sinners; there was every reason to hope for great things among his compatriots. We can only begin to imagine his dismay when he observed the unbelief of so many.

The early years of the gospel in Jerusalem and Judea were indeed times of great blessing so that almost thirty years on from Pentecost James could say to Paul, 'You see, brother, how many myriads of Jews there are who have believed.'[4] There was every reason to be hopeful. Christians too easily forget this obedience and remember only the rejection. However, as time went on it was clear that the nation, as a nation, was not turning to Messiah Jesus – it was failing to fulfil its destiny. Paul himself experienced this firsthand during his ten years of preaching among the Gentiles when, despite there always being some Jews who believed, it was his own people who most often led the charge against the gospel. He saw this national failure and grieved deeply. I am not suggesting he was naïve, for Jesus had warned of how things would develop, but Paul had within him the hope for his nation which every patriot possesses for his own people – honour and achievement, peace and security, health and provision for all. He could see those things slipping away from them.

Israel's Privileges Today

In what sense do these privileges of Israel still influence them today? The fact that they are broken-off branches does not mean those privileges lose all effect. They have not become the natural branches of a peach tree or a wild olive! There is a parallel with the loss suffered by a backslidden Christian, who does not lose everything gained from walking with God for months or years, and who certainly does not lose adopted status despite contrary appearances.

I have already drawn attention to some privileges earlier in this chapter. Being Israelites, descended from illustrious forefathers, with a continuing awareness of being a people adopted by God and recipients of his promises are all things which impact the Jewish people today, pointing them to the way of life God requires, and alerting them to their messianic destiny.

Some things, like the temple worship and the manifest presence of God, can be only a memory, as they are not experienced now, and yet that memory can stimulate a hunger and thirst for a living relationship with God today. One thing all Jewish people know is that there is something unique about them and their God-connection simply cannot be erased. All this is reinforced by their national history, which is biblical history and its main events are celebrated in the annual round of Jewish festivals. Every nation has at least one day to which the entire nation relates as pivotal to their existence, and for the Jewish people that is the Passover, reminding them year by year of a great deliverance event in their history. It is theirs to remember and it speaks loud and clear of their indebtedness to Almighty God. Millions of Jewish people now live in the land where so much of this history occurred, and for many of them it is where they were born; which further underlines the history and its significance, creating a pressure to recognize the accuracy of the biblical story.

The hope for the Messiah is repeated every day in the prayers of the synagogue and every Jewish person knows of the promise, even if they make no effort to investigate it. In over thirty years of witness to Jewish people I have never met any Jewish person, young or old, who was ignorant of this hope. Possessing the law of God still has a profound ethical influence on Jewish culture such that Jewish people easily take their place in what we call Christian societies because of ethical beliefs held in common with Christianity: the Judeo-Christian ethic. There is a strong sense of right and wrong, of fairness and justice, among Jewish people, which leaves them far less influenced by post-modernism than others in western societies.

All of these privileges were granted to Israel with the ultimate aim of them being a channel for the knowledge of the one, true God being conveyed to the world. It should not surprise us therefore to see in them the gifts required for good communication. And we do see them. There is no lack of Jewish people among the lawyers, writers, musicians, entertainers, news-show hosts and film producers of the world. And most Jewish people are good conversationalists; in fact, in thirty years' experience of conversations with Jewish people I cannot recall an embarrassing silence! May their day of salvation soon come – they will certainly let everyone know!

Finally, there is the ongoing influence of having had the Son of God, incarnate among them. He is the great unmentionable subject among those who do not believe within the Jewish community, in their institutions and now in the organization of the Jewish State. If he could be easily dismissed there would be little or no tension at the mention of his name. After all, there have been many false messiahs in Jewish history,[5] and the mention of any one of them will not turn a hair but 'Jesus' does. Jesus is the unmentionable name within the Jewish community. To borrow some phraseology from George Eliot, he is the sound on the other side of the silence. God was incarnate as a Jew and the impact on the Jewish psyche is inescapable to this day.

Paul's Response

There is surely nothing like this in the annals of Christian writing. Here is what underlies Paul's heart's desire for the salvation of Israel. Paul knows he is stating something that some might find hard to believe and so he prefaces it by expressions designed to underline to us that he is being absolutely truthful. Paul asserts he is speaking 'in Christ', which means that he is conscious that every word will be weighed by him. He asserts he is certain he is not lying because his conscience is not telling him he is. Paul knows the conscience is an imperfect instrument, due to sin, so he asserts he is conscious of the Spirit's work to ensure his conscience is working accurately. There is really no more anyone can do to check him or herself and assure others that they are speaking truthfully. So what is Paul asserting? There are two things: one concerns the emotions created within him by Israel's loss, and the other concerns what he was willing to do to remedy the situation.

Great sorrow and continual grief

Elsewhere Paul tells Christians to rejoice always,[6] and some may find it difficult to imagine how he could follow his own exhortation and yet profess to always carry about within his heart a great sorrow and never-absent grief over the unbelief of his Jewish kinsmen. Clearly Paul could not wear a smile and a frown at the same time. I think what it meant for Paul was that if you had encountered him in any number of situations in church life, situations in which he, like all others, would express a variety of emotions, and you had asked him something about Israel's unbelief, then the sorrow and grief would have welled up to the surface. It was always there, deep down. There must be something similar in the experience of the president of a nation which is at war. He has to concern himself with other matters, even social occasions, but it cannot be imagined that if on such an occasion he was asked about the war, he would say, 'You know, I'd quite forgotten about it.' It is a burden he will always carry while those he has sent to war are being injured and dying on the battlefield. Likewise, Paul never forgot the spiritual battle, and its consequences for so many of God's people Israel.

Paul shows us how an awareness of the seriousness of Israel's sin, and grief because of it, are not incompatible; they can be held in tension. Some Christians fail in this and develop a condemning spirit, which smacks of James and John's attitude to opponents of Jesus, 'Lord, do you want us to command fire to come down from heaven and consume them, just as Elijah did?'[7] What Jesus said to James and John acts as a warning to us: 'You do not know what manner of spirit you are of. For the Son of Man did not come to destroy men's lives but to save them.'[8]

I could wish

Paul also declares what he would like to do to ensure his kinsmen escape the consequences of their unbelief. What he does is to wish upon himself the condemnation they deserve. This is the force of the expression, 'I could wish that I myself were accursed from Christ.' There is no way to water this down. Paul is expressing a willingness to be separated from Messiah and suffer God's curse, so they might be saved. Here is fervent love! The impossibility of this idea is not lost on Paul, and is reflected in the way he expresses himself. 'I could wish' in our English versions is a use of the imperfect tense to express a wish for something yet unrealized. It is the context that determines whether it is something impossible. For example, in Paul's anguished words over the Galatians' situation: 'My little children, for whom I labor in birth again until Christ is formed in you, *I would like* to be present with you now and to change my tone.'[9] But he is elsewhere so it is impossible. Likewise, Paul knows that being accursed from Christ to save others is something which cannot be; he knows he is a sinner who cannot bear the sin of another. So he is expressing a desire but this does not make him insincere. A retired athlete watching a race might express his desire to be involved again by saying, 'If only I was forty years younger!' He has a deep desire to put his kit on and get out there but he knows he cannot run; yet his desire is sincere. 'What love is this!' we might well exclaim. There is no greater depth of love for the lost that a redeemed sinner can attain. For us it stands as a goal to strive for, and especially for those in gospel ministry. Can I say it? No. Can you? The road to it is surely a thorny one.

And Us?

I want to suggest that Paul's heart's concern for the Jewish people is something all Christians should, to one degree or another, enter into. Paul's feelings are not just due to being Jewish himself but they arise from observing the failure of God's covenant people. The sight of someone backslidden from Christ, who once praised and served God with us, surely grieves us. Seen on the grand tapestry of God's redemption, Israel is that backslider. If we stand back and see the big picture, we should join Paul in his grief.

Prayer to God

It is not surprising to find from his words in Romans 10:1 that Paul's heart's desire for Israel led to prayer for their salvation. It would be surprising if Christians did not follow his example; as branches of the olive tree we cannot but be aware of the broken-off branches. There ought to be prayer by church leaders when the whole church gathers, at church prayer times and in a Christian's private prayers. Over the centuries God has heard and brought in the remnant. May Israel's fullness yet come in answer to our prayers! Maybe you have never prayed for their salvation. May I suggest starting on a Friday night because that is the eve of the Sabbath, a significant time for the Jewish community when many families gather for a meal and some go to synagogue. That is an easy picture to have in our mind, which will remind us to pray for them every week at that time.

13.

Sin and Satan Defeated

God's purpose for Israel has not been allowed to falter because of sin or Satan's malice. And that is not just a matter of history; today they are not cast away, they have not been abandoned to their sin and to Satan. It might appear so, because they have sunk into a state of rebellion against God through hostility to his Son, but the reality is otherwise. To establish this we need first of all to review the victory achieved by Messiah over sin and Satan, and then to consider the outworking of this among the Jewish people in salvation and providence.

The Victory of Jesus the Messiah as Israel

Jesus the Messiah was destined to perfectly fulfil all God's will for his people Israel. In particular that meant becoming God's ideal Israel, for Isaiah calls Messiah, 'My servant, O Israel, In whom I will be glorified.'[1] He would perform faithfully all that God required of his people Israel. He kept the law perfectly and, as Isaiah prophesied, he magnified it and made it honourable.[2] He was tempted, both by Satan and the sinful suggestions of people, tempted to stray from God's purpose for him and choose an alternative and easier pathway; yet he never wavered.[3] As the representative Israelite he triumphed over sin and Satan.

God had promised Abraham that in his seed all the nations of the earth would be blessed; Israel would be the salvation of the world. In Messiah Jesus, the ideal Israel, the core requirement was achieved when he paid the law's penalty, offering himself a sacrifice for sin according to the plan of God. He died crying, 'It is finished!'⁴ He triumphed. Paul expresses this victory at the cross in a unique way: 'Having disarmed principalities and powers, He made a public spectacle of them, triumphing over them in it.'⁵ By dealing with the divine charge against sinners of 'guilty before the law' by paying the law's penalty, Satan's hosts are disarmed; unable to make accusations stick, they are defeated.

The Gentiles need to hear of this salvation and be obedient, and that too is a role fulfilled by the Messiah as Israel when, as a 'light to the Gentiles', he becomes God's salvation to the ends of the earth.⁶ He fulfils that role to this day as he directs the work of his kingdom and the nations continue to hear and obey.

The Triumph of Salvation in Israel

But how has the victory of Messiah worked out among his brothers after the flesh, the people of Israel – victory or defeat, success or failure? Isaiah foresaw a decisive victory. In Isaiah 59:9–21 he describes the coming of God's Redeemer to a people sunk in sin. The Redeemer will bring salvation and the gift of the Spirit to ensure future faithfulness. Verse 19 is Isaiah's summary, 'When the enemy comes in like a flood, The Spirit of the LORD will lift up a standard against him.'⁷ Isaiah does expect many to be delivered from the penalty and power of sin by the Redeemer. This does not mean that Isaiah expects victory to be the experience of every person in the nation, for in a subsequent prophecy he addresses those who forsake the Lord, 'Behold, My servants shall eat But you shall be hungry',⁸ and to the faithful he writes, 'I will bring forth descendants from Jacob, And from Judah an heir of My mountains; My elect shall inherit it And my servants shall dwell there.'⁹ This is exactly how Paul describes the Jewish situation of his day: 'What then? Israel has not obtained what it seeks; but the elect have obtained it and the rest were blinded.'¹⁰ God made it plain beforehand that some would believe and some would not; some would receive grace to believe and some would be judged for their wilful unbelief. In both cases he is magnified. Sin and Satan are defeated.

Christians are accustomed to read and hear of 'the failure of Israel', especially in sermons or commentaries, but the expression strikes me as unhelpful because it implies the failure of God's purposes for them. But the reality is otherwise. Despite unbelief, many were obedient and the Gentiles heard and believed. This is not a failure but a glorious triumph.

To put this into perspective it might be useful to consider how we react to the expression 'the failure of the church'. It is not meant to indicate that God has failed but that there is far too much sinful behaviour among God's people. However, when I read the expression 'the failure of Israel' it does not always come over in the same way but rather, they rejected the Messiah so that is it, Israel failed. The fact that many of Israel repented and took the good news to the world is not imputed to Israel but to Christians. Christians did the good bits and Israel did the bad ones. But the fact is it was men and women of Israel who did the good bits! Why does this happen? Well, for 'Christians' in the above read 'Gentile Christians'. It is not a misperception I have found among Jewish Christians. It seems to be another example of that boasting over the Jews which is condemned by Paul in Romans 11:18. God has not been defeated by sin or Satan. He planned to bless Israel, and to use them to take the message of redemption to the world. They did that centuries ago and they are still doing that through the Scriptures today.

God's future blessing for Israel is connected to this same theme of victory over his enemies. The chapter of Isaiah quoted above, which spoke of Israel's deliverance from the power of sin by the Redeemer,[11] is quoted by Paul when he reveals future blessing in Romans 11: 'And so all Israel will be saved, as it is written: "The Deliverer will come out of Zion."'[12] In other words, future salvation blessing for the Jewish people is to be seen in terms of God's determination that sin and Satan will not lord it over his people but that God himself will have the last word.

It is also worth considering how every Jew who comes to faith today is a triumph over Satan's lie in the Jewish community that Jesus is not the Messiah. The reaction of the Jewish community to one believing in Jesus testifies to this. No one says, 'Oh, that's just one person.' Statistics are not the issue. Just one who believes challenges their position, challenges the lie. Each one who believes effectively declares, 'You were wrong two thousand years ago and you are still wrong today; you believed a lie.' And as Paul revealed, there will always be a remnant to expose and defeat the lie of Satan.[13]

The Triumph of Providence and Promise for Israel

The Jewish people as a nation are still with us. That may sound self-evident but it should be remembered that they survive despite some very determined and barbaric efforts to destroy them. Over the last two thousand years the efforts of Roman armies, the Crusades, fundamentalist Islamic rulers, national expulsions, the Inquisition, pogroms, the Holocaust, and now Israel's neighbours in the Middle East and fundamentalist Islamist terror movements, have all desired their harm and even their annihilation.

The New Testament presents these assaults in terms of sin and Satan and promises their defeat. I want to consider two ways we are assured of this: Satan's defeat in the book of Revelation and God's promises to Abraham.

A satanic conflict

Chapter 12 is the point in the book of Revelation at which we are introduced in more detail to the church's conflict with Satan. In a vision John sees a woman who gives birth to a male child. She is clothed with the sun and has a crown of twelve stars on her head. Immediately a great, fiery red dragon (which verse 9 reveals to be Satan) attempts to destroy the child, but the attack is thwarted. Verse 5 describes the child as the one who will 'rule all nations with a rod of iron' and is obviously the child Jesus. Verse 6 describes the woman fleeing for safety to the wilderness. Satan immediately sets about destroying the woman. Failing to destroy her, he widens the war to include an attack on 'the rest of her offspring, who keep the commandments of God and have the testimony of Jesus Christ'.[14]

Who is the woman? Some suggest the New Testament church, but such a view is difficult to square with the distinction made in verse 17 between her and 'the rest of her offspring', who are the church. There is also the problem that the New Testament church did not give birth to Christ. Others have suggested that she is the faithful Israel of the Old Testament through whom Christ came. But that has two difficulties. Firstly, Jesus' genealogy is hardly a list of the faithful, and secondly the woman continues on and is persecuted at the same time as the New Testament church. The woman has to be the nation of Israel. This being so there is a prophecy here of her survival, indeed her triumph over Satan, by God's grace.

Her survival is certain because a place of refuge for her in the wilderness is 'prepared by God'.[15] Whatever attack comes against her the Lord already has a place of escape which will enable her to avoid extermination. Verse 14 describes her as 'nourished' during this time, indicating her needs will be met. This has certainly been the case for the Jewish nation on many occasions during the last two thousand years. They have been and are in a wilderness, but they have survived Satan's attempts to destroy them. By God's grace he is a defeated foe.

What do these images tell us about how Satan will attack, and how God delivers Israel from annihilation? There is no impression of obviously supernatural means of attack or deliverance. The image of floodwater in verse 15 is probably meant to portray Satan's use of people in hordes or in concert, as water frequently portrays people in Scripture.[16] History would certainly bear that out. Similarly, God uses earthly means, portrayed by the earth opening up to swallow the flood. Pressure from foreign governments and organizations restrained the hand of Russian persecutors of the Jews in the late nineteenth century, and every survivor of the Holocaust has a story to tell of 'coincidences' which meant they survived but others did not. By very ordinary means God has ensured the survival of the people of Israel.

God's covenant promises to Abraham

I understand this preservation of Israel as rooted in those original promises to Abraham,[17] promises still in force as part of their covenant status. At this point I want to briefly review how those promises are being fulfilled so that they are not defeated by sin or Satan.

They remain a *great nation*, not perhaps in numbers but certainly in ability, as the number of Jewish people who have won a Nobel

Prize testifies.[18] God has *blessed* them in his providential care, as Mark Twain's famous description testifies,

> the Jew ought hardly to be heard of, but he is heard of, has always been heard of ... his contributions to the world's list of great names in literature, science, art, music, finance, medicine, and abstruse learning are also way out of proportion to the weakness of his numbers ... exhibiting no decadence, no infirmities of age, no weakening of his parts, no slowing of his energies, no dulling of his alert and aggressive mind. All things are mortal but the Jew; all other forces pass, but he remains. What is the secret of his immortality?'[19]

The secret is God's faithfulness and blessing. The name of Israel is still *great* despite being disliked by many, and aside from the spiritual blessing they have been, they are *a blessing* in many other ways; witness the medical research by Jewish people which has led to cures for polio, typhus, tuberculosis, diphtheria, diabetes and syphilis.

As to God's promise of *cursing those who curse* and *blessing those who bless* Israel, I find evidence of this more difficult to pinpoint. It seems to me that this promise functions more like a warning on a parcel, 'Handle With Care!' or like one of those marketing letters we all get which has on the envelope 'Open today for your free gift!' The promise tells us to think carefully about our attitudes to Jewish people. However, I believe there is one way in which we can see evidence of God's curse or blessing, and that is by observing the effect of shunning Jews or of welcoming Jews. There is a story about a sultan of Constantinople who declared the king of Spain to be very foolish because the latter had expelled all the Jews from Spain in 1492. Why? Because many of those Jews fled to Constantinople and brought increased prosperity to the sultan's domains! When Oliver Cromwell argued for the Jews to be permitted to return to England and resettle, part of his reason was the benefits it would bring to the national economy. This has been repeated time and again through history. Those who have shown favour to the Jewish people by welcoming them have benefited from their education, expertise and industry. This is one means by which God blesses those who bless and curses those who curse. More than this is, I think, very difficult to say. God's providential dealings with people and nations are frequently a mystery to us; they are the 'secret things' of God.[20] Too many Christians seem to think they know God's secret things when it comes to blessing and curse related to the Jews. My advice to them would be to desist from thinking they know God's secrets, and stick to what they can see of cause and effect.

One final comment, which relates this issue to a Christian's personal spiritual growth: I am sure that the humble attitude which is necessary to esteem Israel and seek their good brings its own blessing to the soul, and the lack of it produces a hardening.

The Almighty has determined to preserve Israel, even though in a wilderness; sin and Satan will not defeat them. And as that wilderness period has a time limit[21] then we have every reason to hope they will emerge, as a nation, from a dry and barren place to one of fruitfulness for God – a victory for the God who saves.

The Middle-East conflict

I cannot leave this subject of conflict for the Jewish people without some comment on the ill winds which swirl around the State of Israel in the Middle East. It is not my intention to take sides on particular details of the conflict but to look at the broad picture. God's providential care has been obvious in the failure of attempts to destroy her (such a comment is not intended to justify all Israel's actions). The 'Handle With Care!' label should be carefully noted by all who enter the conflict or comment upon it. I believe that those who would deny any right for Jewish people to live in their ancient homeland with some form of self-government, and those who seek their annihilation, are manifesting the antagonism of sin and Satan. Satan is having no difficulty stirring up murderous intentions against them, particularly through the negative attitudes to Jewish people embedded in Islam. Those who oppose Israel while having principles that would lead them to support her democratic values and civil liberties are manifesting sin's hatred of a people linked to God. Yet, out of the whirlwind God does speak and I cannot but think that he is doing so to Israel, and to others living within this conflict; something I will discuss further in my chapter on the return to the land.

Christian Responsibility

Christians are those who have an insight into the satanic origins of the troubles which the Jewish people have endured, and also they have been blessed by Israel's spiritual blessings. How should they respond when they see Jewish people in trouble? Prayer for their salvation is assumed here, but what other prayers and actions should Christians consider?

Prayer

Surely we should pray that Satan's purposes will be thwarted; that Jewish people will be preserved. We should intercede on their behalf and pray for the Lord's name to be glorified in their preservation. This does not mean we have to take their side in all that they do, agreeing with their every action, or always assuming their opponents are in the wrong. It simply means we must stand back and see the wood for the trees – when Satan sends out a flood to destroy the woman who brought the Saviour into the world then we should pray for them.

Words and actions

However, there are times when we should get involved in the details if we are able. If we see anti-Semitism rear its ugly head in our community surely we should have something to say, to authorities and to the Jewish community. Regarding the Middle East conflict, Christians should be careful about getting embroiled in debates on details unless they are well informed, because situations are often very complex with much misinformation circulating. However, we do not have to be experts on all the details to speak or write on their behalf to drive home the basic point that they, like all other peoples, have a right to exist and a right to live in their ancient homeland with secure borders. I was in Sydney, Australia, in 2002 and saw a leaflet advertising a 'Solidarity with Israel' meeting. Its slogan was, 'We have a right to exist!' I was stunned. I never thought I would again see the Jewish people being reduced to such a basic defence. Christians cannot remain silent when such an atmosphere develops.

A simple expression of sympathy to a Jewish friend counts for more than we often realize. I once had a regular correspondence with a management consultant who was a leading figure in London's Jewish community. When it came to a close I wrote to express my readiness to help should things turn for the worse for the Jews in Britain. The reply I received was full of a sense of relief and thanks. Not at the thought of what I might achieve, but at the thought that a non-Jew had some sensitivity to the sense of isolation he felt.

Responding to Christendom's Past

Many of the troubles which Jewish people have suffered at the hands of sinners and Satan took place within what is called 'Christendom', at the hands of people that the Jews would understand to be Christians. Are all those who take the name 'Christian' responsible? Do we need to respond in some way?

Sadness

Christians should be deeply sorrowful that so much persecution of the Jews took place in the name of Jesus. They may bear no personal responsibility but they should be saddened by it. It is no good saying, 'It's nothing to do with me', because it is perceived as such and that has to be taken into account. There is no doubt that most of this persecution was inspired by baptized Gentiles, nominal Christians with no love for God and his ways. That is not to say that true Christians have not held wrong attitudes and said wrong things regarding the Jewish people. When that is brought to light it should be confessed to God and, where appropriate, to fellow men and women. Christians today have to live with the damaging effects of what some true Christians said about the Jewish people hundreds of years ago – statements by church leaders such as Chrysostom and Luther. We need to be careful about joining in with the blanket condemnation of such men which is often meted out by Jewish leaders. Some of the criticisms by those men of the Jewish people of their day, and of rabbinic Judaism, were no different from those of the Lord Jesus. However, other things they said were unworthy of a Christian in both content and tone, things of which we should be ashamed because they have dishonoured the gospel. From such things we need to disassociate ourselves, while being aware of our own proneness to speak hastily and sinfully when angered and under pressure.

Repentance

What about repentance on behalf of others who sinfully persecuted Jews in the name of Jesus? I have already noted above that if we are guilty of anti-Semitism ourselves then we need to confess it and repent, but here I am considering our responsibility because of our association with others who bear the name 'Christian' and who have persecuted Jews. For example, some nominal church bodies were implicated to one degree or another in the Nazi persecution of the Jews and have issued formal expressions of repentance. Do we have to follow their example because we are part of a Christian church and are lumped together with them in the perception of the Jewish community? It seems to me that the answer is, no. There is a pressure from within evangelical church circles for this to happen but I believe it is more inspired by emotion and sentiment than clear biblical thinking. Repentance is a change of mind, and it stands to reason that we cannot be asked to change our mind if we do not have an anti-Jewish mindset, and we certainly cannot be asked to have a change of mind on behalf of another.

This argument for repentance has been fine-tuned by some in pointing to men like Daniel, who associated himself with the sins of Israel and sought forgiveness,[22] even though it is assumed he was not personally guilty. Should we not therefore do the same? We can only answer affirmatively if there is a genuine sense in which the people concerned can be called our people. Daniel was a member of the covenant people then, and as they suffered God's judgement he suffered with them. It was impossible for him to divorce his own personal sins from their experience and so he identified with them in confession. In New Testament times, sin in the covenant community is dealt with at a local church level, for example in the letters to the churches in Revelation 2 – 3. That is because the responsibility of the members for each other is a real one. If there is sin in a church then the sinner is guilty and the others are responsible to act against it; they sin if they fail to do so. Anti-Semitism would be one such sin. We do not read anywhere in the New Testament of the sins of one church, say Corinth, being charged on any other church, although it is possible to extend this responsibility for acting against sin to a group of churches when they have bound themselves in some form of disciplined fellowship. Therefore I would say that the response of repentance can only be expected of a Christian if he or she has been personally guilty of wrong attitudes to the Jews as a people, or of a Christian church if it is failing to deal with such wrong attitudes in its midst.

Sorrow and shame

The response I would encourage in Christians and churches is that of sorrow and even shame. Sorrow should be stirred in us from a feeling of common human compassion because the Jews have suffered so much, but also because such things were done in the name of Jesus. There should also be shame. Now shame implies guilt, and that requires repentance. Am I contradicting what I said above? We need to consider that there are examples in Scripture of the experience of shame where there is no personal failure in the one feeling shame. For example in Ezra 9:5,6 we read of Ezra's shame at the marriages taking place between Israel's leaders and Canaanite women.

Maybe an illustration would help to show the contrast between shame for the actions of others and that of repentance. If a group of supporters of our national football team should go on the rampage while abroad, and lives were lost, we would see a threefold response from within the nation: repentance, apology and shame. The ones who repent in such a situation are those who were violent. The ones who apologize and condemn the evil will be those in positions of leadership, because there is a sense of identity and responsibility which demands it. The ones who will feel sorrow and shame are the ordinary members of the nation because they strive for integrity and good behaviour in national life, and they feel that somehow the nation has failed when such events take place. No one suggests that they are all personally responsible, but they feel that somehow, somewhere, something has gone wrong in their national life, they are a part of that, and they feel ashamed. In a similar way, whether we like it or not, we are identified with all who call themselves Christian, and with the influence of Christianity in world history. Our response to the fact that so many who have taken that name have hated Jews must include some degree of shame. Somehow, somewhere, something has gone wrong in the spread of Christianity into the world, and we should feel ashamed.

Are there ever any circumstances in which repentance or apology, shame and sorrow should be expressed formally and publicly? I believe there are. All the possibilities cannot be covered here, but a general point can be stated. When hostility to Jews has been publicly and officially encouraged in a community, and a publicly recognized church or church body in that community has either kept silent or even approved such official anti-Semitism, then some form of public statement is surely necessary.

The sufferings of the Jews at the hands of people called Christians is a major issue for Christians and churches because the Jews are a people with whom we have a unique relationship. I have no doubt that church bodies should have an official statement of their attitude, especially if they have Jewish neighbours. Does yours? What is your own personal attitude? Do you feel some degree of sorrow and also shame? Surely we should be grieved that there have been times when the Jews have seen Christianity as their worst enemy.

14.

I am of Peter: the Apostleship to the Circumcision

If there is one word which unifies the whole Bible from Genesis to Revelation, I would say it is 'mission'. Yahweh is on a mission to rescue his fallen, rebellious creation. He planned it before the foundation of the world and the book of Revelation portrays its successful completion. Pivotal to it all is one person, the Anointed One, the Messiah, whom Isaiah calls 'the Servant of the LORD'. His role is twofold, 'to restore the preserved ones of Israel' and 'a light to the Gentiles, That You should be My salvation to the ends of the earth'.[1] His mission is twofold because of the radically different states of the two groups to whom he ministers. Israel has light but needs to be brought back to obedience; the nations are in spiritual darkness and need light.

Jesus is the Servant of the Lord and his ministry reflects this prophetic pattern. It could be said that it was not only twofold but in two stages. During his earthly ministry his main focus was Israel, as he said to a Canaanite woman living in Syro-Phoenicia, 'I was not sent except to the lost sheep of the house of Israel.'[2] He was calling them back and many came. Yet Jesus was not careless of the spiritual need of non-Israelites, as that same woman discovered when he heard her request and delivered her demon-possessed daughter. It was a matter of when, not whether. The time for an earnest start to be made on his mission to the Gentiles came some seventeen years after Pentecost. However, it would be a mistake to think that that marked a closing of Jesus' ministry to Israel. At the start of Acts, Luke describes his earlier work, Luke's Gospel, as an account of 'all that Jesus began both to do and teach'.[3] What we see in Acts is therefore Jesus continuing his work as the Servant of the Lord – restoring Jews and giving light to the Gentiles. Far too often our view of mission post-Pentecost is one which focuses on the nations and overlooks the Jews. Read any book on mission and you will find there is almost no discussion about how the church should continue Jesus' mission to Israel as it engages in his mission to the nations. The apostles knew better and they established a division of labour, some to the Jews and some to the nations.

An Apostolic Division of Labour

Paul tells us about this division in Galatians 2:1–10. In the early part of his letter Paul relates to the Galatian believers a visit to Jerusalem during which the other apostles received him as an equal. He describes how they recognized each other's ministries, but also a fundamental difference between them.

Paul's summary of the discussion mentions a gospel of the uncircumcision and a gospel of the circumcision, and an apostleship of the circumcision and to the nations.[4] At the end of this encounter Paul describes how they agreed among themselves that 'We should go to the Gentiles and they to the circumcised'.[5] Clearly this was not just a wise strategy, the sort of thing which leads some to focus on particular groups for reasons of language, culture, religion or social organization. The terminology of 'circumcision' and 'uncircumcision' is deliberate – one group was in a covenant relationship with God and the other was not. Circumcision was the sign of the covenant between God and Abraham and his offspring through Isaac and Israel.[6] Some English versions use 'Jew' instead of 'circumcised', which unintentionally weakens the reason for the distinction, failing to draw attention to the covenant issue.

In fact, the apostles were not themselves creating a division of labour, they were simply recognizing what God was already doing, as Paul wrote, 'He who worked effectively in Peter for the apostleship to the circumcised also worked effectively in me toward the Gentiles.'[7] Jesus was still at work as the Servant of the Lord, through his chosen instruments, reaching out distinctively to Jew and to Gentile.

An Apostleship to the Circumcision Today?

Are these two apostleships in force today? I do not mean do we have apostles today but are there those whose ministry puts them in one role or the other? When we think of mission today the bulk of the personnel are devoted to mission to the nations, which is not surprising, it is a huge task. Whether they and their churches think of their ministry in this way or not, those thousands of missionaries are of the apostleship to the nations. It seems to me that it does not occur to most Christians to think the apostleship to the circumcision even exists today. But why not? The New Testament does not cancel it, and Jesus remains the servant with a commission to Jew and Gentile, so an apostleship to the circumcision still exists. Commenting on these verses Calvin quipped that if the Pope was indeed the apostle of Peter he should focus on the Jews: 'If the Pope would establish any claim to his primacy, let him gather churches from among the Jews.'[8] He was making a serious point, and implicitly acknowledging an ongoing apostleship to the circumcision. Commentators on this passage acknowledge the division's relevance for those days and see God's hand in it; only a few go on to discuss its relevance beyond the days of the Judean state. Yet 'the circumcision' still exists today, and God's covenant with them remains in force.[9] We should therefore expect a distinct ministry to them.

In practice

Throughout the gospel era there have been those who have experienced God's call to focus on the Jewish people. In the age of modern missions some organizations have been founded to focus on Jewish people and they plan their activities to maximize contact with Jewish people. I have no doubt that these are today's 'apostleship to the circumcision'. It seems to me that churches in Israel that are situated in predominantly Jewish neighbourhoods, and necessarily focus on Jewish people, are also part of the apostleship to the circumcision.

In New Testament days it appears that this ministry was engaged in only by Jewish preachers so, is it a ministry only for Jews today? To argue that would also require arguing that only Jews should go to Gentiles, as Paul, the apostle to the Gentiles, was a Jew. Experience proves that God calls both Jews and Gentiles to this ministry. However, we would expect to see Jewish believers beginning to take the lead in ministry to their own. This has happened: some of the great medieval debates were led by highly competent Jewish believers; the first minister and evangelist of an Anglican church in Jerusalem in the 1840s was a converted rabbi; in the nineteenth century many missionary organizations to Jews were founded by believing Jews, and today they are taking the lead in evangelism and apologetics to their own. It is a joy to see. However, I have no doubt that Gentiles are still needed, because there are many situations where they will be given a hearing and the Jewish believer will not.

The Gospel to the Circumcised

I have written on this elsewhere in this book, and in my book on witnessing to Jews,[10] so I will make only some brief comments here. However, some explanation of this phrase is needed.

Are there two gospels? Paul goes out of his way to say an emphatic 'No' to such an idea in the first chapter of Galatians, 'I marvel that you are turning away so soon from Him who called you in the grace of Christ, to a different gospel, which is not another.'[11] Yet in Galatians 2:7 he refers to a gospel of the uncircumcised and one of the circumcised. It could be that he omits the word 'gospel' in his second phrase (it is supplied in the text) to avoid any impression of two gospels, while at the same time stressing there was a distinction. What is that distinction? It can be readily seen in the gospel presentations in Acts. To the circumcision Peter spoke to his hearers as 'sons of the prophets, and of the covenant which God made with our fathers';[12] likewise Paul spoke to them of 'that promise which was made to the fathers'.[13] To the Jewish people the gospel was the fulfilment of the promise Yahweh had made to them as a people. However, to Greeks gathered to listen to Paul on Mars Hill the idea of a promise fulfilled would have made no sense. To them Paul said, 'Since we are the offspring of God, we ought not to think that the Divine Nature is like gold or silver or stone, something shaped by art and

I am of Peter: the Apostleship to the Circumcision

man's devising',[14] and then went on to speak about Jesus. With the Gentiles, Paul starts with the very basics about God before going on to the gospel; with the Jews, he and Peter called upon them to respond to the good news of the fulfilment of promises of which they were well aware. Clearly, there are not two gospels but the content and context which leads up to the good news of Jesus is so different that Paul could actually write of a gospel of the circumcised. That difference between the circumcision and the uncircumcision stands to this day.

Setting Apart to This Apostleship

We should expect to see some called to this ministry. Jesus taught us to pray to the Lord of the harvest for labourers in his harvest field,[15] and that surely includes asking God to raise up missionaries to the Jewish people. It seems to me that anyone called to such ministry will already have a zeal for the lost and be showing it by involvement in personal witness and some form of church outreach. At some point they will develop an interest in the Jewish people, an understanding of them and an empathy with them. They will begin to read about them. They will pray for them, and those who are spiritually discerning will note this prayerful interest. They will eventually reach the point where they see this is something they must do; it is a divine pressure on their soul.

The preparation required has much in common with that for any other form of ministry of God's word. They need to study widely and engage in various forms of Christian service. But there is also the need for something specific. There are few full-time courses which prepare for Jewish evangelism in our Bible colleges, but universities with Jewish studies departments usually offer very useful one- or two-year courses in relevant subjects of Jewish history, Judaism and so on. There are short-term opportunities and the possibility of training alongside experienced missionaries, including supervised academic studies. On top of such studies a year or more living in Israel will create an understanding and empathy which cannot be gained in any other way.

There is no virtue in hiding the fact that it is a hard ministry, and those who do it must endure much rejection and see relatively little fruit. Those called to it need much support from their home church. One natural compensation is that it is an endlessly fascinating work. The Jewish people are full of interest and their history is full of great themes. Spiritually, it is an immense privilege to be called to Jesus' own nation, the people of promise. There is no higher calling. Those with this calling need our prayers.

15.

Provoking to Jealousy

'To provoke them to jealousy, salvation has come to the Gentiles.'[1]

Here is the ABC of witnessing to Jewish people, whether you are Jewish or Gentile. Here is the secret and, what is more, it's not really a secret because it's plainly stated by the apostle Paul. In other words, all Christians can do this. They can provoke unbelieving Jewish people to jealousy by ensuring they present their faith as Jewish in its origins, and that Gentiles are enjoying the blessings promised to Israel.

A word like 'provoking' might indicate a pugnacious attitude but that is not the tone intended here. It follows the method Jesus often used to arouse his hearers to think by using thought-provoking statements like, 'You shall know the truth, and the truth shall make you free',[2] to people who viewed themselves as free already. If love motivates us, then challenging statements will come out right, even if they are not well received.

There is an interesting implication here: Paul does not envisage a time in the future when this approach will be redundant. Israel can always be provoked to jealousy because they are always the people of promise.

Jealousy – a Brief Word Study

Some word study is necessary to grasp Paul's point here. It is especially necessary because some English translations have the expression 'provoking to envy' rather than 'provoking to jealousy', which is a serious point of difference.

Is jealousy a good thing or a bad thing? The problem is that 'jealousy' is often misused to describe undesirable envy, so it gets a negative press, but jealousy properly understood is a good emotion. In the Old Testament the adjective 'jealous' is only ever applied to Yahweh himself: 'I, the LORD your God, am a jealous God.'[3] What are the Hebrew and Greek words being used?

The Hebrew noun is *qinah* and it means 'zeal' or 'ardour'. Depending on the context it can be translated: 'jealousy',[4] '(good) zeal',[5] 'envy'[6] or '(zealous) anger'.[7] The word 'jealous' is used when describing how someone feels when the affection due to him or her is being placed elsewhere. An obvious example is a husband when his wife is unfaithful, and vice versa. Spiritually, it describes God's response when his people turn away from him to idols. As far as our verses in Romans 11 are concerned, the key Old Testament verses are Deuteronomy 32:16,21. Paul has already quoted verse 21 in Romans 10:19, and he is using its leading idea in Romans 11:11,14 without quoting Deuteronomy again. In Deuteronomy 32:16 Israel's sin is described by Moses, 'They provoked Him to jealousy with foreign gods; With abominations they provoked Him to anger.' Clearly the word 'jealous' is appropriate because the affection God deserves is being directed elsewhere by Israel. Then verse 21 describes God's response. First the charge is repeated, with the extra nuance that what caused the provocation was 'not God', and what moved to anger was 'foolish'. Then God's response is revealed, which is a like-for-like judgement. He will provoke them to jealousy by those 'not a nation', and to anger by a 'foolish nation'. As they did to him, he will do to them. But, as we shall see, Paul sees a road to mercy in this judgement.

When we come to the New Testament the Greek word translated jealousy is *zeloo* but again, like its Hebrew equivalent, it can be translated: 'jealousy',[8] '(good) zeal',[9] 'envy',[10] and 'indignation'.[11] In the translation of our Deuteronomy passage quoted in Romans 10:19, and referred to in Romans 11:11,14, we would expect the word 'jealous' to be chosen and that is so in most English versions. The NIV uses 'envy' and as many readers may use that version I will briefly comment. It is a puzzling choice because in other verses where affection due to another is being misdirected the NIV uses 'jealous'. For example in 1 Corinthians 10:22, where some

Christians are attending idol feasts, Paul warns, 'Do we provoke the Lord to jealousy? Are we stronger than He?' It seems to me that the NIV has failed to grasp the significance of 'jealous' in Romans 10:16 and 11:11,14. 'Envy' catches something of Paul's meaning, but not all of it. It misses the point that what Gentiles have come into is more than just a good thing, it was originally promised to Israel.

To Provoke to Jealousy

So, if we take Deuteronomy 32:21 and Romans 11:11,14 together, what is the evangelistic strategy Paul is describing? Moses wrote that the Jews will be provoked to jealousy by those who are 'not a nation', and Paul says that the Gentiles receiving salvation provokes Jews to jealousy. The thought here is that the believers from among the nations will appear as 'not a nation', to Jews, especially religious Jews. They will lack a common history, especially Yahweh at the origin and centre of their history, a body of learning, glorious edifices and respected institutions, and yet they will possess all Israel seeks – a relationship with God, joy, righteousness, love and hope. This produces jealousy because it was all promised to Israel.

We should be careful to note that Paul does not teach that being provoked in this way will inevitably lead to salvation. In Romans 11:14 he writes, 'and save some of them'. This indicates the provoking is a means to get people responding and thinking and then, by the grace of God, they will press on to salvation. Without that grace they will only get angry and become resentful, something the Christian who does the provoking will have to bear.

Orthodox Jews are especially prone to being angered by 'a foolish nation', as Moses put it. They are aware of their own great traditions and wise teachings, and see others as needing help from them. I was once invited into the home of an Orthodox Jewish man as I visited to share the gospel. I was asked to sit down, and then politely informed that I had nothing to teach him. However, many among them are far less polite! The very suggestion that they have something to learn from a Gentile makes them angry and I have been on the receiving end of that on many occasions. How does this provoking take place today, and what is the difference for Jewish believers and Gentile believers?

Impersonal Provocation

There is an unspoken provoking of Jewish people taking place when they live in a society deeply influenced by Christianity because they know it claims to be the inheritor of Israel's blessings. The impact was well expressed by Rabbi Dr Sidney Bricto:

> We Jews, however, remain as negative as ever about the Christian faith. We are always alert to any Christian claim of superiority to our own faith, but without giving up our own claim to chosenness. We totally ignore the contribution of Christianity to human culture. We will not read the New Testament nor take any interest in understanding why it succeeded in conquering the western world where we failed. I appreciate that our reaction is conditioned by centuries of persecution under the cross, but has not the time come for us to move on?[12]

The phrase, 'always alert to any Christian claim of superiority', describes a community in a permanent state of provocation. I remember a thoughtful Jewish young man whom I met many times to discuss the Scriptures, whose interest was stimulated by the existence of Christianity. He could see its value, the way the world had been bettered by it, its adherence to many biblical things and the good lives of Christians, so what was God doing? It had provoked him to jealousy.

Jewish Believers Provoking to Jealousy

It is understandable that when Christians consider this issue their first thoughts are of Christians from a Gentile background being the means of provoking Jews to jealousy. However, what provokes is the fact that salvation has come to the Gentiles, whether that knowledge is brought to Jewish people by Christians who are Jewish or by Christians who are Gentile.

Paul's example

The one example we have in Romans 11 is, in fact, of a Jew provoking his own people to jealousy. How was this done? Paul's words in verse 13 are, 'I magnify my ministry.' He was the apostle to the Gentiles and proud of it, but others were infuriated. The religious crowd in Jerusalem saw Paul as worthy of death for going to Gentiles: 'Away with such a fellow from the earth, for he is not fit to live!'[13] We may not think of associating with those of other nations as a capital offence but they did, because they saw Paul's activity of mixing with Gentiles and taking Israel's law to them as sacrilege. He was polluting himself and God's law. Now Paul knew this is how they would respond to any mention of going to Gentiles but the point is, he did not hide the fact; rather, he deliberately drew attention to it when he could have downplayed it.

What about on a more personal level? Imagine Paul visiting some of his religious relatives (assuming they would receive him – we do know he had a nephew who was sympathetic to him.)[14] We can imagine that they would greet him with words like, 'How are you, Paul? What have you been doing?' and he replies, 'Oh, you know, teaching the things of our Scriptures, trying to bring our people to be faithful to the Lord, and having some influence on Gentiles I encounter to make them better citizens, and not against us Jews.' Such words from Paul would have impressed them; they were truth but not the whole truth. To magnify his ministry would have meant telling them of the large numbers turning from idolatry, witchcraft, mystery faiths, sensualism and so on, to serve the God of Israel. It would have provoked them and led to hostility in many but Paul understood that in a fallen, self-righteous culture, there is no comfortable way to bring people to repentance.

Jewish believers today

Paul is an example to Jewish believers today. It is a strong temptation for them to keep the peace in family and among friends by downplaying their contact with the church (seen as Gentile) but it is a serious mistake. Jewish believers should follow Paul and magnify to their family and friends that people in darkness are receiving God's light and following his ways. It will not be easy but it is evidence that Messiah has come, and may lead some to reconsider Jesus.

I can imagine some Jewish believers thinking, 'Yes, but things are different now. Look at all that Gentiles, so-called Christians, have done against the Jews since Paul's time. It is much more difficult now.' Is it? Perhaps, to a degree, but we should not underestimate Paul's difficulties. Judging by his letters to churches, especially Corinth, there were some serious flaws in their beliefs and behaviour which would not have been a good example to their Jewish neighbours. Some in Corinth doubted the resurrection of the body and, in Colosse, gnostic ideas were being entertained. Worse still some Christians appeared to have only added the Lord to their idolatry, for they could be seen going into idol temples.[15] Furthermore, Paul's warning to Gentile Christians not to boast over Israel in unbelief indicates there were anti-Jewish attitudes in the churches.[16] Perhaps worst of all in the eyes of devout Jews, these Gentiles were not living under the law of Moses, and the Jews who believed appeared to be picking and choosing from Moses what suited them. However, Paul did not allow any of these things to obscure the big picture of Gentiles receiving salvation and honouring and worshipping the God of Israel; he magnified it. Today's Jewish believers should follow his example. I labour this point because the opposite is happening, and the trend in the Messianic Movement is to distance itself from 'Gentile Christianity', which is a great shame because this movement has contributed many good things. Paul's example was otherwise, he proudly associated with Gentile believers.

Gentile Believers Provoking to Jealousy

For Jewish believers to provoke to jealousy requires a willingness to be looked down upon. For Gentile believers something similar is required: they must acknowledge indebtedness to a people whom the world frequently despises. They have to acknowledge that they have come in from the outside to the blessing of God's promises to Israel. For some Christians this comes as a jolt, because they simply don't think of Christianity as a plant cultivated in Jewish soil. In 2004 French Jewish students conducted a campaign against anti-Semitism, using shock tactics to make their point, one of which was a poster with a picture of Jesus with the words 'dirty Jew' scrawled across it. It was not intended as an attack on Jesus but it was making the point that it is ridiculous to be pro-Jesus and anti-Jewish. It deeply grieves me to say that many Gentile Christians are. They are content to stress their indebtedness to Christ but shy away from focusing on the means he has used to bring that salvation into the world. It seems to me that remaining fleshly pride inhibits many Gentile Christians from acknowledging their debt but the sooner they deal with it the more fruitful will be their witness to Israel.

What does it mean in practice? How can a Gentile believer's testimony provoke a Jewish friend to jealousy? This is not a book on witnessing but let me mention a few basics. The Gentile believer must communicate to a Jewish friend that he is blessed by what is 'theirs', that is, what God promised to the Jewish people. Without wanting to get you tongue-tied over terminology, try to refer to 'God' as the 'God of Israel', speak of Jesus as the Messiah promised to Israel, and describe the Old Testament as 'your Scriptures'. Talk of the New Testament as a Jewish book and Jesus as Jewish. You might use his Hebrew name, Yeshua. Please do not interpret this advice slavishly, as if whenever you use the word 'God' you must say 'God of Israel', but mix up your terminology so as to bring this Jewish flavour in and underline that you are blessed by what is theirs. Some Gentile Christians may feel inhibited by the history of Christian anti-Jewishness and other failures. Paul knew such problems would continue but it did not weaken his conviction that salvation for the Gentiles will provoke Jews to jealousy.

And there is one further point which Jewish and Gentile believers can make when challenged about the weaknesses within Christianity. Messiah's kingdom is presented as a development of Old Testament Israel, so it should not cause surprise that the same problems, originating from sin, continue in Messiah's day. His people are presented as willing, not sinless.[17] The failures of Israel in Old Testament days did not mean they were not God's people; neither do the failures of Messiah's people.

All this raises issues of oneness in Christ for believing Jews and Gentiles, and issues of how Jewish believers express Jewishness. I want us to consider them in subsequent chapters.

16.

One New Man from the Two

Has it ever struck you that there would be something seriously deficient about the church if there were no Jews in it? It would have all the appearance of an unwanted gift, rejected by the original recipients. More than that, it would proclaim Jesus had failed in his purpose that the church should be 'one new man from the two', the two being Jew and Gentile.[1]

The continued presence of some Jewish people in the church underlines that Jesus is the Messiah, the one who fulfilled God's promises to Israel. That presence is certainly a challenge to the Jewish community. In Ephesians 2:11–22 Paul describes the glory of Christ's church in terms of the unity of Jew and Gentile; it is a glory that must be seen in every generation.

Jew and Gentile: Then and Now (Ephesians 2:11,12)

We have already looked at the Jew/Gentile distinction in some detail, so in this chapter we will simply look at how Paul expresses it in Ephesians 2. First, we will consider the distinction in those early days of the gospel, and then what it is now. In verses 11 and 12, Paul is addressing believers from a Gentile background in the church in Ephesus. This mention of different backgrounds causes some Christians to react: 'We are all one equal in Jesus, so why differentiate between the Jews and Gentiles?' The simple answer is, Scripture does. Elsewhere in Ephesians Paul addresses husbands, wives, children and servants, so here he has something specific to say to Gentiles. Background is not irrelevant in church life, even though it makes no difference to receiving salvation or our status in the body of Christ.

Paul's description in Ephesians 2:11–22 makes an interesting contrast to the description in Ephesians 2:1–10, where his focus is the individual experience of believers – what they have been delivered from, and their position in Christ. In Ephesians 2:11–22 Paul turns to focus on their experience as Gentiles coming into the people of God. His language indicates that the vast majority of the church in Ephesus must have been Gentile in background: 'Therefore remember that you, once Gentiles in the flesh'.[2] Paul's purpose is pastoral, to assure Gentiles of their full acceptance, on an equal basis, into God's people. Does that strike you as odd? Why was that a problem? The fact is, when Paul wrote, Gentile believers were Johnny-come-latelys. For the preceding two thousand years the story of God's people had been an exclusively Jewish story, and that was also true in the first twenty years after Messiah Jesus had come. This is reflected in Paul's words, 'that *we* who first trusted in Christ should be to the praise of His glory. In Him *you* also trusted, after you heard the word of truth, the gospel of your salvation'.[3] Our tendency is to quickly pass over those first twenty years as a small blip before entering the 'gospel to the world' period. But that smacks of the arrogance of the 'new kid on the block' who takes no account of the shoes he steps into. But the new kid – the Gentiles – came into what was promised to and prepared for others – Israel – and the first batch clearly needed reassuring that they were fully in. That is what this passage in Ephesians is all about.

In Ephesians 2:11–12 Paul details the outsider status of Gentiles by describing their hopeless position compared to Israel's. These are his words: 'Therefore remember that you, once Gentiles in the flesh – who are called Uncircumcision by what is called the Circumcision made in the flesh by hands – that at that time you were without Christ, being aliens from the commonwealth of Israel and strangers from the covenants of promise, having no hope and without God in the world.'

Christ was not with them either before or after his incarnation; they were outside the community which God was blessing; God had made no covenant with them and had given them no promises. The end result was people living in God's world with no sense of God being with them, or for them. This meant they had no hope, and many of them felt it. The desperate rituals in many pagan religions are an evidence of that sense of hopelessness.

The practical reality

How did this Jew/Gentile distinction operate in day-to-day terms? In Ephesians 2:15 we read of 'the law of commandments contained in ordinances'. The Mosaic law acted as a 'middle wall of separation' (v. 14), keeping their lives divided. You may do business with someone, but if you cannot share a meal with him or her, then a social bond will not form. That is just what the food laws in Leviticus were intended to prevent. In the temple of Jesus' day, there was a literal wall securing the area where only Jews could enter. There was a stone sign with these words in the Greek language: 'No alien may enter within the barrier and wall around the temple. Whoever is caught is alone responsible for the death which follows.'[4] Not exactly a doormat saying, 'Welcome'! The result of this division was enmity. I understand this to have a good and a bad component. The law was meant to produce in God's people a holy enmity – a righteous hatred of idolatry and godlessness living. That was a good thing. But the sinful heart created an unholy enmity, leading to resentment, hatred, anger and contempt between Jew and Gentile. Both sorts of enmity can be found described in the pages of the New Testament.

This is all very interesting, but what about today? Surely things have changed. Are the Jew/Gentile categories relevant any more? Sadly, there are still multitudes in the world today that fit Paul's description of Gentiles in Ephesians 2:11,12 – their people have no promises from God, they have no hope and are without God in the world. As for the Jewish people, they remain an identifiable people, an elect people having God's promises but, for the most part, rejecting them and suffering the consequences. There are still these two groups in the world – and they are two by virtue of the distinction God made. The Jew/Gentile distinction is not just one among a list of human differences: rich/poor, black/white, urban/rural, etc. It is a spiritual distinction which God created as part of his purpose to save sinners. Only he can tamper with that distinction by bringing Gentiles into his righteous community on an equal basis with believing Jews. However, outside of Christ, these two distinct groupings, Jew and Gentile, continue to exist, one in a covenant relationship with God but mostly disobedient, and the other without God in his world.

And they are still at enmity, most of it unholy. Anti-Semitism has been described as 'the longest hatred' and it is still alive and well. Gentiles and Jews have not buried their animosity since Jesus came; indeed many Gentiles have used the name of Jesus to justify their enmity towards the Jewish people. Religious Jews continue to view themselves as somewhat superior to Gentiles (Christians or otherwise). Secular Jews tend to stick together, for understandable reasons, mistrusting Gentiles. Muslims continue to resent and reject Jewish chosenness. Others simply hold on to their negative stereotypes of Jews, choosing to ignore all the good contributions Jewish people have made to civilization. It is still a particular purpose of Christ, through the gospel, to make peace between them. And only the gospel can do this. As far as I know, there are no Jew–Gentile clubs in the world, with the specific aim of uniting them! The nearest I have found was a Jewish social club in Bondi, Australia, which welcomed non-Jews as members. In a sense, the church is God's Jew–Gentile club. So, how does he unite them?

The Means and Experience of Unity (Ephesians 2:13–18)

Jew and Gentile are only reconciled to one another because they are first reconciled to God. In Ephesians 2:16 Paul describes how Jesus reconciles them to God by the cross so that those who repent and believe in Jesus are forgiven and reconciled to God. Those who are reconciled to God in such a way, by the one body of the Saviour, crucified for them, simply cannot remain at enmity with each other; it is put to death. Jesus is their peace.

But that holy enmity, which arises from the law, also needs to be removed. Now, this could have been done by putting all Gentile believers under the law, but God's way is to abolish the law: Jesus abolished 'in his flesh the enmity, that is the law of commandments contained in ordinances' (v. 15). The uniqueness that the law gave to one nation (Israel) has gone in Christ. Jews and Gentiles are to receive one another as they are; Gentiles should not expect Jews to become Gentiles, and Jews should not expect Gentiles to become Jews. This is not just a friendly wave from a distance, but they are being united in 'one body' and a new covenant directs their life together.

The daily, God-ward expression of this reconciliation is their equal access to God. In Ephesians 2:18 Paul describes the new means of access for both to the Father, which is through Messiah by the Spirit. Previously, access was only via the temple but now there is no need to be a part of Israel and travel to Jerusalem; wherever worshippers are Jesus will bring them into the presence of the Father. Note the wording, '*one* spirit'. There are not two spirits aiding them to draw near, but one, the Spirit of God, emphasizing their oneness, which is to be a daily experience as they pray together.

The New Community (Ephesians 2:19–22)

Paul's final words in this passage lay out the welcome mat for believing Gentiles, assuring them of their equal citizenship in the new covenant community; they possess full membership. Anyone who has been refused membership to a club or association knows how second-class it can make you feel. Paul is anxious to dispatch any such feelings and assures them the welcome sign is on display, the door is wide open, there is no ante-room for late-comers and the table they are at is a round one.

Paul's description of the new community in verses 20–22 draws on Old Testament temple terminology, making it clear that this is not a completely new start but a fulfilment of Israel's experience. As God dwelt among Israel by the visible manifestation of his presence in the temple, so he now dwells within the totality of those who believe in Jesus by the Spirit. He is in all and working among all to fulfil God's purpose. The teaching of the apostles and prophets is the foundation of this new community, not the law of Moses, and the cornerstone is Christ, not Moses. This does not consign the law to irrelevance, for the teaching of the apostles and prophets reveals how the righteous requirement of the law is to be fulfilled in believers.[5]

A new name?

Strange to say, nowhere in this passage does Paul give this new community a name. The closest to a name would be 'the household of God' but that is more of a description. Interestingly, Paul does not do what many Christians do – name this household 'Israel'. For example, if Paul had written in verse 19, 'Now, therefore, you are no longer strangers and foreigners but fellow citizens of Israel with the saints', it would have confused Gentiles; were they now Jews? What about the expression 'Israel of God'? I will discuss this in detail in the next chapter, but if that expression refers to the church then surely this was an ideal place to introduce it. Certainly this passage reveals the new covenant community as the glorious fulfilment of all God promised Israel, but we need to recognize that this new community is not given the name 'Israel' here. We need to go back to Ephesians 1:22 to find one. There, Christ is described as 'head over all things to the church'. The new name is 'church', the *ecclesia*, which means 'the called-out ones', who are called out from Israel and the Gentiles. This underlines both the continuity with Israel, in that Israel was a called-out people in the Old Testament, but also the newness through the bestowal of a new name. And this is the term Jesus himself used when speaking of his followers: 'I will build My church, and the gates of Hades shall not prevail against it.'[6] Jesus' emphasis on '*My* church' clearly pointed to a new body of called-out ones, distinct from Israel as a called-out body. To have referred to this body as 'my Israel' would have been confusing to say the least.

This new body will always be drawn from the two groups, Israel and the Gentiles, hence there will always be an Israel from which Jews will come to faith in Jesus. To use the word 'Israel' in a title for the church simply confuses things, and the New Testament never does it.

One New Man from the Two (Ephesians 2:15)

What are the implications of newness and oneness for the life together of Jew and Gentile in Christ? Is it just an inner, spiritual reality which leaves Gentile and Jewish Christians living separate church and private lives, or does it require more of them?

'Man' here is a metaphor for a community. Jew and Gentile each come from a 'man', a community with a religious way of life. Before the gospel it was impossible to unite Jew and Gentile without at least one of them changing but the words 'one new man' require that both change when coming to faith in Messiah and following his way; it is new for both. For Jews who believe, there is no longer any obligation to keep the law of commandments contained in ordinances, and Gentiles leave the unrighteousness of paganism and come into truth. In a word, both now walk according to the law of the Spirit of life in Christ Jesus.[7] Clearly, the new conditions are not *two new men* – Jews following Jesus via the ordinances of the law, and Gentiles living righteously apart from the law. Under such conditions joint worship gatherings, fellowship and many joint service activities would not have been possible. It was 'all change'. Difficult, no doubt, but Jesus expected it.

One old man? Two new men?

The early believers had their struggles with this process of change. For instance, when Gentiles believed some of the believing Jews were adamant they should be circumcised and keep the law.[8] That would have led to one old man from the two, with Jew and Gentile united in an old covenant lifestyle. The Apostle Peter certainly rejected such an approach, but he was not immune to the pressure of his previous Jewish lifestyle. During a stay in Antioch, his behaviour could have led to two new men. Paul tells us:

> Now when Peter had come to Antioch, I withstood him to his face, because he was to be blamed; for before certain men came from James, he would eat with the Gentiles; but when they came, he withdrew and separated himself, fearing those who were of the circumcision. And the rest of the Jews also played the hypocrite with him, so that even Barnabas was carried away with their hypocrisy.[9]

For Peter to go along with Jewish and Gentile believers eating separately was a backwards step, which would have pressured

Gentile believers to take on a Jewish lifestyle. If Gentiles refused to take such a step there would be two groups, two new men: Gentiles with a lifestyle unencumbered with Mosaic ordinances and Jews observing them.

Working it out: one for both; new for both

Staying united was not going to be easy, which is why James made his practical suggestions to ease tensions, 'I judge that we should not trouble those from among the Gentiles who are turning to God, but that we write to them to abstain from things polluted by idols [food], from sexual immorality, from things strangled, and from blood.'[10] The purpose of most of these requirements was to make table fellowship between Jews and Gentiles easier. Jews who had all their lives steered clear of certain foods could not be expected to bury such scruples in five minutes. Even if their heads said it was acceptable, their stomachs might not. A missionary colleague of mine had been brought up in a traditional Jewish way, and he had never eaten pork but, strange to say, he was usually offered it when on preaching tours. He could not eat it. His head said 'yes', but his stomach turned over at the thought.

Paul's principle for fellowship between believers with scruples was accommodation: 'It is good neither to eat meat nor drink wine nor do anything by which your brother stumbles or is offended or is made weak.'[11] Are we thinking about it when we entertain Christians from a Jewish background, or from other cultural backgrounds different from our own?

The easy option?

What is very clear from all we have considered is that the easy option is not the valid one – the easy one being the forming of separate churches for Jews and Gentiles. Paul's account of his confrontation with Peter at Antioch shows that there was table fellowship in the church between the Jewish and Gentile believers.[12] There is no doubt that this was the area of greatest tension for their fellowship, but they were succeeding, so we can safely assume they were worshipping and serving God together in all other ways. Here is the first church among the Gentiles, and Scripture sets it before us as an example of the practical outworking of the one new man in Christ. They did not choose the easy option and establish separate churches.

Paul's church-planting clearly followed this pattern. His churches were described by their location, not the ethnic background of those in them. In Thessalonica there were Jewish and Gentile converts[13] but Paul perceived only one church there – 'the church of the Thessalonians'.[14] This does not necessarily mean they had only one meeting place but they were all the one church of the Thessalonians, and there is never a mention of an ethnically defined sub-group. With no examples in Scripture of ethnic churches, but only examples of inclusiveness, there is no warrant for ethnically defined churches. The obvious problem is when the converts cannot yet speak the language of a country or region, but such churches should be viewed as a temporary phenomenon.

When I was in New York in 1983, I visited a church which was located in what had been a WASP suburb (white, Anglo-Saxon, Protestant) but where Jews, and many other ethnic groups with no Christian tradition, had moved in over a period of time. The pastor brought in ethnic workers to conduct sensitive evangelism in their own languages, and then services were started early on Sundays in the church building for new believers from the different language groups, with the goal of feeding people into the main English service when they were ready, although it was accepted that some never would be. He did not opt for forming a church for each group. The oneness of the church was preserved, and church life was enriched by having people of so many different backgrounds, Jews being among them. Believers maintained their own cultural traditions in their homes and community. I believe that such a church reflects the New Testament pattern.

Why have I focused on this oneness and newness so much, and stressed Jew and Gentile together in local churches? Because today there is a strong movement which says otherwise.

Jewish Churches

My concern is for believers to appreciate why some Jewish believers start their own churches by exploring below four of the issues they have with churches, and then to go on to examine particular issues connected to messianic congregations. I also want to suggest alternative answers which meet their needs but which are more consistent with Scripture. Initially I will be directing my words to Gentile Christians, but I trust Jewish readers will be helped by my analysis of their situation.

Anti-Semitism

Because of centuries of anti-Semitism within Christendom, and the rift between Judaism and Christianity, new Jewish believers will anticipate it is not easy to be Jewish in a church, and bad experiences may prove it. An understandable reaction is to start their own show. For centuries that was not really possible, but it is today. For Gentile Christians who observe this movement, and are inclined to be dismissive or unsympathetic, a dose of humility is in order, coupled with a search for any beams in their own eyes.

Culture

Most Christians simply fail to realize how much of their own culture moulds their church life and Christian expression, and they fail to put themselves in the position of those who belong to minorities among them. Such insensitivity can drive the minorities away. Jewish believers are a minority who have grown up in a significantly different culture and may feel like a fish out of water. It is tempting to want to be part of a church that is mostly Jews.

Evangelism

Jewish believers want other Jews to believe in Jesus, but where to take them to hear the gospel? For most Jewish people, churches are seen as the enemy, as per the above paragraph. An elderly Jewish lady I knew was brought up to cross the road rather than walk near a church building. It is tempting to start a Jewish-style church where seekers will feel more at home.

Israel's commission

The *raison d'être* of the Jewish people is to be a blessing to the nations via the Messiah. So it is not surprising that when Jewish people come to faith in Jesus they long to see their people fulfilling that destiny, but how to do it? Should they somehow work within the community: a Christian synagogue perhaps? It is an understandable consideration.

Messianic Congregations and Messianic Synagogues

'Messianic congregation' and 'messianic synagogue' are the two terms most frequently used for a church which is culturally Jewish in ethos and adopts practices from rabbinic Judaism. They are not exclusively for Jews and most have about 50 per cent Gentile believers attending. It is not easy to be precise about why some Jewish churches choose one of these terms and not the other, as there is a lot of overlap. If you visit them you will discern two main types: some will feel like an evangelical church with a Jewish feel about everything, probably with a charismatic flavour; others will make you think you have accidentally arrived at the local synagogue. The latter is usually because they have taken a much larger step towards rabbinic Judaism, worshipping according to the pattern of a synagogue, and teaching a lifestyle which observes Mosaic and rabbinic customs. Many of these congregations and synagogues are independent, but there is a trend to group together. By 2003 three umbrella organizations had been formed: the Union of Messianic Jewish Congregations (UMJC, 70-plus congregations), the International Alliance of Messianic Congregations and Synagogues (IAMCS, 50-plus congregations), and the Association of Messianic Congregations (14-plus congregations).

I believe that, despite all their good intentions, these churches fall short of the New Testament pattern because they have effectively created a second new man. Furthermore, their whole practice encourages externals in the spiritual life, contrary to Paul's exhortation: 'Therefore, if you died with Christ from the basic principles of the world, why, as though living in the world, do you subject yourselves to regulations . . .?'¹⁵ No doubt other churches are prey to these failures but that does not justify messianic congregations doing the same thing; two wrongs do not make a right. All their additional Jewish customs have to be adopted by Gentile Christians or they will feel out of it; Gentiles have to behave like Jews, which is not the newness Paul had in mind for them. This deserves to be considered more fully

So, what's a Gentile doing in a Jewish church?

I have given reasons why Jews might start Jewish churches but it is worth asking why Gentiles want to be there? It cannot be because of anti-Semitism or a desire to express their Jewish culture. Some attend because they have a particular concern to see Jewish people saved, or because they want to support Jewish believers in their desire to fulfil Israel's commission. Other reasons given are:

- to learn about Jewish festivals;
- a preference for liturgical worship;
- an enjoyment of Jewish-style song and dance;
- a belief that the teaching brings them into contact with a wisdom inherent in Jewish people; and
- a desire to return to the worship of the 'original church'.¹⁶

I have no doubt that other ways can be found for Gentile Christians to enjoy Jewish-style songs, learn of Jewish festivals, and sensitively evangelize Jewish people, but what about the other matters?

Is it biblical to think that a church life with Jewish festivals and Jewish people is somehow more spiritually enriching? In Colossians 2:16 – 3:3 Paul tells the believers not to be intimidated by those who pretend there is something superior about certain observances and mystical insights. Jewish observances belong to an age of immaturity; they are but shadows of Messiah. In Galatians, Paul goes further and doubts the very Christianity of Gentiles who take up such things thinking that it helps their acceptance with God: 'You observe days and months and seasons and years. I am afraid for you, lest I have labored for you in vain.'¹⁷ Paul is quite clear, either spiritual immaturity or spiritual disaster will be the result when Gentile Christians observe such traditions.

On the matter of the 'original church' in Jerusalem, what we know of their practice does not encourage the practice of Jewish traditions. In Acts 2:42 we read, 'And they continued steadfastly in the apostles' doctrine and fellowship, in the breaking of bread, and in prayers.' There is nothing there that would encourage Jewish traditions. The only tradition mentioned is the breaking of bread. Elsewhere it is mentioned that there was the practice of pooling everyone's possessions but, interestingly, those who admire the original church do not appear to be proposing this practice for today. Attendance at the temple obviously involved traditional practices, but that was only for Jews.

Finally, Jewish mission is the best way to identify with God's end-time purpose for Israel. Salvation through faith in Jesus, and joining in a local expression of the one new man, are Paul's desires for his people in the last days as he expresses it in Romans 11 and Ephesians 2. There is no mention of a return to the land or of an earthly messianic kingdom.

Messianic Judaism

The term 'Messianic Judaism' was coined by the Union of Messianic Congregations and Synagogues to express the conviction that Jews who believe in Jesus should band together in linked congregations to be a fourth branch of Judaism (the others being Orthodox, Conservative and Reform).

However, let me first clear up a misuse of the term. 'Messianic Judaism' is increasingly being used to describe the faith of all Jews who use the term 'messianic Jew'. This is inaccurate or dishonest. Many Jewish believers use that term on a regular or occasional basis yet they do not attend a messianic congregation or synagogue, or understand their faith as a Judaism. It is an uncomfortable fact for proponents of Messianic Judaism that the vast majority of Jewish people who believe in Jesus, probably around 90 per cent, attend churches. It is more accurate to use the term in a narrower sense, which is explained in these quotes from one of its leading exponents, Richard C Nichol:

Messianic Judaism is an expression of Jewish faith built upon the essential truth that Jewish people who embrace the risen Messiah of Israel, Yeshua, are obliged to partner with God in securing the ongoing existence and vitality of the Jewish people worldwide while simultaneously upholding Yeshua's message of love and redemption for the world.

So how does Messianic Judaism respond to the demands and privileges of divine-human partnership? By forming Messianic Synagogues . . . modern Jewish believers in Yeshua can survive as Jews. Messianic Judaism is primarily a congregational movement.

Our faith is a Judaism.[18]

It is important to point out that many who are supporters of messianic congregations are opposed to this philosophy of being a fourth Judaism, and the hope of being accepted as such by the wider Jewish community.[19] As might be expected, the stress on identity with the Jewish people has led some within Messianic Judaism to place that identity before identity with the wider church:

For a messianic Jewish group:

1. to fulfil the covenantal responsibility incumbent upon all Jews,
2. to bear witness to Yeshua within the people of Israel, and
3. to serve as an authentic and effective representative of the Jewish people within the body of the Messiah,

it must place a priority on integration with the wider Jewish world (my italics), while sustaining a vital corporate relationship with the Christian church.[20]

Those committed to Messianic Judaism are not a tiny, disparate, disorganized and poorly educated group of people. They have established a Messianic Jewish Theological Institute (MJTI), founded in 1997, made up of a school of Jewish studies; a training programme dedicated to training a new generation of messianic Jewish rabbis and leaders; educational centres; Hashivenu, a messianic Jewish leadership forum; and *Kesher*, a messianic Jewish theological journal. Some have created a *Halakha*[21] to govern their personal and congregational life.[22] Such groups speak of a bilateral ecclesiology,[23] that is, two churches: the wider church of Gentiles and one primarily for Jews, though Gentiles are usually welcome. At present the majority would oppose a conversion process for such Gentiles to become Jews, although a minority in their midst advocate it and want their congregations to be entirely Jewish ones. Some would advocate Gentile believers observing *Halakha*. As might be expected serious error is beginning to be taught, as can be seen in this quote from Mark Kinzer: 'Because of the validity of the Abrahamic covenant, I believe it's still as possible for a Jew who doesn't know Yeshua to have a living relationship with God, just as a Christian. But of course Yeshua is still the Messiah and any Jew who knows him is in a better place and has more access to God than before.'[24]

While those associated with Messianic Judaism as a congregational movement no doubt see themselves on the cutting edge of God's purposes for Israel, I can see them only as a Christian sect, akin to Seventh Day Adventists, destined to be little more than an irrelevant sideshow in God's global purposes, including his Israel purposes, and a waste of the talents and energies of those believing Jews involved. The fact that they will see people saved when they preach the gospel is not evidence they are on the right track, only of the promise of Jesus to save all who hear and believe.

Main criticisms of Messianic Judaism

I would make the same criticisms as above in the section 'Messianic Congregations and Messianic Synagogues': they have effectively created a second new man, their whole practice encourages externals in the spiritual life, and they are encouraging Gentiles to behave like Jews. However, I have a further criticism of their effort to be a fourth Judaism within the wider Jewish community. Hebrews exhorts Jewish believers, 'Therefore let us go forth to Him, outside the camp, bearing His reproach.'[25] The camp is the wider Jewish community in a state of rebellion against her Messiah as she had been against Moses; the camp imagery is taken from Moses' experience with Israel.[26] Jesus was crucified outside the gates of Jerusalem as a sign he was rejected, and those who believe on him have no choice but to follow him there. All attempts to remain within will inevitably lead to a watering-down of a distinctive declaration of Jesus as Messiah and Son of God.

I believe the leaders of Messianic Judaism need to take a warning from the experience of King Jehoshaphat. Messianic Judaism desires to play a part in Israel fulfilling her commission by being a part of Israel in an organized religious sense. This means taking the name of another religion, one which opposes Jesus the Messiah, and making it a part of their name; that has to be syncretistic. King Jehoshaphat is an example of the dangers inherent in Messianic Judaism. He was a godly man whom Scripture commends highly.[27] He had a concern to heal the division between Israel and Judah, and that led to joint ventures in war, trade and even marriage,[28] all of which were disastrous. The latter even led to the introduction of Baal worship to Judah. The rest of his story shows that he never really learnt the lesson and never quite gave up hoping for some form of unity with the northern kingdom. Undoubtedly he was well motivated – he wanted to bring them back to the Lord – but his policy nearly led to disaster for Judah seven years after his death. The leaders of Messianic Judaism have similar motives, to see their people obedient to Messiah, but Israel as a people is one that, like the northern kingdom, has apostatized. It is a high-risk strategy, threatening to wreck the faith of many.

The Significance of Eschatology for Messianic Congregations and Synagogues

Israel's commission is one reason why some start messianic congregations and synagogues. They aim to be an influence within the community. At this point eschatology is a significant factor because most who attend these groups hold to an eschatology which understands that Israel will yet regain her central place in God's purpose of redemption when Jesus returns to reign in Jerusalem. Many within these groups believe the time is near, and therefore priority should be given to their association with their Jewish people. Even if such eschatology were correct it should never be allowed to weaken the need to go outside the camp, to be one new man and to put mission responsibility before prophetic speculation.²⁹

Church and Para-Church Alternatives

How do we respond to all these reasons for Jewish churches? I have presented the valid concerns which motivate those who form them, and I hope that readers will understand them and sympathize with them. I hope they will also rejoice that another reason for it all is that there are many more Jewish believers in Jesus in our days. However, I believe these concerns must be met in other ways because Jews and Gentiles ought to be worshipping together in local churches and not forming ethnocentric ones. The solution is twofold: to have a proper perspective on the church, and to consider the help which can be given by para-church organizations. I want to consider the latter first.

Para-church assistance

Missions to the Jews

Churches need to engage in sensitive evangelism to Jewish neighbours and friends and if they feel ill-equipped for this then they can get help from experienced missions to the Jews like the one I work with, Christian Witness to Israel (http://www.cwi.org.uk). Likewise such missions can help with teaching on Jewish culture and festivals.

A messianic fellowship

Something which meets all the four concerns mentioned earlier (anti-Semitism, etc.) is a messianic fellowship: a gathering for believers and unbelievers, Jew and Gentile, that is not a church but has a ministry to present the gospel as a Jew to the Jews, and also to have a teaching ministry which focuses on Jewish themes. It can be organized on an independent basis or linked to a particular church as part of the church's ministry. The evangelism is sensitive; Jewish believers enjoy fellowship with other Jewish believers, and the ambience is culturally Jewish: Jewish-style music, decor and food. There will also be opportunities for the children of Jewish believers to learn about their Jewish heritage together with their peers. Such groups can be organized so that it is quite clear they are not a church nor will they develop into one. There will be regular meetings and also specials at festival times, etc. The Jewish believers attending may feel a need for an occasional 'Jews only' fellowship time when they can discuss the issues of special concern to them.

Fellowship groups

Jewish believers in a locality sometimes arrange to meet to achieve some of these things without being as formal as a messianic fellowship. They may link to an umbrella organization like the Messianic Jewish Alliance in their country.

Jews and Gentiles in a Church

An antidote to 'Jewish churches' is to have a proper perspective on the local church. A church of Jews and Gentiles with a minimum of cultural trappings from either can work – it did in New Testament days. I want to make a few observations which I hope will help that process.

For Jewish believers to consider

A mixed-culture local church will help Jewish believers to keep the whole matter of Jewish rituals and observances in perspective. They are not essential to spiritual growth and the lack of them in the new covenant underlines that. When David Baron, a leader among Jewish Christians in the United Kingdom a century ago, wrote against the advocates of Messianic Judaism in his day, his concern was the danger of spiritual immaturity by observance of customs.[30] That same danger looms today.

While it is understandable that the experience of anti-Semitism leads Jewish believers to be cautious about churches, they need to remind themselves that there is a rich history of philo-Semitism in the churches. As long as Jewish believers do not act like spoilt children who expect special treatment, they will surely be able to find a fellowship of Christians who will welcome them and encourage them as they live in a world which is increasingly anti-Semitic. If they detect anti-Jewish attitudes, they should not throw a tantrum and head for the door, but see it as one sin alongside many others in their brothers and sisters, and play their part in helping them to recognize and repent of it.

Is not every church Jewish? What I mean is, the core elements of any New Testament church came through the Jews. The Scriptures, which are read and taught, were written by Jews and their history is a Jewish one. The apostles, whose teaching is the foundation of the church, were all Jews. The only two ordinances commanded – the Lord's Supper and baptism – both evolved from Jewish practices: the Passover and ritual washings. There are other ways for Jewish believers to enjoy their unique heritage without insisting it be a part of the life of the one new man. That life is new for all; it is spiritually but not culturally Jewish and Jewish believers should recognize that.

Jewish believers need to beware of those Christians who give them special respect because of their Jewishness. Such people will puff them up and make them arrogant. Our ability to be a blessing to others in the church is related to one thing – our likeness to Jesus. This does not mean I discount the value of Jewishness. I would like to be reading the history of my nation when reading my Bible but that will never happen because I am an Englishman. Jews who believe do have that privilege. It should help to draw them into the earthly dimension of the text and give a unique feel for those experiences recorded there, which they themselves have known as Jews.

On the matter of Israel's commission, there is a need to recognize that the church, for all its failures, is the body through which it is being fulfilled. The fact that God has called Gentiles to be part of it should not be allowed to obscure the fact that Israel's commission is now being fulfilled. Furthermore, Israel's commission also continues to be fulfilled through the Scriptures. Through them Israel continues to be a light to the Gentiles until the end of time. For example, when a preacher teaches he often uses a phrase like 'Isaiah tells us', and in that way a Jewish person is teaching the nations. Now is the time to join together with all who are children of Abraham by faith, to fulfil Israel's commission to tell the nations through the preaching of the gospel.

Some general considerations

Churches should welcome Christians from a minority cultural background, and among such would be Jewish believers. Most churches will have a way of doing things which derives from the majority culture in the church, and the temptation for that majority is to assume their cultural preferences are best. That is all the more so in a culture where the gospel has influenced it for centuries. In James Mitchener's novel, *Hawaii*, he examines the issues raised when the gospel impacts a culture. At one point he describes a missionary, who had no medical training, acting as midwife to his wife rather than asking help from local midwives, who had centuries of accumulated wisdom. Why take such a risk? It was due to his understanding of the verse, 'Do not learn the way of the Gentiles'![31] Clearly, nothing good could come out of Hawaii for that missionary. Such an attitude is ridiculous but is often mirrored in churches which will learn nothing from those Christians who are among them from a minority culture, who can usually see such foibles and lesser errors much more clearly. 'Outsiders' can distinguish more readily what is a practice clearly taught in Scripture and what is only an inference which has led to a cultural norm; dress being an obvious example. Jewish believers are one such minority, and their input should be valued without having to accord it divine status.

Jews are Jews and will always be Jews. Why should things be otherwise? Jewish characteristics are not somehow sinful because Judaism rejects Jesus, and therefore something expected to die away in time. Jews eat Jewish-style food, which is full of the variety of the many cultures they have lived in; tell Jewish jokes and have their own mannerisms. Jews care about the State of Israel; not 'my country right or wrong', but a simple human desire to have somewhere they can call 'home' and organize themselves. Believe it or not, Jewishness is important to them! Jews have been scarred by history due to the frequently oppressive attitudes of those among whom they have lived. They have been put down, so it is quite natural that they work hard to get up again; if you push a cork down, it bobs up with force. They are accused of sticking together; well, wouldn't you if your school-friends or neighbours called you 'Christ-killer' from time to time? Their humour is often a response to this mistreatment, and they are good at using words precisely, almost to the point of legalism, because they have had to defend themselves with words so often. Some of these reactions to bad treatment can rub others up the wrong way, but let him who is without sin cast the first stone. All experiences can be sanctified by God's grace. If we step back and observe the benefits Jewish people have brought to any nation where they have been able to give full reign to their talents and energies, we should want as many in our church as we can get.

One special contribution Jewish believers bring to church life is due to their people being the people of the old covenant. The churches of the nations neglect the Jewish (Old Testament) roots of their faith at their peril, and the presence of Jewish believers will act as an antidote to that. Furthermore, their presence is a simple reminder of the faithfulness of God – he has promised at least a remnant, and there will always be one. The presence of Jewish believers reminds us that all we believe took place in the context of a real people, in a real place, over a definite period of time. Our faith is not ideas but history.

I have already mentioned the phenomenon of over-the-top Gentile Christians who fawn on Jewish believers but suffice it to say here that the effect of their behaviour is to discourage Jewish believers from staying in their church. Jews want to be Jewish but not theatrically so, nor as pets or gurus. Gentile believers should not be too accommodating either. A minister friend told me the story of some theologically astute ministers visiting his church at a time when a few of the Jewish believers in the church were experimenting with wearing various items of Judaica, one noticeable item being a tallit (a prayer shawl). The visitors were apprehensive of what was going on but as soon as they were told the people concerned were Jewish believers it seems all was well. But was it? A little more exploring of the issues would not have been out of place.

One New Man from the Two

For preachers and teachers to consider

Finally, let me make a point for those who teach the word of God in churches. It is possible to make Jewish believers very uncomfortable by giving the impression their people are especially sinful. The question to ask yourself is, do you tend to refer to the bad guys of a story as Jews, and the good guys as God's people? Do you use blanket terminology like 'the Jews failed'? It is too easy to overlook the many Old Testament instances of true zeal for God (e.g. Asa), or that it was Jews who took the gospel to the Gentiles. Imagine being a Jewish Christian listening to those expressions – and slowly sinking in the pew or getting angry. He or she, as a Jew, identifies with the faithful and obedient Jews, but by your terminology he or she is being put in the sin bin. This approach spills over into the way the promises and judgements of Scripture are handled. Too often the Jewish people are viewed as the object of all the judgements, and the church the object of all the promises. But if we see the church as the fulfilment of God's dealings with Israel then, as with Israel, she can expect both judgements and promises.

One further question on this issue of terminology for preachers concerns how to refer to the land of Israel. This is a tricky one, and care is needed. The term 'Palestine' came to be adopted in scholarly circles because it conveniently covered the whole area of ancient Israel. However, the word was first used to describe the Philistine region, and then the Roman historian Herodotus adopted it in the fifth century BC to describe a region which broadly covered biblical Israel. Rome included the word in its official name for the region, after they had finally crushed a Jewish revolt against their rule, in AD 135. The term was designed to reflect Jewish humiliation and deny them any rights to the land. Byzantium followed suit when the Roman Empire declined. All this is equivalent to a French atlas naming England 'MiniFrance', to draw attention to the Norman Conquest in 1066!

It is probably fair to say that this pejorative use of 'Palestine' from history has faded from the minds of most non-Jews and it is just a convenient term. However, its revival as the name of a people whose leaders deny Jews any right to create a political state and govern their own affairs in their ancient homeland has again made it a very loaded term. One Christian publisher has a gospel leaflet called 'Postcard from Palestine', a name which not only is inaccurate in its attempt to express the historical roots of the gospel but also, in the present conflict, gives the appearance of taking sides. It will be as red rag to a bull for a Jewish seeker.

There was a time when the term 'Palestine' was just about neutral but it is not now, and Bible teachers should not use it when referring to the land of the Bible. It is not a biblical term and should be avoided. So what term to use? Whatever biblical term is appropriate to the passage under consideration is surely the safest approach. In a more general discussion of biblical matters, whether Old Testament or New Testament, the phrase 'land of Israel' is accurate. It was the term of an angel to Joseph telling him to return from Egypt.[32]

This has been a long chapter, but that is not inappropriate. This book is not meant to be only exegesis of relevant Bible texts, but also to explore their practical implications. Inevitably, the theme of the one new man is a crucial one and a very practical one. This chapter has focused on Jew and Gentile in the church but what about Jewishness for Jewish believers in their private, family and friendship circles? That is the subject of a later chapter.

17.

The Israel of God

Jews who believe in Jesus have two spiritual identities. Within the church they are one of the two groups, Jew and Gentile, who make up the 'one new man'; within Israel they are the remnant according to God's election of grace. What terms are used to describe them in these two contexts and how important are they?

Jewish Spiritual Identity in the Church Context

When churches first began to be more mixed bodies, as in Antioch, Jewish believers would have been one group among many; a new name was needed and the term 'Christian' was created. However, there are places in the New Testament where there is a focus on the Jewish contingent within the church and these are the sort of names we come across: 'Jews who believed in Him';[1] 'those of the circumcision who believed';[2] 'myriads of Jews there are who have believed'.[3] Jews who believed were certainly understood to remain Jews and their faith was indicated by the use of the word 'believer'. 'Jewish believer' is still popular today but others have been coined through Christian history, like: 'Hebrew Christian', 'Jewish' Christian and the more recent 'messianic Jew'. All that is in the church context.

Jewish Spiritual Identity in the Israel Context

In the context of Israel there are two biblical terms which Christians use to distinguish those of Israel who believe in Jesus: 'the remnant' and 'the Israel of God'. The former is not especially contentious – it is used in the Old Testament,[4] and Paul uses it in Romans 11.[5] The other term, 'Israel of God', is more contentious and so I want to devote more space to examining its use by Paul in Galatians 6:16, where he writes: 'And as many as walk according to this rule, peace and mercy be upon them, and upon the Israel of God.' Is this important? I believe so, because we need to get our terms for the church right, and because Christians need to be clear about the role of Jewish believers among their people.

Israel and the Church: a Bone of Contention

Galatians 6:16 has become a bone of contention. The contention is all connected to the goal of God's purpose in this present world. Some Christians understand that Yahweh's goal in the present age is the gathering together of Jews and Gentiles in the church, the body of Christ, through believing the gospel, and that this body is 'the Israel of God'. Others understand that the goal is Israel and the Gentiles believing in Christ but with Israel living in their land ruled by Jesus from Jerusalem, and the Gentiles serving God in their lands. Some fine-tune that a bit but the basic difference in the goal remains. Those with the latter viewpoint emphasize strongly the uniqueness of Israel, and so the phrase 'the Israel of God' is not the church. My understanding leads me to emphasize both the ongoing uniqueness of Israel and the church as the fulfilment of God's promises to Israel but to question equating the church with the Israel of God. Galatians 6:16 has become something of a lightning rod for the whole debate, so I want to look at it carefully.

The Broader Context of Galatians

I want to try and come at this text in Galatians as if the last two thousand years of church history and theology had not happened. Why? Because I believe that much of the misunderstanding of it emerges from a failure to take account of the context. I want us to try and be Galatian Christians for a while.

The Israel of God

First we need to travel back in time to the churches of Judea and Jerusalem, and then to Antioch and the new churches in the south of Galatia. It is a world very different from the world of our churches today.

The believers in Judea and Jerusalem in those heady early days of the gospel were mostly Jews and, alongside the Roman laws, the law of Moses, as interpreted by the Jewish leaders, was the Jewish law of the land and of religious life. Any suggestion of diminishing that status quo was greeted with violent opposition, as Stephen discovered to his cost when he was accused of teaching – 'Jesus of Nazareth will destroy this place and change the customs which Moses delivered to us.'[6] Jews who came to believe in Jesus in such an atmosphere did not suddenly become twenty-first-century Christians, who generally never contemplate keeping the law of Moses, but all the indicators are that those early believers continued to live by the law. At the end of Acts we find James describing the believers in Jerusalem in this way: 'How many myriads of Jews there are who have believed, and they are all zealous for the law.'[7] Imagine being a converted Pharisee with many unconverted Pharisee friends. Even if you saw yourself as not under law, would you not live as under the law to win those under the law? Keeping the law would have been further encouraged by the fraught relationship between the generality of Judeans and their masters, Rome. As far as Judeans were concerned their superiority to their conquerors was demonstrated by a life lived by the law of Moses, therefore any suggestion of watering down such a lifestyle would have implied a descent into pagan licentiousness. This was evidenced by the contempt in which those were held who associated with Gentiles.

Into this atmosphere of deep reverence for the law of Moses came news of Gentiles coming to faith in Antioch. The Judean believers rejoiced but its implications were uncomfortable – these Gentile believers were not being circumcised or keeping the law of Moses and, furthermore, the Jews who believed were mixing and mingling with them. At about this time Paul and Barnabas were sent on their first missionary journey among the Gentiles and it is likely that at this time some churches were established in the southern part of the region called Galatia. What is certain from Acts and Galatians is that both Antioch and the Galatian churches received an unsolicited visit from some Jews from Jerusalem, who professed faith in Jesus and purported to have authority from there, and who began teaching the new Gentile believers that they needed to be circumcised and keep the law of Moses.[8] To combat the influence of these teachers Paul wrote his letter to the Galatian churches.

What must be understood from all the above is that, viewing the church as a whole, Jews were by far the majority and also its heavyweights. Paul was one of them. When he appeared among the pagan Galatians preaching the gospel one thing would have been obvious – the source of the message was the Jews. From a Jew they heard the message of salvation, a message that was indissolubly connected to the Jewish people and their history. The Galatians surely sensed their indebtedness to the Jews. After a period of time Paul would have ordained elders and moved on, but it was not long before some other Jewish heavyweights arrived, from Jerusalem no less, the place where so much of God's truth had been revealed – the premier theological centre of the day. They had something new to say, which they obviously presented as the full gospel, some of which Paul had apparently omitted, being an inferior apostle who had received his understanding from others. I am sure the Galatian Gentile Christians would have felt some unease but can you imagine them boldly resisting such teachers? These were professors of theology from Jerusalem! They listened and started to conform. It would seem some were circumcised and many started to observe days and months and seasons and years.[9] When Paul heard about it he wrote a letter, which must have burnt holes in the parchment at some points, so intense was his spirit and language.

It is not our purpose here to analyse Galatians in detail but one thing is very striking: Paul's arguments constantly hark back to Abraham. He wants the Galatian believers to relate to Abraham, the father of all the faithful, Jew and Gentile. Everything between Abraham and Jesus is interim and passing. This means he never uses the word 'Israel'. When he refers to the body of the faithful his terms are: 'sons of Abraham', 'Abraham's seed', 'sons of God' and also 'church of God'. Within his argument he makes almost no use of the institutions of Israel, or of Israel itself, to make his point. Hence there is no focus on Israel at all.

The Israel of God

So, what body of people would we expect the Galatian Christians to call to mind when suddenly, and without any introduction, Paul uses the word 'Israel' at the very end of the letter? Has anything in the letter prepared them to think 'Israel' meant them? Surely, nothing at all. Who would it make them think of? The Jewish nation, no doubt. To them Israel was a group of people, quite distinct from themselves, from whom they had heard this glorious message of hope.

The 'Them and Paul' Context of the 'Israel of God'

Later in his letter Paul directs his attention more particularly to those who had misled the Galatian believers. His contrast between himself and the other teachers becomes more and more pronounced in chapters 4, 5 and 6. Paul urges the Galatians to become like him,[10] and not to give way to the zealous courting of the others.[11] He sees them as hindered by these others, and could wish they were cut off from them.[12] They boast in the flesh but Paul boasts in the cross of Christ.[13] The point is this: Paul's comparison is revealing two groups within Israel; those, like Paul, who taught that, for salvation in Christ, circumcision availed nothing, and those who stressed the value of circumcision in salvation. When, therefore, Paul mentions, out of the blue so to speak, the 'Israel of God', it is natural to think he is referring to one of these groups within Israel; the one for who circumcision avails nothing.

This fits with Paul's other use of 'Israel' in this way. When he is explaining in Romans 9 why all of Israel had not believed he writes: 'They are not all Israel that are of Israel.'[14] I would paraphrase this as, 'They are not all people of faith like Israel (Jacob) who are descended from him'. This points to two groups within Israel. Both are descended from Israel, that is from Jacob, whose name was changed to Israel at the moment of his greatest trust in the Lord.[15] One group is described as 'not . . . Israel', i.e. not people of faith, not princes with God, not like their father Israel. The other, by implication, is like their father Israel, people of faith.

The Danger of Identity Theft

It is also worth noting at this point that when the New Testament uses a term that originated in Israel (e.g. 'circumcision') to stress that believers in Jesus (Jew and Gentile) are the true ones of God, it never uses the word 'Israel' itself. It especially uses 'circumcision' – 'we are the circumcision, who worship God in the Spirit',[16] and other terms like 'children of God', 'children of Abraham', 'saints', 'people of God', 'temple', 'holy nation', 'kingdom of God'. But Israel is confined to the Jewish people.

Why so? Because the word 'Israel' is the ethnic and national name of a particular people, a people who will never disappear off the map because they are a covenant people of God. To take that name from them is a form of identity theft. We are familiar with 'identity theft' today, when someone has all his or her details stolen, like bank and passport numbers, and then used by someone else. As far as the various authorities are concerned that person has ceased to exist and they find themselves stymied, marooned, unable to do many of the familiar things of daily life. They are like a non-person.

Non-people and non-nations get forgotten. And this is the great danger which concerns me. It has happened for Israel in the minds of many Christians. Israel became a non-nation. Jews are aware of this as was shown by an article in the *Jewish Chronicle* by the British Chief Rabbi, in which he was exulting in *Am Yisrael Chai!* (the people Israel lives!). In the process he made a negative comment about Christianity, that it was in error to have written the Jews off; they were still very much alive. In mission terms this has meant that mission to Israel has taken a back seat instead of a front one, because non-people get forgotten. To give an example: think of married couples you know; in how many cases do you know the maiden name of the wife? Not many, I imagine. Something new has begun and the old is of little significance to most who get to know the couple after their marriage. To Christianity's great shame this has happened with Israel. The princess has become Cinderella.

The Israel of God (Galatians 6:15,16)

But to come back to our text. In verse 15 Paul lays down again his summary rule in this particular context – in Christ neither circumcision nor uncircumcision avails anything, either for access to salvation or once saved. In verse 16 he invokes peace and mercy on all who hold to this. The words we are interested in are 'peace and mercy be upon them, and upon the Israel of God'. The main difference of translation in English versions is 'even to', rather than 'and upon'.[17] Both translations are valid, and because Paul's statement in verse 16 is so abrupt it is difficult to decide which translation is best solely from that verse, so we need to consider which translation best fits the context and argument of Galatians.

The effect of 'even to' is to provide a connection between the 'them' who walk according to the rule and the 'Israel of God' so as to emphasize that they who walk by this rule are truly God's people (the 'real Israel'), and the Judaizers who are leading them astray, although Jews, are not. Certainly that is consistent with the message of Galatians. However, as I have pointed out above, this understanding makes nothing of the stress in Galatians of two groups within Israel, and it takes no account of the fact that 'Israel' has not been used earlier in Galatians. It is a view which Christians readily accept because they are so used to equating the church with the word 'Israel', but they fail to ask whether the Gentile believers in Galatia would have readily made that connection. I have sought to show that they would not.

The effect of 'and upon' is to direct the reader to another entity upon which Paul invokes peace and mercy; it is somehow distinct from the 'them' who walk according to the rule and yet it is also a valued part of it.[18] What might this be? What group is there which is part of those who keep the rule and yet has another identity which distinguishes it within that group, and can also have the word 'Israel' tagged to it? The only answer to that is Jews who believe in Jesus. Yet, more than the word 'Israel' is needed to describe them, because they alone within Israel are following God's rule for the new covenant – they are the 'Israel of God'.

Does this fit the larger context? It is perfectly in keeping with a situation in which Jewish teachers are leading the Galatians astray that Paul would urge the Galatians to listen to the right Jewish teachers. It is as if he is saying, 'If you are going to respect Jews as your teachers then listen to the right ones, those who follow this rule – they are God's Israel – not these troublers who are false teachers – they are no more than the circumcision.'

Conclusion

Is it really important to spend so much effort looking at it? Yes, because it helps Gentile Christians to recognize the unique identity of Jews who believe, and strengthens the identity of Jewish believers, which promotes their testimony to their people. For the sake of the salvation of Israel all Christians should encourage Jewish believers to hold on to their identity as the remnant and to creatively find ways of maintaining it and expressing it. More of what that involves in a later chapter.

18.

Pay Attention!

Jewish believers in Jesus face unique pressures to drift away from their faith. An entire epistle, Hebrews, is devoted to the problem and is specifically addressed to them, although its teaching is obviously relevant to any Christian tempted to become sluggish. They need understanding, teaching and encouragement from fellow believers, Jew and Gentile; hence this chapter.

All believers face the temptation to be sluggish, so in what way are the temptations faced by Jewish believers unique? The focus of Hebrews is more pointed than mere sluggishness; it is concerned about a believer drifting back into the situation he or she has turned away from when coming to Christ, and in that regard the Jewish situation is like no other. It is the only one where the old situation is that of a national entity and religion that has the stamp of divine revelation upon much of it. In fact, when Hebrews was written and the temple was still standing, the 'old situation' was truly one that Yahweh had revealed and commanded. Today things are not the same, rabbinic Judaism is not Old Testament-revealed religion but, on the surface of things, it makes a passable attempt at it. It is not paganism or idolatry. With a bit of chutzpah[1] Judaism today can claim to be God's original; which is what it does claim. This acts as a tremendous pressure on those who have left it and have begun to have doubts.

The Pressures Faced by Jewish Believers in Jesus when Hebrews was Written

Some of these are plainly mentioned in the text of Hebrews but others are not spelt out; they are implied by the way the author seeks to help his readers.

Indications of pressure

Here are some of the words of the author which indicate the pressures. 'Let us therefore be diligent to enter that rest, lest anyone fall according to the same example of disobedience.'[2] 'Do not become sluggish.'[3] 'Let us hold fast the confession of our hope without wavering.'[4] 'Let us lay aside every weight.'[5] Clearly, these Jewish believers of temple times were struggling to keep their heads above water.

Pressure to go back to an earlier divine revelation

An obvious question is, why? What wrong ideas and preferences, what experiences, what false hopes were pressurizing them? Some of these are explicitly mentioned in Hebrews: 'Therefore we must give the more earnest heed to the things we have heard',[6] and, 'Lest there be in any of you an evil heart of unbelief in departing from the living God.'[7] These two statements indicate a failure to take proper account of what they had heard, presumably from their first teachers. The consequence was that they were beginning to disbelieve it and believe something else. Because of this the author refocuses their attention on the basic truths about Jesus, and especially his superiority to the various Mosaic institutions. This indicates what they were tempted to return to – the whole Mosaic economy of law, temple, priesthood and sacrifice, as well as a respect for angels and the revelation they had given to Israel. I do not believe this necessarily means they were turning to a works righteousness. It seems that they were getting themselves into a confused no man's land where the things of salvation could be received through the Mosaic alone, or through something from Jesus and something from the Mosaic.

The pressure of disappointed hopes

The exhortation to be diligent to enter God's rest for his people is connected to turning back to the Mosaic,[8] with its hope of rest in the land of promise. But I wonder if there is also an indication of disappointed hopes here. The apostles' question to the Lord Jesus in Acts 1:6, the one about restoring the kingdom to Israel, indicates the desire of many devout Jewish people in those days: the hope for a situation of peace and rest in the land of promise under the reign of Messiah. Jesus had not only failed to achieve this but those who followed him were being hounded and persecuted in the land. Something seemed to have gone dreadfully wrong. Furthermore, it was looking increasingly like Jesus' followers were in the minority. No doubt in the early days, with thousands coming to faith, there were many among them who expected things to just roll on until most of Israel believed because the prophets surely indicated such a triumphant Messiah. Perhaps Jesus was not the Messiah after all. Disappointed hopes were causing them to turn back.

The pressure of suffering

There is no doubt that following Messiah Jesus continued to be costly and difficult. We are told, 'You endured a great struggle with sufferings . . . reproaches and tribulations . . . the plundering of your goods.'[9] But the author tells them they needed to endure, indicating the situation was ongoing. Not an easy one to endure; it was much easier to drift.

The Pressures Faced by Jewish Believers in Jesus Today

Things are not so very different for Jewish believers in Jesus today, although, as indicated, rabbinic Judaism is not the religion of the Old Testament. When someone Jewish tells unbelieving family and friends of their new faith in Jesus, the pressure begins.

Pressures historical, emotional and material

It will probably start in a way not experienced in Second Temple times because of something new which has entered in – the fraught relationship with Christianity, due to the persecution of Jews within Christendom. Christianity has become the enemy. In one sense it always was, as a quick read of the conflict between Jesus and unrepentant Jewish leaders shows, but the persecution within Christendom has created a deep scar. It is best summed up by the one word which entered Stan Telchin's mind when his daughter told him over the phone of her faith in Jesus – 'Betrayed!' She had joined the enemy. The assumption is that the one who has believed has turned their back on being Jewish, so psychological pressure will be brought to bear – 'How can you do this to your grandparents, your ancestors, those who died in the Holocaust because they were Jewish? How can you do this when others died rather than renounce their faith?' A rift with family and friends opens up, which may not be so difficult to bear in the first flush of spiritual blessing, but is wearing as time goes on. There may be a loss of employment or of future help from within the Jewish community.

Strong intellectual pressures

At some point a rabbi or trained anti-missionary may be brought in and then will begin the more pressing intellectual arguments. I was once asked by a friend to suggest a way to challenge a Jewish work-colleague, so I made a suggestion, which he took up. The email reply to my friend from his Jewish colleague was quite obviously 'cut and pasted' from one of the many web sites created by religious Jews to challenge the claim that Jesus is Messiah. The arguments are backed by superficially impressive knowledge and are intimidating to the average, new Jewish believer, who has probably not investigated every objection imaginable but has been impressed by the basic fact of Jesus as the one promised in the Hebrew Scriptures, who has saved him or her from sin. The battle for the Jewish mind is being hotly contested and the arguments about the Messiah are readily available. It will also be pointed out that, although the church claims to be Jewish it does not really look or feel it. And then the question will be asked, who came first? They should trust the original with its thousands of years of tradition, experience and scholarship. Can so many Jews and so much learning be wrong?

Loss of the familiar

Later on the more sentimental may come in. A Jewish believer may find church life to be somewhat different from expected, disappointing in some areas, and very different from religious life in family and synagogue. It is easy to forget the inadequacies which made them more open to Jesus, and to develop a nostalgia for the past. The TV drama, *Disputation*, portrayed a debate held in 1263 in Aragon, Spain, between Rabbi Moses ben Nachman and Pablo Christiani, a notable convert from Judaism. At one point the rabbi is portrayed as exerting this sort of emotional pressure when he asks Pablo if, when walking past the synagogue, he felt drawn back by the singing and the whole atmosphere he grew up with. Pablo confesses that he does.

The same pressure exists today and there are two types of Christian who are no help to Jewish believers under such pressure. One sort is those who talk to them as if they are no longer Jewish and speak in disparaging terms of Judaism, as if everything about it and about Jewish life is of no value. The other sort is those who prepare a new believer for church life by giving them the expectation that they will experience anti-Jewishness at every turn. Both sorts of Christians do them no favours, and make it difficult for them to feel they belong.

Put all these pressures together and it is not difficult to see how doubts may arise, especially for single people. Church attendance becomes less regular, broken Jewish friendships and family ties are tentatively re-established – Jesus not being mentioned – and they may even begin to take a critical look at all that has happened to them.

The Response in Hebrews

This falls into four broad categories: doctrine, spiritual perspective, exhortations and warnings, and encouragements to remember personal past faithfulness. They are valid and valuable despite today's differences.

Doctrine

The author's basic assertion is the superiority of Jesus over all the Mosaic institutions because of who he is, and because he fulfils it all.

God speaks by the Son
In the past God spoke to Israel by angels and prophets, and that was a great privilege. But now he speaks by his unique Son, the description of whom makes clear his divine nature, being the 'express image' of God's person.[10] A superior revelation has come. That does not make all earlier revelation redundant but it is to be understood through the teaching of the Son. The question this raises is, why go back, confining yourself to a preparatory revelation, when the one who gave it, who now interprets it authoritatively, has come?

A lowly saviour
The lowliness of Jesus as one like us, living in a world under the curse, diminishes him in the eyes of some Jewish people. Is not Messiah to be a glorious figure, conquering with majesty and brooking no opposition? How can he appear lower than angels? Because there was a good reason: that he might make propitiation for the sins of the people and be prepared for a high priestly role in which he is fully able to empathize with his people.[11] Nothing has happened to change that requirement. The day will come when all will see him in his glory but it is a day for which his followers must wait patiently.

Greater than Moses
Moses stood head and shoulders above all subsequent prophets because he mediated the covenant within which they worked. He was head of house, so to speak. That house was God's house, and Moses was God's servant in it. But a new house has now appeared, which fulfils and replaces the first one, and its mediator owns it; it is his house, and hence his superiority is plain.[12] The message is: respect Moses, but worship the Son.

Rest and a heavenly country

Enjoying life in God's promised land was a lot more restful for Jewish people than life in Egypt, and obedience ensured a little piece of heaven on earth, according to what Moses promised.[13] Good as it was, it was not the true rest but only a shadow. The patriarchs understood this and anticipated something more – 'Now they desire a better, that is, a heavenly country.'[14] Today's Jewish believers may have a hope of returning to the land of Israel (if they are not already there), even of Messiah reigning there, but it has to be subservient to the fullness of rest in the new earth and the new heavens. To put anything before that hope is to invite disappointment and risk slipping back. However, there is a rest of God we can and must enter into now if we are to be ready for the fullness of the promise. It is that rest which, as with God's rest on the seventh day, involves a rest from our works. This is a spiritual rest of soul which trusts God alone for salvation and puts no trust in our efforts, as Hebrews puts it: 'For he who has entered His rest has himself also ceased from his works as God did from His.'[15] Judaism lacks this rest, so why return to restlessness when Messiah Jesus promises, and gives, 'rest for your souls'?[16]

The law made nothing perfect; Jesus did

Inheriting the promise of God is something that ultimately depends on Jesus. Promises were indeed made to Abraham and to the people of Israel, and they definitely enjoyed God's faithfulness, but the kindness of God was not enough to secure the promised inheritance; it depended on the one to come. Their sin was not dealt with by temple sacrifices but by Jesus: 'And for this reason He [Jesus] is the Mediator of the new covenant, by means of death, for the redemption of the transgressions under the first covenant, that those who are called may receive the promise of the eternal inheritance.'[17] And what confirms this to believers is that Jesus is in God's presence now: 'This hope we have as an anchor of the soul, both sure and steadfast, and which enters the Presence behind the veil, where the forerunner has entered for us, even Jesus.'[18] Without Messiah Jesus, nothing in the Old Testament can come to fruition.

The author of Hebrews could safely assume his readers understood the need for a blood sacrifice if sin was to be covered. A life had to be laid down in death to pay the penalty the sinner deserved. At one point he spells it out: 'And according to the law almost all things are purified with blood, and without shedding of blood there is no remission.'[19] Such an assumption cannot be made today when speaking with Jewish people. If a Jewish believer is starting to wobble and head back towards Judaism it will be not only because of doubts about the sacrifice of Jesus but also because of doubts about the need for sacrifice at all. But the arguments of Hebrews still stand. The negative statements expose the weaknesses of Old Testament religion and how it expects something better, though cast in the same mould. This demolishes the pretensions of rabbinic Judaism to be the heir of Moses and the prophets because it is not cast in the same mould. The positive statements present the superior priesthood and sacrifice of Jesus, fulfilling all the Old Testament expected. They build on the Old Testament and, by default, demonstrate how far Judaism has departed from it on the all-important matter of atonement.

The order of Melchizedek
The Old Testament expects Messiah to be of a priestly order quite distinct from the Levitical. He is a 'priest forever According to the order of Melchizedek'.[20] The argument of Hebrews 7 presents this priestly order as one which, according to the record of Scripture, was in existence before the Levitical, continued over and above the Levitical, and ultimately fulfils it. It only had one priest before Messiah – Melchizedek – and, according to the Scripture record, he had no end of life and remained a priest continually.[21] Of course, we are not meant to understand that Melchizedek did not die, but that the record of Scripture presents him like that (normally the record of significant figures is very clear about their parentage, birth and death). To David it was revealed that Messiah would be a priest of that order and he states it in Psalm 110. This indicated that the Levitical had a 'use by' date. Hebrews draws attention to this weakness of the Levitical – it made nothing perfect.[22]

The Melchizedek priesthood requires a priest who has an endless life. Melchizedek himself only had that in the record of Scripture – no parents, no genealogy, no beginning or end of life. Jesus has it by nature; he has the power of an endless life and continues forever.[23] Because of this he always lives to make intercession for those who come to God through him.[24] The same person is always there on our behalf, having no limitations. It is always dissatisfying to go to see our doctor and find he or she is unwell and we can see only a stand-in. If this goes on for a long time, each time with a different stand-in, it is very unsatisfactory. This was the case with the Levitical priesthood but it is not so with Jesus; he has an unchanging priesthood. Furthermore, as a divine person he has all power in his ministry to his people, who can come to him with complete confidence. How tragic that Judaism has no one to go to. The claim of the rabbis that Jewish people can go straight to God is totally out of sync with the whole system of priest, sacrifice and altar. Mediation was always needed, due to sin.

A high priest seated in heaven
Another point made in Hebrews is that the location of Messiah's high-priestly ministry is vastly superior. The Levitical all took place in an earthly sanctuary, which though beautiful and full of rich symbolism, was man-made and therefore only temporary.[25] Jesus ministers as a priest at the right hand of God, seated in the heavens, in what Hebrews describes as the true tabernacle.[26] Indeed that true tabernacle is his human nature.[27] Because of this there is no limited access, he is always in the presence of God the Father, but the Levitical high priest had only a once-a-year opportunity to appear in God's immediate presence.[28] This limitation was connected to the difference in efficacy of the sacrifices presented under Moses and the once-for-all sacrifice of Jesus.

Sin removed
Hebrews is emphatic that the Levitical ordinances – food and drink, washings, blood of bulls, goats and calves, ashes of a heifer – could not cleanse the conscience but only the flesh so that the worshipper was ceremonially acceptable.[29] Sin was covered only in a ceremonial sense. Hebrews makes the obvious point that the sheer repetition of the sacrifices demonstrated that they were not making worshippers perfect:[30] 'For the law ... can never with these same sacrifices, which they offer continually year by year, make those who approach perfect.' By contrast, 'Christ was offered once to bear the sins of many.'[31] His once-for-all sacrifice on the cross of Calvary 'obtained eternal redemption'.[32] Therefore he cried, 'It

is finished!'[33] No repetition was needed, there was nothing to add and there was no need to point to something better to come; Jesus had 'put away sin by the sacrifice of himself'.[34] How immeasurably sad to see most of his own people offering charity, repentance and prayer as an atonement when Messiah has laid down his life in death.

An argument from prophecy
The prophecy is Psalm 40:6–8, and is quoted to demonstrate that the Levitical sacrifices were not something in which God had pleasure but he had planned something better. That may seem odd, seeing he ordained them, but it demonstrates they had value as a shadow but not to take away sin. What he desired was a person who did his will and offered his body as a perfect offering. That one was David's greater son, Jesus. Because some struggle with the way Hebrews uses Psalm 40 let me attempt a brief explanation.

David is describing his own experience of deliverance from desperate trouble. As he reflects on how to respond to God's goodness he knows that what is most important is to listen to God, be a devoted and willing servant, keep God's law from the heart, and speak of God and his ways to others so that they too will obey. By contrast, he sees rituals, such as sacrifices, as inconsequential. David's words, 'In the scroll of the book it is written of me', most probably refer to the prophecy of Baalam, which describes, 'A Star shall come out of Jacob, A scepter shall rise out of Israel . . . Out of Jacob One shall have dominion.'[35] This prophecy of Balaam describes Israel subduing the nations around them, something that was accomplished by David. Scripture reveals time and again that David is a type of Messiah and that events in the life of David are a shadow of a greater spiritual reality in the rule of Messiah. Hence the things David writes of himself in these verses will be so of Messiah too. He comes according to prophecy, he has the law in his heart and does the will of God; he is delivered from death and proclaims the good news of righteousness to many. For all this to be possible Messiah has a body prepared for him.[36] The will of God for him is to offer sacrifice, not anything Levitical, but himself. All of which was so of Jesus. This presents a clear congruity between the shadow of salvation presented in the law and the life of David and the actual salvation in Messiah Jesus. There is no difficulty in seeing one as the fulfilment of the other. But a quick glance at rabbinic Judaism tells another story because the entire Levitical system, which pointed forward to the messianic deliverance, is absent.

An argument from covenant
The law was also a shadow because God had promised a new covenant, in which 'Their sins and their lawless deeds I will remember no more'.[37] What God forgets has gone but under the law sins were being remembered, not removed.

Earlier in the letter the author has mentioned a 'better covenant', meaning better than the Mosaic. It is better because its priest, Jesus, was appointed with an oath of God, making everything more certain, which was not so of the Levitical.[38] It is better because its promises are better: God puts his law in the hearts and minds of those in the covenant (it was on stone in the Mosaic with no promise that all covenant members would have it in the heart; some did but many did not). The promise is that all in the covenant will know the Lord, and will have their sins forgiven (again, not promised in the Mosaic, though experienced by some).[39] It is better because its mediator, Jesus, has himself obtained eternal salvation for his people, and is therefore fully able to dispense it to them.[40] In Hebrews 9:15 the term 'new covenant' describes this better covenant, recognizing the existence of another but declaring it obsolete.[41] Rabbinic Judaism fails to discern this obsolescence, so evident through the vanishing away of the Second Temple and all that was connected to it, and continues to strive to live according to the Mosaic when most of it simply cannot be observed.

The existence of a new covenant also speaks to confused Jewish believers who imagine some of the commands of the Mosaic are still obligatory for them as Jews. That is to be under it as a covenant, something that is no longer possible.

Spiritual perspective

Here I want to address the issue of the unseen. Much of the Mosaic covenant focuses on the seen and the tangible, and this is so in rabbinic Judaism; even the hope of the Messiah is connected to his visible reign in Jerusalem, where all will be comfortable for Israel. Hence it is difficult to get used to a faith which expects a great deal of focus on the unseen and a high likelihood of troubles in this life.

A focus on the unseen
Hebrews draws attention to the experience of the heroes of faith in Israel's story and describes them as 'strangers and pilgrims' on the earth, people who believed God's word concerning promises of things which were 'afar off'.[42] Some suffered and some died rather than deny this faith and hope.[43] When Jesus was rejected and crucified it might have appeared at first sight to be completely out of tune with what God's Messiah would experience but Hebrews presents it as all of a piece with those faithful Israelites. He mentions: Jesus also suffered; he endured the cross and despised the shame, keeping his eye on the joy before him.[44] So Hebrews exhorts Jewish believers not to focus on the passing: 'It is good that the heart be established by grace, not with foods which have not profited those who have been occupied with them.'[45] They need to be prepared for reproach and to engage in some degree of separation from the unbelieving Jewish community: 'Let us go forth to Him, outside the camp, bearing His reproach.'[46]

It doesn't look Jewish
Some Jewish believers struggle with the issue of the Jewishness of the church. When considering the gospel they will have recognized its Jewishness in terms of the promises to Israel fulfilled in Jesus the Messiah. However, to be told the church is Jewish is not so easily recognized. The form of church services will not feel like the prayers, songs, liturgical chants, Scripture reading and the sermon of a synagogue service. The social interaction after services, and at other times, will feel different. If they have had a struggle to come to a church, and perhaps have been told 'it's Jewish' so as to encourage them, it can be very disappointing to find it does not feel very Jewish; and the disappointment can re-emerge later, perhaps after a time of disappointment. The answer is to have a proper perspective on Jewishness.

Jewish believers should not expect a church to be culturally Jewish. Why should it be? As a rule there are only a few Jewish people in a local church, so how can it feel culturally Jewish? A church takes much of its cultural feel from the people in it, its location and the leadership style. Jewish believers who want to express the cultural side of their Jewishness must find other ways to do that, and I have written on that elsewhere in this book.[47] By that I do not mean they should suppress their Jewish character in church life; far from it, diversity is part of the glory of the church. However, it is natural to want to express the cultural side of Jewishness with other Jews.

From a spiritual perspective the church is Jewish, but that is due not so much to its external religious forms as to its spiritual reality. Gospel churches worship the God of Israel through the Messiah of Israel. They read the Scriptures written by Jewish people. The songs they sing are either paraphrases of Israel's psalms or will frequently use terminology drawn from Israel's experience. There may even be the occasional Hebrew word, like 'Hallelujah'! The spiritual realities of being a Christian are drawn from the types, which were real people, events and ordinances in Israel's history. For example, circumcision, the feasts, the pillar of cloud, the temple sacrifices and priesthood. Christianity is Jewish. A focus on externals may diminish the sense of that but a spiritual focus will reinforce it.

Exhortations and warnings

There are many of these in Hebrews, so I can only pick out the main themes. Those drifting away need to pay attention to what they know: 'Therefore we must give the more earnest heed to the things we have heard.'[48] There is a perfection to which they need to press on, 'Leaving the discussion of the elementary principles of Christ, let us go on to perfection.'[49] Hindrances must be recognized and put aside, 'Let us lay aside every weight, and the sin which so easily ensnares us, and let us run with endurance the race that is set before us.'[50] However, those who seek help to stop drifting will not be alone. The author encourages them that help is at hand, 'Let us therefore come boldly to the throne of grace, that we may obtain mercy and find grace to help in time of need.'[51]

For some, serious warnings are necessary, and they all add up to one thing: demonstrate the genuineness of your faith by persevering: 'For we have become partakers of Christ if we hold the beginning of our confidence steadfast to the end.'[52] The final evidence that what has happened to us is the real thing – genuine regeneration, repentance and faith – is that we persevere to the end. The warning is this: do not drift away thinking your past profession of faith is some sort of insurance policy, as if you can afford to dabble with doubt and denial, you must sort things out before you go beyond the point of no return. And there is such a thing as no return: 'For if we sin willfully after we have received the knowledge of the truth, there no longer remains a sacrifice for sins, but a certain fearful expectation of judgment, and fiery indignation.'[53] To 'sin willfully' in this context means to defiantly reject Jesus as Messiah. That may seem unlikely to the person who has just begun to have doubts and, in their eyes, is just a little less enthusiastic than they once were, but such should note that the process of decline is rarely dramatic but incremental. Hebrews exhorts Jewish believers to demonstrate the genuineness of their profession by being diligent and pressing on. It also gives a warning: 'It is a fearful things to fall into the hands of the living God,' because, as stated elsewhere in the letter, 'Our God is a consuming fire.'[54]

Encouragements to remember past faithfulness

Those who have faltered and grown sluggish but then repent should not despair of recovery. The writer reminds them of all they suffered in their early days and then says: 'You have need of endurance.'[55] That is, there is no sense of them needing to do penance or complete a re-entry test, they must simply pick up and press on. The writer also encourages them that their former faithfulness has not been wiped off the record but remains valued by God: 'God is not unjust to forget your work and labor of love which you have shown toward His name, in that you have ministered to the saints, and do minister.'[56]

Exhort one another
We are not to be loners in God's kingdom; we are to enjoy fellowship with one another and encourage each other. Jewish believers are strongly tempted to be loners: they do not feel welcome among their own, and in the church it is possible to feel like a fish out

of water. The writer of Hebrews encourages Jewish believers to consider one another – to take note of each other's circumstances and struggles – to stir each other up to love and good works, and to meet together.[57] This is an in-house, Jewish, Christian responsibility, as well as one which falls to all those in a local church to which a Jewish believer belongs.

In a local church, Jewish believers will probably need more fellowship than others in the early days of their faith, and in later days if they remain single. It would be invaluable if one home in their church is 'open house' for them, and others are hospitable. They should be part of a church home group. Someone should mentor them and keep in touch. I do not want to give the wrong impression, as if all Jewish believers are perpetually fragile, but they are likely to be more vulnerable than they appear, especially in early days.

I believe Jewish believers have a special responsibility to encourage each other, and I have written more on this in other chapters of this book. But to repeat the basics here, Jewish believers from local churches should get together regularly, or from time to time, with other Jewish believers, formally and informally, to study relevant truths, share experiences and pray for one another. Other Christians should not look askance at this as if they are being elitist or separatist, but recognize this is what all churches or inter-church bodies do to meet the needs of different groups among them.

19.

Culturally Jewish

There is such a thing as Jewish culture, and it is more than Judaism. That needs to be underlined because too many Christians still think Jewish culture is all down to Judaism, and because of that they act cautiously when Jewish believers speak of their Jewishness.

Culture

What is culture? Culture is as easily learned as our native language; we never stop to analyse it, we just know and do it. Culture is a human creation. Humans develop methods of agriculture and make artefacts; they communicate and create social institutions to order family and community life; through their arts they communicate their thoughts and feelings about hope and experience; and they create religion to give expression to the metaphysical realities they sense. Different people groups have done these things differently. And I do not think the differences are simply due to external influences (nurture) but also to something embedded in their nature, somehow connected to the natural character of those who began the group way back in their history.

Only one national culture has ever existed which has had God's imprint on it through the revelation of a law regulating life and that was the old covenant Israelite culture. Today's Jewish culture is by no means identical with it but draws a great deal from it. Much has been added over the years as Jewish people have lived in other cultures and adapted elements from those cultures into their own. I remember sitting down to a meal at a home in Belarus with a Jewish friend of mine from New York who exclaimed, 'Hey, look at all this Jewish food!' But it was typical Belarusian food, which Jewish people had taken with them to New York years earlier and there it became 'Jewish food'. However, there would be many Jewish people who would not recognize it as 'Jewish food' at all, having been brought up say, in North Africa. Jewish culture has many variations due to the different influences upon different communities over the centuries.

And there is a 'nature' element to Jewish culture too. However, the moment this subject is touched upon there is the danger of stereotyping, and Jewish people are extremely sensitive to it, almost to the point of saying that there is nothing different about Jews. However, when Jews themselves produce TV and radio programmes about Jews being Jews, then there has to be something Jewish about Jews which transcends all cultural variations! It is an interesting exercise to try and find one word to sum up the character of a people. The English are often described as diplomatic, the French as having flair and the Chinese as industrious. The Jews? I see them as a people marked by ingenuity. Speaking generally, there is an inventiveness, intelligence, energy and creativity about Jewish people. And that ingenuity is frequently productive because of other qualities like openness, personableness and humour. Because of these things Jewish people have made significant contributions to human society.

The New Testament and Jewish Culture

The New Testament believes there is such a thing as Jewish culture. Paul wrote about becoming as a Jew to the Jews.[1] And that is not just a religious matter because he addressed that specifically when he wrote about becoming as under law to those under law. For Paul, Jews in his day fell into two broad categories: those who were devout and lived by the law of Moses, and those who were Jewish but not devout. There was obviously a Jewish way of life which was not dominated by the law, although it could not have been completely divorced from it; and it was not Gentile. It is the same today: Jews, and Jews under law.

For Jewish people who become believers in Jesus it is inevitable that they bring their Jewishness with them. No bad thing because churches always need a healthy dose of ingenuity. But what about those cultural practices which owe their origin to the law of Moses and rabbinic Judaism? Here is where the difficulty arises. If Jewish believers retain some of those practices, are they just weak believers, incurably attached to their old ways? What New Testament examples do we have?

New Testament Jewish believers and Jewish religious practices

Many of the early Jewish believers continued to eat only food which was allowable under the law. When Peter was challenged in a vision to eat any sort of food he protested that nothing unclean or common had entered his mouth.[2] Up to that point, before and after faith, he had eaten only kosher, and that was so for many of those early believers, which is why they created a few rules to aid fellowship between Jewish and Gentile believers, especially table fellowship.[3]

During Paul's first stay in Corinth we read that he had taken a vow, 'He had his hair cut off at Chenchrea, for he had taken a vow.'[4] We are not told why but it may have been an act of special consecration, due his great apprehension at preaching there. Something about the form of it – the cutting off of his hair – resembles the Nazirite vow, a Mosaic ordinance aimed at aiding a special time of consecration to Yahweh.[5] However, there is something different. The Nazirite was to cut off his hair at the temple and burn it on the fire of the altar which was burning under the peace offering that the Nazirite was commanded to bring.[6] Paul clearly did not do that. It would seem to me therefore that he is adapting a Mosaic custom familiar to him from his days immersed in Judaism as an aid to devotion in his service of Messiah Jesus.

When Paul and Silas headed off into the region of Paul's first missionary journey they met Timothy, and Paul wanted him to join them in the work. At that stage they were delivering to the churches the Jerusalem decrees regarding Jew/Gentile fellowship in the churches but they would soon be entering unevangelized fields, and perhaps Paul felt they needed another in the team. But there was a problem with Timothy; he was not circumcised, so: 'He [Paul] took him and circumcised him because of the Jews who were in that region, for they all knew that his father was Greek.'[7] It would seem that Paul anticipated that this would be a hindrance to evangelism, a diversion from the main spiritual issues, because his Jewish hearers would be more interested in the issue of Timothy's status than the gospel. His action cleared the air of any unnecessary debate that would have hindered his presentation of the gospel. Bearing in mind that this was at a time when he was delivering decrees about Gentile believers not having to be circumcised and keep the law, it probably created confusion in the minds of some. Paul no doubt took the opportunity to clarify the issues. For Paul, a smooth path for the gospel was crucial and if the performance of a particular Jewish custom would help, without any compromise of the gospel, he would go ahead.

The final example is Paul in Jerusalem, accompanying four Jewish believers to the temple to assist in the conclusion of a vow, involving ritual purification for them and for him.[8] The aim of James and the elders was to defuse the tension caused by Paul's presence, due to the understanding among Jerusalem believers that he taught diaspora Jews to abandon Moses, circumcision and Jewish customs. That was obviously a distortion of what Paul taught but Paul was prepared to go along with the suggestion so as to help keep the peace. This act would demonstrate, as James put it, 'that you yourself also walk orderly and keep the law'.[9] Some have wrongly concluded from this that Paul continued to keep the law, however that was simply impossible for one who was the apostle to the Gentiles, as he wrote himself, '[I became] to those who are without law, as without law.'[10] He adapted himself to a Gentile lifestyle when presenting the gospel to them, and that would have included eating non-kosher food. What Paul did in Jerusalem was practising what he preached in Romans 14: 'Receive one who is weak in the faith, but not to disputes over doubtful things.'[11] Rather than get into a heated debate about all the issues, and his practice, he simply went along with the four men's act of genuine devotion to the master who had received them. It was an act of keeping the peace between believers.

These examples from Paul's life and ministry cover three key areas of Christian living: personal devotion, evangelism and fellowship, and provide examples for today's Jewish believers. However, before considering today's situation it would be helpful to remember some history.

Historical Developments

In the post-apostolic churches it seems that, to begin with, the churches understood Paul's practice. About AD 150, Justin Martyr wrote his *Dialogue with Trypho*, and he makes reference to the way that some Jewish believers attempted to retain their Jewish identity. To different degrees some continued to keep the law, and Justin had no problem with this, but those who insisted that Gentile Christians kept the law were not accepted by him. However, as time went on, in the days of the church fathers (first to fifth centuries), the dispute between the church and the synagogue sometimes became very sharp, placing Jewish believers in the churches in a difficult position. Their love for their people, coupled with any expression of their Jewishness, made them suspect; and one church in the fourth century required the following declaration of them: 'I renounce all customs, rites, legalisms, unleavened breads, and sacrifices of lambs of the Hebrews ... in one word, I renounce everything Jewish.'[12] Astonishing, but clearly that church was in no mood for subtle distinctions. While it is not clear that other churches adopted such a declaration, the growing anti-Jewish feeling among church leaders produced the same effect. Leadership in the churches had become mostly Gentile, which meant that the natural sympathy which had once tempered attitudes was gone. In addition to this we can see a reaction in the churches to the way the Jewish leaders had opposed the first preaching of the gospel. Furthermore, the waters were constantly being troubled by both sides winning converts from each other.

This situation for Jewish believers went on for many centuries but eventually winds of change began to blow. The first was the Reformation. One truth, rediscovered at the Reformation and held by good numbers of the leaders, was that God had not cast away the Jews. This was further developed in the Puritan era and was strongly taught in eighteenth century in the English-speaking world by men like Jonathan Edwards, John Wesley and George

Whitefield leading to the commencement of many missions to the Jewish people in the nineteenth century, as well as to strong support from many evangelicals for Jewish people to be restored to their ancient homeland.

A second wind of change was the emancipation of Jewish people from the ghettos of Europe. The Enlightenment of the eighteenth century, with its emphasis on reason and human equality, and the political movements it spawned, enabled Jewish people to play a part in society as Jews. This was more than an individual matter; a reviving of the national consciousness of the Jewish people began. A third wind of change was the large number of Jewish people coming to faith in the nineteenth and twentieth centuries as they were more exposed to the gospel.

A fourth wind of change, developing from the second and third, was the formation of a Hebrew Christian Alliance in Britain in 1866, and later, in 1925, the International Hebrew Christian Alliance. Jewish believers were organizing themselves as a body within the church. A fifth wind of change was the creation of the State of Israel, reviving Jewish national consciousness even more strongly, and enabling Jewish people to have a focus for expressing their Jewishness apart from the synagogue and the traditional Jewish institutions in the diaspora.

A sixth wind of change was the emphasis of the Church Growth Movement, which taught that, 'Men like to become Christians without crossing racial, linguistic, or clan barriers',[13] leading to a stronger emphasis on culturally sensitive evangelism and particularly giving encouragement to ethnic churches in multicultural cities.

A seventh, and final, wind of change was the emergence in the 1970s of the Messianic Movement, which resulted from all these things. This is more than a modern term for Jews who believe in Jesus; the movement gave new impetus to Jewish believers being culturally Jewish, and especially with regard to the use of Jewish religious traditions in the practice of their faith. For a minority it has led to the creation of Jewish ethnic churches, normally termed 'messianic congregations'.

This brings us back to a New Testament situation in which Jewish believers feel free, as Paul did, to use things which belong to their Jewish religious culture as a part of their Christian faith. I do not mean to suggest that nothing of the sort happened between Justin Martyr's days and the 1970s. I am sure Jewish believers did more of such things than we know but the point is, things are now very open and accepted; at least by many Christians. I say 'many' because I know that, despite such examples as I have given from Paul, there are many Christians who see such religious practices by Jewish believers as a reversion to Judaism or a failure to get out from under the law. Such need to think harder about the issues. They may find it helpful to consider how much of their own Christian practice derives from the culture of Christendom and how much of it has a New Testament justification.

Culturally Jewish Today

Jewish believers in Jesus have a cultural background which is distinct from the national culture in which they live. It will have borrowed from that national culture but it remains distinct. They have a national history going back to Abraham, a unique religious book (the Hebrew Scriptures), the Hebrew and modern Hebrew languages, religious and social customs that draw on the Bible and their historical experience, a family network, a style of music for communal events, a unique cuisine and a distinctive sense of humour. On top of all this is the cultural development taking place in Israel, which influences all other Jews, and Jewish believers living there are a part of it. To one degree or another this is the cultural milieu of Jewish people who come to faith in Jesus. However, when they join a local church they find it is not the cultural milieu of most of the people there, unless that church is in Israel and made up mostly of Jewish Israelis. Church life will soon take up a large slice of their time, so they start to find that they are spending much more time with non-Jews than previously and are in danger of losing that easy Jewish rapport with fellow-Jews.

Reinforcing Jewishness

So, can Jewishness be lost? Never objectively, but our focus is on the subjective. In one sense, it cannot be lost subjectively. Most people know who they are and where they belong and Jews know they are Jewish. For some who come to faith in Jesus that is enough, that awareness is strong within them and they feel no need go out of their way to do Jewish things which reinforce that. I have no quarrel with that, except to point out that, in fact, they are doing things which reinforce Jewishness every day. They know and love Israel's Messiah, they are reading a Jewish book full of the history and spiritual experiences of their people, they are praying to the God of Israel, and their praises to God draw upon a biblical, Jewish spirituality.

Beyond such inevitable things, Jewish believers can continue to delve into Jewish history and current events, maintain or improve their knowledge of Hebrew, show support for Jewish causes and for Israel, eat Jewish food, enjoy Jewish music, celebrate Jewish festivals and customs, and meet with other Jewish people. The latter would include family and communal events (where possible), and meeting with other Jewish believers. For some, the contrast between their close involvement with fellow-Jews before they believed and the sense of isolation subsequent to believing is very hard to bear. To solve this some choose to go and live in Israel. Many Jewish believers marry non-Jews, and although it is certainly more important to marry a fellow-Christian than to marry someone Jewish who does not believe, I can understand those who have a strong desire to find a Jewish spouse who is a believer and develop a home life which is both Jewish and Christian. That is not necessarily a recipe for instant harmony but for some it is important and should be understood.

If we review all the suggestions made above it is worth asking how much of that reinforces the Jewishness of the average non-believing Jewish person? For most Jews, meeting with other Jews, having some familiarity with Hebrew, supporting Israel, and having a Jewish home are quite enough. They do not regularly read the Scriptures or attend a place of worship, but try telling them that their Jewishness is weakening or that they are not Jewish! How much stronger is the position of the Jewish believer, who lives in the Jewish Scriptures and who loves the Jewish Messiah.

The Non-Jewish Jew and the Jewish Gentile

Some Jewish people have been raised all but Gentile. This happens less nowadays, but some Jews of the generation that survived the

Holocaust decided not to burden their children with Jewishness and raised them with very little contact with the Jewish community, and some never told them they were Jewish. I have met Jewish believers who did not know they were Jewish by birth until after coming to faith in Jesus; their Jewish parent or parents deciding that, at that point, they ought to know. It is understandable that Jewish believers with such a background want to learn more about their people and being Jewish. Some of them go overboard in this, perhaps wanting to prove something by the 'zeal of a convert' as we say, but they usually settle down when they have 'been there and done that' and learnt to develop a mature Jewish and Christian lifestyle.

And then there are Christians who have in every way grown up in their Gentile culture but they get bitten by the 'Jewish bug'. They hear about the Jewish roots of their faith, they think they have been missing something for years, they look into all things Jewish and they start to investigate if they have any 'Jewish blood'. Some find it in a great-great grandfather or -mother and decide they are Jewish. Certainly the Jewish community would not count them as Jewish, as they require a Jewish mother, meaning a mother who had Jewish parents, giving some living contact with the Jewish community. They are declaring that it is a matter of what you pick up first-hand at home. It reminds me of the story of a Jewish young man wanting to explore his Jewishness and visiting a synagogue to learn about God. The rabbi's response was, 'Go home!', which sounds perilously like 'Go away!' but was meant to make the point that the Jewish home is where Jewishness is learnt, because it is all about learning by experience. If a person's Jewish relatives are further removed than a mother, or they have none at all then Judaism requires a conversion process, which gives the understanding they have not been able to pick up in the home.

I am elaborating on this because I would say to such 'Jewish Gentiles': 'OK, you have someone Jewish in your family line. Enjoy exploring that, learn about them and their life, learn more about Jewish people. Love them, pray for them, enjoy mixing with them if you want to, but do not say you are Jewish. Do not become another frustrated "Jewish wannabe"; be secure in your Christian and Gentile character. Time is precious, maximize it by setting your mind on things above.'

Jewish believers and Jewish religious practices today

I want to make some suggestions within the four New Testament areas I have mentioned. I want to underline first of all that these things are essentially cultural, by which I mean Jewish believers are in no way obliged to do them. It also needs to be underlined that they are not somehow more spiritual. It should go without saying that any practice adopted must be consistent with the gospel, and certainly not be something which developed within Judaism in opposition to the gospel.

A core cultural practice

In the land of Israel the first Jewish believers ate kosher, as other Jews would have done. Today, one thing all Jews do, worldwide, is to circumcise their male offspring. That is a good thing for Jewish believers to have done for theirs too; otherwise they will simply not be accepted as Jews.

Devotional

What Jewish practice today might be profitably copied or adapted by a Jewish believer for devotional purposes? One suggestion would be to fast and pray during the Ten Days of Repentance,[14] engaging in a period of self-examination and intercession. Another, for married couples, would be to observe Judaism's laws of family purity for a season, which would mean no sexual relations for seven days after the wife's menstrual period. There would be value in the self-discipline, and there could be a greater focus on meditation and prayer.

Witness

For evangelistic purposes there are many things which could be practised, occasionally or permanently, depending on Jewish family and friends. It might be essential for entertaining Jewish relatives to keep a kosher home. There would be value in having a regular Friday night, Sabbath meal as a means of keeping up social contact, including the hope of sharing Messiah at some future time.

Fellowship

Jewish believers who keep kosher in their own home should not give the impression others must provide kosher food if they invite them for a meal. Hopefully their hosts will ask about their preferences but they should not be so picky that no one wants to invite them back. And then, as an internal Jewish believer matter, some Jewish believers are weak and feel they must eat kosher, so if other Jewish believers invite them for a meal they should not tell them to lighten up and serve them pork chops; they should accommodate themselves to their weak brother or sister.

20.

The Return to the Land

Every year, at the close of the Passover celebration, Jewish people throughout the world shout out, 'Next year in Jerusalem!' In some periods of history it was only a hope, today it is an option. A lot could be said about what Jewish people have achieved there in the last one hundred and fifty years but that is not my purpose. Likewise, a lot could be said about the rights and wrongs of the current Middle East conflict but it is not my aim. This much can be said: it is a conflict which the world cannot ignore; it is one which is constantly in the news. There are other conflicts across the globe that barely get noticed, despite having much higher death tolls, but this one is noticed, and for the simple reason that it threatens to escalate out of control into a much wider conflagration, and one which, because of oil, threatens to disrupt the lifestyle of millions. There are very large numbers of anxious spectators.

The religious dimension adds to the complexity of the issues and the commitment of the spectators. Most Orthodox Jews see a messianic dimension, and the interest of Christians is drawn because the arena of conflict is within the lands of the Bible. What is God doing? Should they support God's plan, whatever it is? And then, Islam has awoken, not that it was ever really asleep, but its concern is much more noticeable now that some of its more radical adherents are proactive in their opposition to the State of Israel.

Whereas the return to Zion began as a vision of peace and security for a people who had frequently been harassed, persecuted and killed as they dwelt among the nations of the world, it has now become a place where another genocide threatens them. Christians must surely ask themselves how they can help to prevent it.

The fact that the conflict trammels the lives of uncounted helpless sufferers on both sides, and that Christian brothers and sisters on either side of the conflict are also caught up in the consequences, must deepen a Christian's concerns.

In fact, it is not necessary to read too many Christian magazines or visit very many web sites to discover that Christians certainly are alert to what is happening, and that their responses are very much connected to the significance they attach to the return of the Jewish people to the land of the Bible, ranging from insignificant to highly significant. Inevitably, questions of fulfilment of Bible prophecy are raised, connections made to the millennium of Revelation 20, and end-time scenarios created. Which is all very interesting but probably not a priority for those on the ground, who are more concerned with the here-and-now power of the gospel to change people and situations.

Like many, my imagination is stirred and my fears aroused as I watch the swirling, and frequently unexpected events of the Middle East conflict. In this chapter my main concern is to ask what the New Testament has to say about the Jewish people and their ancient homeland. Does it anticipate a return? Does the conflict we now observe loom large in New Testament references to end-time events?

Name and Location

It is so difficult to choose a name for the biblical land of Israel! 'Canaan' is too far in the past; as discussed earlier, 'Palestine' as used by Bible scholars means something quite different today; 'Holy Land' belongs to another era; and 'Israel' can be confusing as to exactly what is meant. I am starting with the term 'promised land' because that is where things began and it is still a term used today, even though people disagree as to whether it is still promised to the Jewish people.

The area originally promised by God to Abraham and his descendants was described by God to Abraham: 'from the river of Egypt to the great river, the River Euphrates'.[1] In the absence of the sort of maps we are used to, it would seem that the use of two rivers to describe the region of what God was promising was clearly meant to convey a general impression to Abraham. It was followed by a list of the lands dwelt in by the then inhabitants, which no doubt made the boundaries clearer to Abraham and certainly falls short of the exact geographical space between the Nile and the Euphrates. We get a much clearer idea of the area intended by looking at the land allotted to and settled by the Israelites after driving out the Canaanites. This area is surely what we are meant to understand by the land of promise. That there was an element of flexibility in it all is indicated by the request of some of the tribes to settle on the east side of the Jordan, something Moses had clearly not expected but which he did not view as ruled out. He obviously did not have lines drawn on a map within which Israel had to reside at all costs. The description of the extent of Solomon's reign uses the same general terminology as God used with Abraham, and in so doing gives the distinct impression that the promise was first fulfilled at that time. We are told that, 'He reigned over all the kings from the River [Euphrates] to the land of the Philistines, as far as the border of Egypt'.[2]

The Promised Land in the New Testament

What does the New Testament have to say about the land promised to Abraham? Very little, is the short answer; certainly a lot less that we might expect and, disarmingly, there is no mention of the land in the passage where we would most expect it to be mentioned, Romans 11. Whatever may be suggested to explain away this silence, the bottom line is that what the New Testament does and does not say about the land gives a doctrine of the land for the Jewish people in the new covenant period.

Some might think it is impossible to consider this issue without making some investigations into Old Testament texts. I sympathize with such a sentiment but as the New Testament is the authoritative interpretation of the Old then its view of the land promise is sufficient, and gives us a template by which to interpret Old Testament texts. My approach will be to try and come to the relevant texts in a straightforward way.

The Land as a Type

The land of promise was a place for the people of God to enjoy God's presence and blessings, sing his praises and walk in his ways but there can be no doubt that the land promised to Abraham and his descendants was meant to picture a greater reality, which Hebrews describes as, 'a better, that is, a heavenly country'.[3] Hebrews tells us that Abraham was aware that the land of promise where he sojourned was not the goal; rather that goal was, 'the city which has foundations, whose builder and maker is God'.[4] That hope is not an ethereal one but a new heavens and a new earth, where God's people will enjoy God's presence and blessings, sing his praises and walk in his ways for evermore.

Paul demonstrates a similar understanding when he describes the promise to Abraham as, 'the promise that he would be the heir of the *world*'.[5] By using the term 'world' here Paul goes beyond any expression God used with Abraham and he is clearly looking to the fulfilment in Messiah. The inheritance is for all who have that faith, circumcised and uncircumcised, and with such a focus it is natural that he should use the term 'world', because the inclusion of the Gentiles breaks the bounds of the old economy and leads into the hope of the messianic kingdom. All believers inherit with Christ and will one day enjoy the new world he will create. The promised land was a type of this inheritance.

The Land as a Divine Space, a Holy Land

Building on what I have written in the above section, the question obviously arises as to the status of the land when the covenant changes. Allow me to repeat a point made earlier in this book. We can picture the original covenant with Abraham as like a foundation. When God's people grow and are in need of a form of national organization, God puts another covenant on that foundation, the Mosaic. It can be thought of as an administrative covenant for God's people, suited to those particular circumstances. When new circumstances are introduced for God's people, those of a worldwide nation of believers under Messiah, then something new is needed to administer God's people, which is the new covenant.

This is how Hebrews puts it: 'In that He says, "A new covenant," He has made the first obsolete. Now what is becoming obsolete and growing old is ready to vanish away.'[6] The writer presumably describes the old covenant as not yet gone because he wrote before the temple was destroyed – that destruction would be the sign above all signs that the old covenant was obsolete. Because of this obsolescence, the land can no longer be a covenantal divine space, an area vital to the playing out of the divine purpose in the world. That space is now the entire planet earth and the new covenant administration pertains to it. Hebrews makes it quite clear that the new covenant is the final administrative covenant for the Lord's people by calling it the 'everlasting covenant' in the closing doxology of the letter.[7] This is the only place in the New Testament where this phrase is used, and it clearly picks up on the phrase as used by the prophets to point to God's new arrangement in Messiah's days.[8] There is no indication of something further, and certainly nothing about a revived Mosaic covenant. The land of Israel is no longer a divine space but that does not rule it out as a place for Jewish people to live.

For some Christian authors, because the type has disappeared and Messiah's worldwide kingdom has begun, then the land is simply not relevant. I am sure that such authors are saddened to see Jews and Arabs fighting over it but for them the land is not of any especial concern to Christians. I consider this an appalling indifference to a people who have lacked the satisfaction of living in their own land for about two thousand years, and have all too often suffered the antipathy of those Gentiles whose national comforts they have sought to share. I do not believe Israel's covenant God is so indifferent.

A Return to the Land – a New Testament Hope? God's Promises to Israel

In Romans 9:1–5 Paul lists out the privileges of Israel and among them is 'the promises', which would include the land. In Romans 11:29 Paul refers to God's gifts and calling with regard to Israel as 'irrevocable'. Again, one of those gifts would be the land. It might be argued that as it was a type, and the type is now being fulfilled, then that promise is fulfilled and as obsolete as the Mosaic covenant. I am happy to agree that its typological significance is fulfilled but not that the promise is obsolete, because Paul says the gifts are irrevocable. However, the giver has set conditions for its enjoyment.

A return of the Jewish people to the promised land is by no means certain because there is a connection between enjoying what God has promised and walking in God's ways, as God said to Abraham, 'For I have known him, in order that he may command his children and his household after him, that they keep the way of the LORD, to do righteousness and justice, that the LORD may bring to Abraham what He has spoken to him.'[9] As long as Israel fails to keep the way of the Lord, which is to believe in and follow Jesus, then there can be no certainty, on the basis of the promise and gift alone, that they would ever dwell there again.

But is the land not essential to their survival as a covenant people? The reality is, they can survive and even prosper as a people without the land; the last two thousand years testify to that. Of course, it can be objected that there has been so much insecurity and suffering in those two thousand years that surely they need their own land to experience something better. Present experience would seem to contradict that. It is almost ironic that there are many places on earth a great deal more secure for Jewish people than the land of Israel. It would seem that being in the land no more guarantees their survival and prosperity than being scattered among the nations.

Ask Jesus about it

Ask Jesus? Would we not just love to have such an opportunity? Then it would all be clear and we could relax. Well, the apostles took their opportunity and did not appear to end up much the wiser. After the resurrection they were together with the Lord Jesus and, knowing something special was afoot – the gift of the Spirit – they asked him, 'Lord, will You at this time restore the kingdom to Israel?'[10] Jesus' answer has been the springboard for much debate: 'It is not for you to know times or seasons which the Father has put in His own authority. But you shall receive power when the

Holy Spirit has come upon you; and you shall be witnesses to Me.' Many would like to think that Jesus' words – 'It is not for you to know times or seasons' – implies that such a restoration will take place but the timing of it is not for them to know. That is an argument from silence and deduces too much, and it certainly flies in the face of what he had previously said about the kingdom being taken away from Israel. Bearing in mind what Jesus had said to them previously about his having many things to say to them but they could not bear them at the time,[11] it could equally be argued that to start elaborating on the kingdom being taken away at that moment would be to say things they were unable to bear at that time, and so Jesus dampens any further discussion by moving on to what their priority was to be. That seems to me to be a valid explanation of Jesus' response. He was not quietly hinting at a restored kingdom, and an inevitable return to the land. However, perhaps the mention of 'times and seasons' in the context of Israel indicates there is a time and a season for them which includes the land; maybe.

A Chink of Light from Jesus?

All three of the Synoptic Gospels record the words of Jesus about the destruction of Jerusalem but only Luke gives us these words: 'And they will fall by the edge of the sword, and be led away captive into all nations. And Jerusalem will be trampled by Gentiles until the times of the Gentiles are fulfilled.'[12] It is those few words, 'until the times of the Gentiles are fulfilled', that may be a chink of light on a return. Jesus is making clear that the nations will have political control over Jerusalem in the future, such that the Jews will have no control. That has certainly happened over the last two thousand years. Although Jewish people have always lived in Jerusalem they have never ruled there. The expression 'until the times of the Gentiles are fulfilled' indicates an end to the period set for the Gentiles to trample Jerusalem, and would imply that the Jewish people have returned there and regained political control.

However, some have objected that there is something unusual here in that we are not told what the new situation will be after the 'until'; we are simply told there is an end to the trampling of Jerusalem by the Gentiles. Hence they conclude that the end of Gentile trampling is concurrent with the return of Jesus, which is the main focus of the passage. They have a point. It is strange that Jesus does not say what happens next. In response, two points can be made. Firstly, bearing in mind his purpose – to reveal the coming desolation of Jerusalem as an act of God's vengeance – it is not surprising that, even if he was aware of a future return, he does not specifically mention it here, as it would certainly blunt his message. Secondly, if the end of the period of trampling is his personal return why not say so, using language he has used elsewhere in the passage: words like 'until the time of the end' or 'until the Son of Man comes'?

I want to draw attention to one other point of interest. If Jesus meant to indicate a future return then it is strange he does not indicate there is something written about it. He does that very emphatically concerning the coming judgement, 'that all things which are written may be fulfilled', which was spoken just a few sentences earlier.[13] He is silent with regard to an Old Testament reference to a return. Again, this may be explained by his purpose in his discourse. Yet, it leaves us with nothing certain.

I believe this uncertainty is why many commentators who wrote about this passage before the present-day return of Jews to the land of promise saw nothing in it for Israel regarding a return to the land. However, I think it is significant that Jesus did not use a phrase like 'until the time of the end'. It does leave us with the possibility of a return but any certainty on the matter awaits the event. The fact that it has happened, that the land is not trampled and desolate any longer but is loved, fruitful and prosperous, points to the interpretation that Jesus was hinting at a future return, and yet in a very undramatic way.

Jesus' underplaying of things, his lack of drama, is significant. It is in stark contrast to the way in which many speak and write about the present-day return of Jewish people to the land. For them, it is as if all history has been tending to this point, a major fulcrum in the plan of redemption has been reached, and a totally new phase in God's plan is commencing. Such a perspective is totally absent from Luke 21 and the rest of the New Testament, where only one major fulcrum remains, the return of Jesus. Such people need to calm down and tone down. For myself, I rejoice to see Jewish people back in their ancient homeland, and I am sure it is significant, but Paul's focus in Romans 11 on their salvation through the gospel means that any significance relates to their conversion.

The New Testament Use of the Old Testament Regarding the Land

If the return to the land is as central to God's kingdom purposes as some think then we would expect something more from the apostles in the New Testament. The considerable use some teachers make of the Old Testament to prove the matter of the return to the land ought to be found in the Acts and the epistles. But, as I noted earlier, there is almost nothing. Two passages which quote the Old Testament are significant, Acts 15:15–17 and Romans 11:26–7 and need to be examined.

The Acts 15:15–17 quote from Amos 9:11–12

The context in Acts is a council of leaders in Jerusalem, which was held to resolve the issue of whether Gentile believers ought to keep the law of Moses. After much discussion James seeks to bring things to a conclusion and is so doing quotes from Amos 9:11–12, a prophecy of the restoration of the Davidic kingdom after a time of severe judgements, including blessing on the Gentiles. James sees this as fulfilled in the events of his day, especially the conversion of Gentiles. Jesus the Son of David had come, he had established his throne in glory and was blessing Israel and the Gentiles. Prophecies such as this, and others like them, are read by many as referring to the present-day return to the land, or yet to be fulfilled in a future return. However, James understands the fulfilment as commencing in his day; I say 'commencing' because it is still being fulfilled to this day. The whole scenario of the return from captivity, spiritual revival among the returnees, a restoration of the temple, city and land, preparation for the Messiah, the coming of Messiah, the gift of the Spirit and the blessing of the nations is all presented in the prophets as one unfolding unit without breaks. And it has happened and is happening. There is no mention of a further return to the land as a key aspect of the whole, and the New Testament authors never present it as part of their understanding of the scenario.

But what about the rest of that prophecy of Amos, the final section after the part James quoted? It speaks of the captives of Israel returning, the land blessed and has the promise, 'No longer shall they be pulled up From the land I have given them.'[14] It seems to me that Amos is viewing the restoration from two perspectives. Verses 11 and 12 give the broad perspective – Messiah's coming to bless Israel and the nations. Verses 13 to 15 give a narrower perspective – events in the land after the return, and his purpose is to encourage the returnees and the generations that followed and waited for Messiah. It is a period of history which many Christians think little about but actually lasted nearly six hundred years! Although the focus is blessing on the returnees yet at some point in verses 13 to 15 the Messiah comes and then the Gentiles are blessed. This helps us to understand how the promise of no longer being pulled up from the land was fulfilled. Clearly it was not fulfilled literally because the Jewish people were pulled up from the land in AD 70. We are faced with the metamorphosis of God's people pictured by the olive tree in Romans 11.

What began as a people composed of repentant Jews who returned, becomes two peoples: those among Israel who rejected their Messiah, and a people composed of Jews and Gentiles who believe in him. The people who believe are those who will never be pulled up from the land. The land stood for a place where God, in the temple, dwelt among his people; it is now the whole earth, where his people are scattered. So the promise of remaining in the land asserts he will ensure he has a people worldwide who will not persist in sin, and so there will never again need to be a separation. To use New Testament words, 'I will never leave you or forsake you.'[15] If it is questioned whether Amos grasped all this the answer is, he did not have to. He is using the concepts and language available to him to describe the future hope.

The Romans 11:26–7 quote from Isaiah 59:20 and 27:9

Could parts of the scenario described above have a further fulfilment later in history? A sort of 'take two'? That is a possibility, but we must have some New Testament confirmation for such a use of the Old. Here is the relevance of the second passage, Romans 11:26–7, where Paul quotes two Old Testament prophecies to prove a point concerning future spiritual blessing on Israel. I do not want to go into too much detail on his use of the Old Testament here, as I will examine it thoroughly in the final chapter, but what is clear is that Paul is using texts that were fulfilled by the coming of Messiah to Israel and giving them a further fulfilment. His use of the term 'mystery' clearly indicates this is not obvious from the Old Testament but that it has been revealed to him as an apostle.[16] The point I want to make here is that the New Testament never does this with a text about a return to the land. In the absence of apostolic revelation indicating a further fulfilment for texts about the return to the land after Babylon, revealing a future return of Jewish people to the land, we simply cannot use Old Testament prophecies in such a way. The fact that Paul used the Old Testament to indicate future spiritual blessing but not for a return to the land must give pause for thought.

A Mini Conclusion

I have argued that the present-day return of Jewish people to the land is not a fulfilment of prophecy, either of the Old or the New Testaments. For some that means it is not on the critical path of God's unfolding plan of redemption so, in that sense, it is irrelevant. It is no more than another movement of peoples, with which history is familiar and, as is often the case, has become another wrestling match between national antagonists. That has to be a false deduction, and perhaps an evidence of Gentile boasting – there are Gentile Christians who just do not like to see the Jews getting up again. We must at least say it is a remarkable providence and seek to understand it. One way to do that would be to see the evidence of something considered earlier, the continuing defeat of attempts by sin and Satan to destroy a significant community of Jewish people. It is not my intention to take sides on particular details of the conflict but to make a comment on the broad picture. Ill winds swirl around the State of Israel in the Middle East but God's providential care has been obvious in the failure of those who should have managed to destroy her by now (such a comment is not intended to justify all Israel's actions). The 'Handle With Care!' label should be carefully noted by all who enter the conflict or comment upon it. I believe that those who would deny any right for Jewish people to live in their ancient homeland with some form of self-government, and those who seek their annihilation, are manifesting the antagonism of sin and Satan.

However, I would go further than the matter of providential care because I believe Jesus hinted at a return in Luke 21:24. I do not see that as a prophecy, as it is so indefinite, but I believe it is more than a hint of a possibility, it is a hint of a divinely planned inevitability. This would give hope of more than survival, a hope of spiritual blessing.

Covenant Graciousness

My use of the phrase 'divinely planned inevitability' is deliberate but it may be an overstatement. I want to go back to the theme of covenant in this matter of return to the land. It has happened, but no one will assert it is due to Israel's covenant faithfulness. It is not that the Jewish people have remarkably turned to the Lord and God has responded by the blessing of a return to the land. The favour is undoubtedly unmerited; God is being gracious, and abundantly so. But because the land is included in his promises to Israel I want to use the phrase 'covenant graciousness'. God is under no obligation to open the door for their return but he has done so. He has decided to give again what he promised to Abraham and his descendants. His gifts are irrevocable and he has decided to give the gift again. It is pure grace.

Covenant Obedience

However, and in apparent contradiction, there is a price tag, which is obedience. I cannot see how the Jewish people can expect to live indefinitely in the promised land without obedience to the promise, that is, the promised Messiah, Jesus. Some may find comfort by thinking, 'Well, from Romans 11, belief and obedience seems to be God's plan, so it will all turn out all right.' I would rather that they thought, 'What should we do?' Hope must lead to action.

Gospel Ministry, Not End-Time Excitement

For many Christians it would seem all we need to do is rejoice in what God is doing for Israel, pray for them and against their enemies, perhaps even give money to help towards rebuilding a third temple and to train Jewish men to be priests. All very exciting. How wonderful to be part of God's end-time plans! Excuse my cynicism but the emphasis I find in the New Testament is a command to get on with the self-denying work of preaching a crucified Messiah to Israel, looking for that day when the remnant becomes a fullness. It is an emphasis I find in the prophets, who not only spoke of future hope but of present sinfulness. It is the latter which is often absent from the message of those who are excited about end-time events. And even when blessing comes it will not be a spiritual holiday; the fight will be all the more fierce, for Satan will be furious.

As Christians observe what is happening in Israel and have a concern for Jewish people (and I hope for all others there too), they must keep their eye on the ball. Not the dancing swirl of current events and tomorrow's possibilities but the ball of the gospel, which needs to be firmly placed between Israel's goalposts. If there is no faith in Jesus the Messiah it is possible that there will be no State of Israel.

Judaism and the Return to the Land

I want to very briefly summarize the views on the State of Israel within Judaism. Judaism has always held out the hope of a return to the land but the creation of a secular state by the Zionist movement was not viewed positively. The various forms of Orthodox Judaism opposed it because the Jewish people ought to wait for the Messiah to come and lead them back and establish a Torah-observant society, which would then be a light to the nations. Other, more liberal, less orthodox forms of Judaism developed a concern for legitimate assimilation into Gentile societies, stressing that they were citizens of their nation, playing down the hope of a return lest it make them appear unreliable citizens.

However, once the state was an accomplished fact most Orthodox Jews took a different view. God in his providence had done things in an unexpected manner; perhaps then the secular state should be seen as a stepping-stone to a Torah-observant one.

At this point it is necessary to understand a basic difference among Orthodox Jews about when Messiah comes. Some believe he comes when there is a measure of obedience among the Jewish people. Others expect him to come when all is hopeless and Israel is disobedient and oppressed. As might be expected, the former tend to see an opportunity in the foundation of the state. Orthodox Jews should work within it to make it more Torah-observant and trust that God will respond by sending Messiah. Hence the involvement of Orthodox Jews in the political process in Israel working for a more Torah-observant society, for example, their efforts to ban public transport on the Sabbath. When it comes to living in the whole of the biblical promised land there are differences among the Orthodox. Most would take the view that righteousness and peace is more important than land. Messiah will come in response to righteousness and peace, and he will sort out what belongs to whom. In the meantime compromises should be made and the rights of others fully recognized. Unfortunately the media are generally only interested in the minority among the Orthodox which insists on Israel possessing all the biblical promised land, and who seem prepared to use unjust methods to obtain it. There is still a tiny minority among the Orthodox who see the state as a secular substitute for the messianic redemption, something which hinders Messiah's coming.

Divine Right and Human Rights

Here is where the rubber hits the road. There is a big difference between saying the Jewish people have a divine right to be in the land today and saying they have human rights as all others.

Divine right

What has been written above has established certain basic truths:

- God promised the land to the Jewish people;
- It played a key part in his unfolding plan of redemption;
- It was a shadow of a spiritual reality;
- Israel's obedience was vital to their enjoyment of the land with disobedience twice resulting in expulsion; and
- The promise and their covenant status have not been withdrawn.

I have also sought to demonstrate that the present return is not a fulfilment of prophecy but that it should be seen as God's covenant graciousness to the Jewish people. In the light of all this it is tempting to say there is a divine right to be there, but this should be resisted. The expression 'divine right' communicates the idea of special authority for actual possession of the land, as in the days of Joshua and Zerubbabel. This would mean that Jewish people can claim their authority to govern comes from God in a unique way and hence all others in the land are guests, so to speak, who may or may not be allowed a say in the affairs of state. This is to say much more than it is a land which has been promised to them. For example, it was promised to Abraham but he never ruled it and he had to purchase land for his own use.[17] When Israel entered the land by divine right it was under a specific command of God to enter, possess and rule; there was no obligation to take account of the wishes of those living there.

Should Christians view the modern return in a similar way, a divinely authorized mission? If so, how would the authorization be communicated? There is only one source – the New Testament writings. Yet, as we have seen, neither the Lord Jesus or his apostles and prophets speak clearly on the subject. I am aware that there are some today who speak on Israel issues and claim special authority but the New Testament tells me their claim is totally false. Paul describes the apostles and prophets as a unique group,[18] who have received new revelation[19] and their role is unrepeatable. Those who make false claims should be rebuked and urged to repent. They should not be feared. Those Christians who teach the Jewish people have a divine right to the land are doing damage because they encourage some Orthodox Jews in their belief that they have such a right, a conviction that all too often leads to a trampling of the rights of others.

Christians and Jews are not the only ones to talk of divine right in the situation. Islam does the same: it views all land that has been conquered by Islamic forces as land which must remain under Islamic control. Without a spiritual change this points to an ongoing conflict. However, for many nominal Muslims the desire for an end to such an unwinnable conflict has led to a willingness to compromise. However, their hopes are constantly being dashed by the fundamentalism of the Islamists who are interested only in a fight to the death. If this element of the conflict is taken seriously it must make many wonder if Israel can survive.

Denying that the Jewish people have a divine right does not mean we are thrown back on only secular arguments. The Bible does provide a model for Israel living in the land of promise but without a divine commission to conquer, and the behaviour of the patriarchs, Abraham, Isaac and Jacob, provides it. They had the promise but sought to live in harmony with those around them by sharing in the benefits of the land with others,[20] purchasing land,[21] making compromises in situations of conflict,[22] arguing what was fair and just so as to achieve change,[23] and concluding mutual agreements to live without conflict and for defence.[24] When violated they acted to defend themselves.[25] If any model is required today for living peaceably in the land with those who differ it seems that here is a good, biblical one. This is the behaviour concerned Christians should support.

Human rights (and responsibilities)

For secularists, rights are their religion but that does not mean Christians and religious Jews cannot use the same arguments when they are based on shared human values. Rights certainly exist in the Scriptures but they are indissolubly connected to responsibilities. Our responsibility to love our neighbour as ourselves acknowledges they have a right to all the things that we ourselves consider basic to existence – a place to live, decent living conditions, employment, food to eat, to be treated equally by authorities and the law, etc. We should endeavour to ensure that others have these things.

What then do we do when confronted with the historic need of the Jewish people for a place to live where they can govern themselves, rather than being subjected to the seemingly endless hatred of others for being Jewish? If we could see some light at the end of the tunnel we might conclude there is no need of help but there is no evidence of it. The world believed it had a responsibility to help and sought a place for them to live, and their need of security gives them a right to a secure place to live. The choice of location was not random but a place where Jews have lived for millennia, giving them a valid claim to return there.

The objection of some in the Muslim world that Palestinians are being made to suffer for western mistreatment of the Jews does not hold water. The Muslim world, and those civilizations of North Africa and the east which preceded Islam, have been equally guilty of persecuting Jewish people, causing the Jews to move elsewhere or suffer in silence. They too have a responsibility to help them. As well as all this responsibility towards the Jewish people, there is an obvious responsibility placed upon the nations to ensure that all others living in the land enjoy those same basics of life mentioned above.

Looking back over the above it might be thought there is little between the requirements of a secular agenda and those demanded by the example of the patriarchs; but there is an additional factor. Holding onto the fact that the land is one which is promised to Israel functions as a potent reminder to the Jewish people, and to other interested parties, that they are under the eye of God. It raises the question, what does the Lord require?

Jewish People and the Land

I have been a missionary to the Jewish people for over thirty years. In that time I have met thousands of Jewish people from across the whole spectrum of Jewish society, in different parts of the world. I have learnt a lot over the years on how Jewish people think about the return to the land and the establishment of the state of Israel.

Forget the Holocaust?

The Holocaust was a big factor in increased immigration to Israel and is a potent reminder of thousands of years of troubles for

Jewish people among the nations. It is still a vivid memory. I make this point because there is an obvious growth in hostility to Israel among liberal elites in western nations and the sense I get is that they do not want any mention of the Holocaust in discussions on Israel. It is as if that is history, it has little relevance to the current tensions, and so it should be left out. I do not believe that such people desire the destruction of the Jewish people but they are seriously underestimating those who do. However, Jewish people do not underestimate them! They have a strong collective memory of the murderous hatred of their enemies and hence Israel is a place they highly value, even though it is none too secure. It is a place where they can defend themselves.

Middle East hegemony?

Jewish people want to live at peace with their neighbours but a number of Israel's neighbours are not reciprocating. Her destruction is their agenda; their destruction is not Israel's agenda. As has been said, 'If our enemies lay down their weapons there will be no war, if we lay down our weapons there will be no Israel.' As I have talked to many Jewish people I do not observe a desire to destroy. There is a total concurrence with the extreme care that Israel's armed forces (IDF) take to avoid civilian casualties. They know what it is like to be a minority and they sympathize with the plight of the generality of Palestinians who have become victims of the conflict. Of course, those who live in Israel can be more hard-nosed about the situation, as they suffer in the troubles, but the understanding is there. I find Jewish people to be a vibrant people who strongly emphasize personal responsibility and care passionately about fairness and justice. They want to get it right in Israel. If their neighbours will accept their existence and determine to live at peace with them then it can happen.

Most religious Jews are preoccupied with living daily life in a Torah-observant way and do not spend hours talking about Israel and plotting a takeover of all Palestinian land. They are aware that the main priority is to get Israel Torah-observant and then Messiah will be revealed and sort out all the difficulties. They are more concerned to attack sin in Israel than to attack Palestinians.

A place with a Jewish culture

Jews want a Jewish-style place to live. Is that such a crime? Most of the people of the world live in a culture of their own making, developed over hundreds of years, and in such cultures others are welcome. Jewish people have an opportunity to create such for themselves for the first time in thousands of years and it is not an easy thing to do. Has anyone ever done such a thing before, in the full glare of hostile observers ready to point out every failure? Jews want to get it right. It is not their desire to oppress non-Jews while creating an impression of civil liberties. Most totally sympathize with the desire of Palestinians for their own state.

Christian Responses

I have mentioned a number of ways Christians should respond to the return of Jewish people to the land but I have a few more, some of which are by way of summary.

Christian gratitude

The attitude of Christians and churches to the Jewish people and the State of Israel as a particular Jewish community should be determined, first and foremost, by past realities, not future possibilities. The latter is contentious, the former is not: Christians have received the gospel from Israel and should, out of gratitude, be supportive of the welfare of Jewish people.

Making amends

Because of the persecution Jewish people have suffered among the nations, Christians should support the right of Jewish people to live in their ancient homeland within secure borders and to govern their own affairs. The fact that such persecution has been done in the name of Jesus should stimulate Christians to want to show what is a true Christian attitude to Jewish people.

A concern for all

Christian support for Jewish people to live in their ancient homeland must go hand in glove with a concern for all living in the land and for stateless Palestinians, that they too should enjoy the same recognition of rights and the same benefits.

A word about what has become known as Christian Palestinianism. There is an increasing momentum among evangelical Christians to support the Palestinian cause and speak critically of Israel's failures. That is understandable and I sympathize with many things they say. What alarms me is what they do not say: they tend to underplay the influence of Islam and Islamism in the situation. They focus on Palestinian Christians or on the more nominal Muslim Palestinians and the impression given is that such opposition is all Israel has to face. This is only part of the truth. They underplay the murderous opposition of the new Islamists but Israel must take account of it in all her political and military calculations. They give the impression that Israel is always taking a sledgehammer to crack a nut but Israel is aware there is another sledgehammer hiding in the nut. Christians who actively support the Palestinian cause must be more open and honest about the difficulties caused by this huge obstacle.

Christian denunciation

Churches and Christians should denounce those who aim at the destruction of the Jewish people.

Christian intercession

Christians should pray for a peaceful resolution to the conflict and for the wellbeing and salvation of all in the region.

Caution and focus

Churches and Christians should be very careful about getting involved in detailed arguments about the rights and wrongs of events in the conflict. The fact is most Christians simply do not know enough so they should stick to the basics. Christians should consider Jesus' response to the man who asked for help in dividing an inheritance with his brother (Luke 12:13–15). Jesus said it was not his responsibility; he would not allow it to interfere with his priorities, even though he could no doubt have provided a wise solution. It seems to me that the average Christian ought to recognize that he or she is not a judge or divider in this conflict – no one has asked them to be and they should feel no obligation to have all the facts at their fingertips; they have other priorities in the situation. Christians have two priorities. The first follows Jesus' example when, in his response to the man who asked for help, he warned of covetousness. We are to address people's motivations in the situation. The second is in the next point.

Christian mission

Churches and Christians should see their responsibility to be involved in calling Jewish people in Israel to covenant faithfulness, that is, faith in Jesus the Messiah.

Knowing the times

We are to take to heart the warning of Jesus not to focus on times and seasons because we have been emphatically told that we are not going to know them in advance. When a season of blessing comes for Israel we will know it because we observe it happening, and that will be because we are preaching the gospel to them and God is granting a season of fruitfulness. That is how we know.

Unequally yoked

We are not to get involved with supporting religious Jews in their programme for re-establishing some sort of Mosaic religious economy in the land, e.g. funds to train priests or rebuild the temple. Theirs is a programme which flies in the face of all Jesus taught and suffered for sinners.

Prophecy and mission

It really ought to make no difference what understanding we have of the millennium and end-time prophecy, and the place of the State of Israel in it all. None of the traditional views teach, 'Something new has now put evangelism on the back burner.' The priority of Christians and churches is to press on with witness to Jesus the Messiah among Jewish people in the land (and elsewhere).

Be hopeful

There is every reason to be hopeful that God has a gracious, salvation purpose for Israel at this time. The early, high hopes of the Zionist dream have indeed faded. After the assassination of Yitzhak Rabin one minister, Yossi Sarrid, said, 'Now we are like everyone else.' The hope that they might not be has been dashed. There is a greater sense of weakness. It is not without significance that an evangelistic outreach in Israel in 2011 offered a free book, *The Power to Change*. Many responded; the need is felt. And then there appears to be no end of the conflict in sight. They have worked hard to provide a safe place to live and it is a place of ceaseless conflict; that is wearing. The Palestinian problem is further eroding any sense of self-sufficiency. It seems to me that the Lord is bringing Israel and the Jewish people low; he is breaking up the fallow ground. When we see it in a national consciousness surely we can be hopeful of a work of salvation? It is an extraordinary thing to observe, and it is happening before our very eyes; it should lead us to pray earnestly for their salvation, and for God's mercy to all caught up in the Middle East conflict.

And yet we must not allow such a hope to obscure the spiritual danger Israel is in. There are signs of changing attitudes but it is no more than a cloud the size of a man's hand. They are living in God's land but are still rebellious. We should fear for them and be urgent about the priority of presenting the gospel to them.

The one new man

We should pray for the churches in the land. We should be especially concerned to see them demonstrate the 'one new man from the two': Jew and Arab worshipping God together in local congregations.[26] They hold the key to the resolution of the conflict; the only one there is – the power of Messiah's gospel to unite, reconcile and heal those who have been in strife. The situation will not just bump along as at present, but it will get worse and worse, the enmity of Islamism guarantees that. Christians have the solution in their hearts and hands and they must pray and act.

As Christians and churches think about Jewish people and the land today the first concern of their hearts must be, 'My heart's desire and prayer to God for Israel is that they may be saved.'[27]

PART 4

The Triumph of Grace

21.

And so All Israel Shall Be Saved

'How unsearchable are His judgments and His ways past finding out!'[1]

Paul's magisterial treatment of Israel and the gospel in Romans 9 – 11 begins and ends with the thought of all Israel's salvation. It is the overarching theme. The failure of all Israel to believe is in his view at the start, where he grieves at their unbelief but asserts, 'It is not that the word of God has taken no effect.'[2] His focus towards the close is the climactic statement that 'All Israel will be saved'.[3] He starts with apologetics, as to why few have come to faith, and he ends with revelation, as to how and when they will. I am aware that those opening sentences beg all sorts of questions – there has been much ink spilt expressing strongly held and differing views over this theme – but I am also confident the main things must be clear. When an apostle sits down and specifically addresses a subject can we not assume it should be straightforward to grasp the main point?

God's Way of Working Humbles Us

All Christians should come humbly to a passage such as this because of Paul's doxology towards the close in which he marvels at the ways of Yahweh, that they are past finding out.[4] Paul is not so much reflecting on what God has done, though that cannot be altogether absent, but how he has done it. And this focus of his doxology gives us one key to interpreting the whole. Our understanding of the main drift of Paul's argument must lead us to the point of marvelling at the unsearchable nature of God's plans –

that is, his ways are not our ways. Time after time he does things in the opposite manner to what we expect. For example, who would have thought that the gospel's assault on mainland Europe would begin at a ladies' prayer meeting outside the important city of Philippi, on the banks of a river?[5] Definitely not the way we organize things!

Israel's Hope for Israel

And what was that expectation? Clearly, that when Messiah came the majority of the Jewish people would believe in him, follow him, and eventually the world would be blessed. And in case that is seen as just carnal Jewish triumphalism it is worth asking what a godly Israelite would be led to expect when reading many of the prophecies of Messiah. For example, when Isaiah writes about the mountain of the Lord's house being established on the top of the mountains, and that all nations will flow to it to learn his ways because out of Zion will go forth the law.[6] Is there not an impression at least that Israel have believed it? That does not nullify the approach to Old Testament prophecy I have taken earlier in this book, that these texts are using Old Testament terminology to describe the blessing of God in the whole gospel era; nevertheless, do they not give some hope that the beginning of the process is great blessing on Israel? Of course, there are other texts in Isaiah which paint a different picture, and Paul quotes some of them in Romans 9 – 11,[7] but did they clearly rule out the hope of a good start for Israel when Messiah came?

Jeremiah's prophecy of a new covenant that is made with Israel and Judah states, 'They shall all know Me, from the least of them to the greatest of them.'[8] I have no doubt that it has been fulfilled through Jews and Gentiles entering the covenant by faith in Messiah, and then experiencing its promised blessings, but is it surprising if a pious Israelite read it to include most of Israel at some point, without wanting to exclude Gentiles?

Do you imagine that the first Jewish believers in Jesus, as they began to preach, had any other hope than such a great turning to Messiah by Israel? Perhaps some were more cautious, like Stephen, but Paul would not have had to explain widespread Jewish unbelief if there were not very many who possessed different expectations.

Remnant and All Israel in the Old Testament

Furthermore, did not God's pattern of working with Israel in the Old Testament period encourage such a hope? Some come to Romans 11 with a distorted paradigm of Israel – the majority forever disobedient but always a faithful remnant. Hence they interpret Romans 11 in such a fashion; but it is an incorrect one. The paradigm is: Israel's history was predominantly a rebellious one (but always with a faithful remnant), punctuated by brief periods of the majority of the nation turning to the Lord, i.e. national revival. I want to make a brief reference to those periods. I do not have space to examine them in detail, only to quote the texts, but if you read around the context I trust you will agree with me that the times mentioned were ones of genuine trust and zeal, usually marked by praise and joy.

The bringing of the ark to Jerusalem by David and all Israel: 'So David and all the house of Israel brought up the ark of the LORD with shouting and with the sound of the trumpet.'[9] The dedication of the temple: 'When all the children of Israel saw how the fire came down, and the glory of the LORD on the temple, they bowed their faces to the ground on the pavement, and worshiped and praised the LORD, saying: "For He is good, For His mercy endures forever."'[10]

Asa's reign was marked by a great turning back to the Lord from idolatry: 'And all Judah rejoiced at the oath, for they had sworn with all their heart and sought Him with all their soul; and He was found by them, and the LORD gave them rest all around.'[11]

A similar turning took place in Hezekiah's days. After the return from Babylon God greatly blessed all the returned exiles:

> So they read distinctly from the book, in the Law of God; and they gave the sense, and helped them to understand the reading . . . And all the people went their way to eat and drink, to send portions and rejoice greatly, because they understood the words that were declared to them . . . Also day by day, from the first day until the last day,

he [Ezra] read from the Book of the Law of God. And they kept the feast seven days; and on the eighth day there was a sacred assembly, according to the prescribed manner.[12]

The same story was seen among non-Jews in Nineveh through Jonah's ministry, with the king leading the people in repentance. Such a public turning to the Lord by most of Israel and their leaders has yet to be repeated in the Messiah's days. Should their old covenant national experience in this respect excel their new covenant one?

Jesus' final public words to the people and the rulers of Israel indicate it will not: 'You shall see me no more till you say, "Blessed is He who comes in the name of the LORD!"'[13] The expectation here is that, as a people, they will welcome him.

The point I am making is that an expectation of many in Israel becoming believers was not necessarily a wrong one. Paul does not actually dampen such a hope but when he finally gets to addressing the subject towards the end of Romans 11 he makes it plain that God has done things differently from all expectations, which leads to his exclamation that God's ways are past finding out. This connects to his use of 'and so' rather than 'and then' in 11:26, because 'and so' focuses on the *manner* in which God does things. He takes the unexpected and indirect approach, and some of his reasons are revealed; but I am getting ahead of myself.

Romans 9 – 10

All that is by way of introduction and overview, and it should be clear from what I have written so far where I am going. I believe that 'All Israel will be saved' points to a great ingathering of Jews to Jesus at some point in history. But it is not enough to describe grand themes in the passage; the details must fit, and so they need to be examined. I want to begin by summarizing Romans 9 – 10.

Romans 8 ends on the high note of the certainty of salvation for those who trust Jesus. Nothing can separate them from God's love; God will keep his promises to them. Exhilarating! And yet, to take note of what had happened to God's people, Israel, could cause doubts to arise. Something appeared to have gone very wrong in their case. The gospel had come and the very people who had had hundreds of years of preparation were not believing it!

God's choice

We have already looked at Paul's answer in some detail in an earlier chapter but I want to repeat the basics here. Paul's explanation can be summed up by one word, 'choice': God's choice and human choice. God made choices at the commencement of his dealing with Israel: Isaac not Ishmael, Jacob not Esau. The point is that he continues to make a choice among the seed of Jacob, so that 'They are not all Israel who are of Israel'[14] – they are not all princes with God who are born of Israel (Jacob). Or to use Paul's expression, they are not all children of promise who are born of Jacob. God's word has been effective to bring those children of promise to faith. The absolute sovereignty of God in choosing who will believe and be saved is asserted.

Human choice

Paul follows this with a focus on the conscious choice made by many in Israel to pursue righteousness by the works of the law.[15] This was a sinful and rebellious choice in the face of the salvation revealed through Messiah Jesus, and they were responsible for it. God cannot be blamed for this failure. They have failed, not his word. Paul goes on to point out that the way of faith for righteousness was nothing new.[16] It should not have taken anyone in Israel by surprise, whether under the conditions of the Mosaic covenant or the new covenant. Under Moses there was a way of living under the law by faith, that is, keeping the law with an attitude of dependence on God, not one's works. It particularly manifested itself in the sense of weakness exhibited by the words of Moses, 'Do not say in your heart, "Who will ascend into heaven?"'[17] But the self-righteous in Israel lacked this sense of need and were marked by self-sufficiency, so that when Jesus proclaimed his message they saw it as opposed to all they stood for, rather than understanding it as a new outworking of the same trust in the mercy of God for righteousness.[18]

By the end of Romans 10, Paul has explained why people's expectation – that most of Israel would follow Messiah when he came – has not been met. As I noted before, he does not expressly criticize the expectation. In fact, although his explanation is especially necessary when few believe, it is also important when many but not all believe.

Romans 11

In one sense Paul could have stopped at Romans 10:21. He has answered the problem and discussed some issues that arise. However, he goes on. And it is soon clear why – he is aware some Gentile Christians in Rome are thinking that God has now finished with the Jews and that God's focus is from henceforth on the Gentiles. He intends to correct that error. He also has further truth to reveal concerning his twin themes: salvation for the Jewish people, and the intertwining of the salvation of the Gentiles and the salvation of the Jews.

Romans 11:1–10 – not cast away

Romans 11 divides into two parts, both of which commence with a question that Paul asks regarding Israel's status. This is the issue that some Christians in Rome have doubts about and Paul raises it by asking, in verse 1: 'Has God cast away His people?' In a sense it is a rhetorical question because the words 'His people' demand the obvious reply, which Paul then gives – 'Certainly not!' or more literally, 'May it not be!' Such a casting away is unthinkable; God does not cast from him those with whom he has entered into a covenant. The word translated 'cast away' here is different from the one translated 'cast away' in verse 15. Here it is much more personal; it speaks of a definite putting away from one's self, a break of relationship. In verse 15 it is not personal, a word that could be used for putting an object to one side. However, it is a strong term, and in the context of verse 15 points to the loss of God's favour and blessing. What is therefore unthinkable is Yahweh's breach of the covenant relationship between himself and Israel, the seed of Abraham, Isaac and Jacob.

The meaning of 'Israel'
It is quite plain from the rest of verse 1, 'I also am an Israelite, of the seed of Abraham, of the tribe of Benjamin', that by 'His

people' Paul means ethnic Israel. This needs to be underlined because, incredible as it may seem, some actually dispute it. It is surely obvious that throughout Romans 9 – 11 Paul is discussing the Jewish people in their relation to the gospel, and when he uses the word 'Israel' in this whole passage that is to whom he is referring. Paul uses 'Israel' twelve times in the passage and apart from the two uses in 9:6 and the use in 11:26 they all refer to failure, ignorance, lostness or blindness. In 9:6 he is using 'Israel' in a specialist sense but it is still a sense that is within the ethnic people Israel. In 11:26 the reference is to salvation. It seems to me that unless Paul makes some form of qualification through the words that he connects to 'Israel' then he means the natural descendants of Abraham, Isaac and Jacob. He does make such a qualification in 9:6, where 'Israel' is used to describe a group within ethnic Israel; also in Galatians 6:16 where he appends 'of God' and again in 1 Corinthians 10:18 where he appends the words 'after the flesh'.[19] However you understand each of Paul's qualifications of 'Israel' in these three texts, what must be agreed is that the very making of a qualification to the word 'Israel' to describe a group within Israel must indicate that when 'Israel' is used alone it is simply descriptive of ethnic Israel. This is an important point in considering 'all Israel' in Romans 11:26.

Always some saved (remnant)
To return to 11:1–10, Paul's basic assertion is that the salvation of a remnant within Israel, people like himself, is evidence that the nation is not cast away. The use of the example of Elijah makes the point that the remnant is bigger than we think. He is saying to those in Rome, 'You think there is all but zero of us, and so perhaps God has finished with Israel. Think again. There are many more than you think.' That situation continues to this day, for Paul writes in verse 25, 'Blindness in part has happened to Israel until the fullness of the Gentiles has come in.' From this we can conclude that up to a certain point in history Israel's blindness will always be 'in part', or, put another way, there will always be a remnant who are not blind but who believe in Messiah Jesus. God is faithful to his covenant and church history bears this out. I have always found it interesting when deliberately mentioning the names of well-known Jewish Christians and drawing atten-

tion to their Jewishness, that my hearers so often respond, 'I never knew he (or she) was Jewish.' Fortunately, most Jewish believers do not go around waving a flag to advertise the fact, and so Christians tend to underestimate how many there are. There are more than we think.

A hardening
This section finishes on the note of judgement upon the majority of Israel. However, Paul writes in verse 7, 'Israel has not obtained what it seeks', and that reminds us that there is still a sense among Israel that there is something to seek, and this is seen in religious activity among the devout, or in the constant questioning about 'What is a Jew?' among others. That seeking will bear fruit when a person turns to the Lord and the veil is taken away.[20]

Romans 11:11–15 – straight talking to Gentile Christians

Paul could have stopped at verse 10 and his point about Israel's status would have been made but he has more to say – more about God's purpose for them, and something more pointed for Gentile Christians to be aware of.

Gentile Christians addressed
It is crucial to grasp that he is addressing Gentile Christians very specifically from this point, as he puts it in verse 13, 'For I speak to you Gentiles.' And this continues in a very specific way until the end of verse 31 where he writes: 'Through the mercy shown you they also may obtain mercy.' All too frequently Christian people read such language as if 'you' refers to Christians in a general way but it is more specific that that, it addresses Gentile Christians in the context of their relationship with Israel.

Israel has not fallen irretrievably
As Paul commences he asks a similar question to verse 1 but using language which picks up on a word in verse 9 regarding God's judgement, that Israel's table will be a stumbling block (literally 'an offence' but sometimes translated 'stumbling block'). Paul's question is: 'Have they stumbled that they should fall?' The words in English represent well the original, in that Paul is asking,

And so All Israel Shall Be Saved

have they tripped up so as to fall flat and never get up again? The answer could not be clearer – no! And it needs to be kept in mind all the time through this section that Paul is referring to Israel as a national unit when he uses 'they' or 'them'. Israel as a unit has stumbled, because although some do believe yet the leadership, the national religion, the institutions and the vision of the people is one that finds no place for Jesus the Messiah, and is in fact decidedly negative towards him. However, although Israel has stumbled she has not fallen irretrievably; God has something more.

The Gentiles provoking Israel
Paul now proceeds to put various arguments before his readers to substantiate his assertion, but it is all phrased vis-à-vis salvation among the Gentiles because of his concern they should have a proper attitude. Hence his very first point, in verse 11, is that a purpose of God in doing things this way, that is, Israel in unbelief and Gentiles coming to faith, is that Gentiles being saved will provoke Jews to jealousy.[21] Clearly, if God works in such a manner he has not given up on Israel. Furthermore, Gentiles should be encouraged that they have a role in the salvation of Israel.

Consider this!
Next Paul uses what could be described as a carrot-and-stick approach, followed by a stick approach.[22] First of all, in verses 12 and 15, the carrot and stick. Here Paul gently encourages Gentiles to take a positive view of Israel's ongoing inclusion by pointing out how it will bless them too. And he ups the argument by putting the thought before them that great blessing on Israel means great blessing for them. In both verses his manner of argument is similar, contrasting the effect of loss with the greater effect of gain. In verse 12 the focus is Israel's behaviour and in verse 15 it is God's. In verse 12 Paul asks Gentile Christians to consider how God has blessed the nations through the trespass of the Jews. Well then, he argues, how much more blessing when many believe – which is the only possible understanding of 'fullness'; it is a word that contrasts with 'remnant', and points to the majority of Israel. He makes the same point in verses 15 but the terms describe God's attitude: he has cast Israel away from blessing and that has led to

the Gentiles being brought into his favour, so how much more when he chooses to accept them again.

A brief comment on other views at this point. Those who see 'all Israel' in verse 26 as the sum total of Jewish believers down the ages connect it to 'their fullness' in verse 12. Israel's remnant will somehow become 'much more' when aggregated over the centuries. It is difficult to see how, when at any one time the situation is unchanged, right up to the end. However, the main difficulty with this view is that 'their' in verses 12 and 15 clearly refers to the nation of Israel. That which is cast away is that which is accepted, national Israel. Others see 'all Israel' in verse 26 as all believers, Jew and Gentile, but many of them, like Calvin, see verses 12 and 15 as pointing to a great future ingathering of Jews to faith, even though they do not see it in verse 26.[23]

Romans 11:16–24 – warnings to Gentile Christians

Paul now uses a somewhat sterner approach, something of a rebuke to Gentile Christians.

Root and branches
We have already considered the olive tree illustration Paul uses here so I will not go into details. Paul has two purposes in using it; firstly to underline that Israel still features in God's salvation purposes – 'If the root is holy, so are the branches' – and secondly to rebuke Gentile Christian boasting over the Jews – 'Do not boast against the branches'. Jews are therefore 'natural branches', and Gentiles are branches grafted from a wild olive into what is described as 'their [the Jews'] own olive tree'. It may be irksome for Gentile Christians to acknowledge their debt to Israel (a frequently despised people in the ancient and the modern worlds) but it is spiritually healthy.

Paul presents four arguments to discourage boasting; three of them I will state briefly, the fourth needs more space. Firstly, in verses 17 and 18, Gentiles are branches supported by a root, they are not the root (the 'root' being all the things Paul lists as belonging to Israel in Romans 9:4,5). Secondly, Gentiles stand by faith, not because they are Gentiles (vv. 19–21). Thirdly, God is well able to graft the natural branches back in again (vv. 23,24).

Romans 11:25–9 – an antidote for ignorance and pride: all Israel saved

Paul's fourth argument is stated in Romans 11:25–7 and its implications are drawn out in the rest of the chapter. His words, 'Lest you should be wise in your own opinion' in verse 25, make it plain that he is still discouraging Gentile Christian boasting.

The mystery
Here we need to consider carefully what is meant by a mystery, what the mystery actually is, and how Paul uses the Old Testament to prove his point. In investigating these issues our understanding must be such that it naturally leads into Paul's subsequent conclusions, of which he has three. Firstly, Israel remains elect and beloved, such that God's gifts and calling to Israel will not be withdrawn. Secondly, there is an intertwining of Jew and Gentile salvation leaving no room for any to boast. Thirdly, God's *manner* of doing these things is overawing.

Paul frequently uses the word 'mystery', which was a familiar word in the ancient world connected to what were called 'mystery religions', to describe something which is concealed from the natural understanding of humans but which can be made known by God when he chooses to reveal it. The whole gospel is a mystery in that sense, as Paul puts it in Romans 16:25,26: 'According to the revelation of the mystery kept secret since the world began but now made manifest, and by the prophetic Scriptures made known to all nations.' Paul's mention of 'the prophetic Scriptures' indicates that, whatever mystery is in view, there is in fact some mention of it in the Old Testament but, again, unaided human reason cannot grasp it. This is why Paul quotes Scripture to prove his point; even an apostle is not allowed to pluck something out of the air, so to speak; there must be scriptural corroboration.

What is the mystery? Paul leaves us in no doubt about it, in Romans 11:25,26: 'Blindness in part has happened to Israel until the fullness of the Gentiles has come in. And so all Israel will be saved.' Which seems clear enough, and yet there has been much argument about it! Paul is clearly saying that there will come a point in time when Israel's dominant condition of spiritual blindness will end, and that will be when 'the fullness of the Gentiles has come in'. That phrase 'fullness of the Gentiles' can mean only when the nations of the world have heard the gospel and many have believed. Clearly, it is something yet future. The end of blindness in part (the major part), can mean only the majority seeing (the truth of the gospel). Or, put another way, all Israel will be saved. Of course, 'all Israel' does not mean every single individual at that time, but, as in 1 Samuel 7:5, when Samuel gathered 'all Israel', we are not meant to imagine every single Israelite was present, so here we are to understand most of Israel. All Israel saved! And this revelation is surely the final nail in the coffin of Gentile Christian boasting.

Other understandings

There are objections raised to this view of 'all Israel will be saved' and so we need consider them. I have already mentioned how, in verse 26, some want to make 'Israel' mean something else other than ethnic Israel, either Jewish believers or the church of Jew and Gentile. I simply cannot see how either is exegetically justifiable. How can 'Israel' mean the Jewish nation in verse 25 and not in verse 26 when there is no indication whatsoever of a change in meaning? And then in the very next verse Paul has no subject in his sentence because it is the same subject as in verse 26, but the sentence is about being enemies of the gospel, so he must be referring to ethnic Israel, so 'all Israel' in verse 26 must be ethnic Israel. It has always seemed to me that to take any other view of Israel in verse 26 is an exposition based on theology derived from elsewhere, and not exegesis of the text.

'Then' or 'and so'?

It is often commented that if the view I am expressing is correct then Paul would have written 'and *then* all Israel will be saved', not, as he does, 'and so'. The latter usually has the meaning 'and in this manner'. That is a valid objection if we consider that the only subject in view in Romans 11, and indeed all of Romans 9 – 11, is God's salvation purposes for the Jewish people, but it is not, as I have already indicated. There is another focus and that is the intertwining of the salvation of Israel and the Gentiles or, put another way, God's *manner* of saving Israel, whether in remnant and fullness. The mechanics of this have already been mentioned,

And so All Israel Shall Be Saved

in terms of Gentile Christians provoking Jews to jealousy, but here the focus is more on the order.

Paul's twin foci of the salvation of all Israel and the relationship of that to Gentile salvation both come to a climax in verses 25 and 26. He reveals that Israel's fullness comes *after* the Gentile fullness. Hence he uses 'and so', because God's *manner of working* is as much in view as what he is actually doing. I alluded to this at the start of this chapter. There was a general expectation of a great turning of Israel to Messiah when he came and Paul needed to explain why that had not happened. As I wrote earlier, that was not necessarily a carnal Jewish expectation of an earthly kingdom (although some had that) but could be valid hope based on Scripture of great spiritual blessing on Israel when Messiah came, followed by Israel taking the gospel to the nations and the world being blessed. I believe that Paul's whole approach to this question of 'all Israel' in Romans 9 – 11 has been to say, 'Not yet'. God's ways are not our ways. He plans that only a remnant believe to begin with, according to his election of grace, that they go to the Gentiles and the nations are gathered in great numbers (all the while provoking Israel to jealousy so that some are always saved), and only after that will great blessing fall on Israel and there will be a fullness saved. This is what Paul is declaring in Romans 11:25,26. It makes me want to just cry out with Paul, 'How unsearchable are His judgments and His ways past finding out!'[24]

And why do things in such a manner? As Paul puts it elsewhere: 'That no flesh should glory in His presence'.[25] By working this way God has ensured that Jew and Gentile do not boast over each other. The Gentiles come into what God promised to Israel and cannot boast over Israel. Israel's remnant comes into what God promised Israel through the instrumentality of Gentiles, and Israel's fullness comes about in the same way. Israel's fullness only comes in *after* the Gentiles' fullness has come in. Israel cannot boast over the Gentiles. If God had asked us for our counsel would we have done things in such a way? Of course not. We would have advised a mega impact by saving many in Israel, leading to a great impact on the world. A marketing executive's dream! But not God's; his ways are not our ways.

As it is written

Paul's use of the Old Testament substantiates both of his points, a future turning of Israel to the Lord and the delayed time for it. Paul's method with the prophecies he quotes here is not a putting together of texts which *plainly* speak of a *further* ingathering of the Jewish people, because such texts do not exist. If they did then this particular mystery would not be a mystery at all; we could open the Old Testament and see it without help from an apostle. That is one reason why I am not a pre-millennialist, because such assert that a future ingathering of Israel is plain in the Old Testament. But if so, why call it a mystery? And why the need to adjust the text in the way Paul does? We need to recall that a mystery, although in the text of the Old Testament, is not crystal clear, and we need apostolic clarity, which comes from further insight given to them by the Spirit.

Isaiah 59 – 60

Paul's method here is to go to words of Isaiah that plainly refer to the coming of Messiah to Israel as Redeemer. They are the focal point of Isaiah's prophecy in chapters 59 and 60, which begins by describing the hopeless state of God's people in sin, concluding with, 'So truth fails'.[26] The only hope is the intervention of Yahweh by his own arm bringing salvation, which Isaiah reveals is the person of the Redeemer who will come to Zion, coming to those who turn from transgression in Jacob.[27] Jesus in Jerusalem fulfilled this, especially on the temple mount, teaching Israel and turning many from sin. Isaiah goes on to describe God's covenant with those who turn, he will put his Spirit upon them, that same Spirit who anoints the Redeemer, ensuring their faithfulness to God's truth. This was fulfilled by the giving of the Spirit at Pentecost.

What follows in Isaiah 60 is a description, using Old Testament terminology, of believing Israel arising and shining now that God has blessed them (vv. 1,2), then the Gentiles being grafted in (vv. 3–18) and concluding with the final state of God's kingdom (vv. 19–22). It is one of those glorious overviews that Isaiah gives us of the whole messianic age leading into a regenerated universe where the redeemed of Israel and the nations will live for all eternity.

The question which arises is, can there be a 'take two' for Israel? Of course, there is no repetition of the incarnation, the atonement, the giving of the Spirit, but there might be of blessing for Israel. That is something which cannot be known without further revelation and this is what Paul is claiming as an apostle. Although he adjusts the wording here and there, he is not using the text to teach anything alien to the main import of Isaiah's words, which is the Saviour turning Israel from their sins. However, we need to briefly examine his adjustments, not just as a defence but because it will help to see the matter more clearly.

Paul has the deliverer coming 'out of Zion'. I would understand a twofold reason for this change. Firstly, because Zion has now moved, so to speak; Jesus cannot come *to* Zion to bless Israel because that is where he now is, ruling from the heavenly Mount Zion; further blessing can come only by his coming 'out of Zion'.[28] But the change does not alter the central idea of blessing for Israel. However, there also seems to be an allusion here to the cry of David in Psalm 53:6 that 'the salvation of Israel would come out of Zion'. The psalm presents Israel as in a poor spiritual condition, with the wicked dominant and the godly excluded. David prays for a change through God's salvation coming to them 'out of Zion'. It is almost as if he envisages God shut up with the ark of the covenant on Mount Zion and doing nothing about this situation. He calls upon him to act, to come out. There were, in Old Testament times, many answers to such a cry, but the greatest answer to that cry for deliverance was the coming of Messiah. Paul's use of 'out of Zion' in Romans 11:26 is because he sees within Psalm 53:6 the possibility of another great answer to such a cry for Israel: a special visitation by the Saviour, by his Spirit, to reverse the ongoing situation of dominant unbelief in Israel.

Paul's other adjustment is to change the description of the blessing of the covenant. Isaiah focuses on the gift of the Spirit but Paul wants to focus on the essence of God's *new* covenant with Israel, revealed to Jeremiah subsequent to Isaiah's time, that he would remember their sins no more. Paul is putting first things first for a situation of unbelief. Therefore he takes words from Isaiah 27:9 and inserts them to express the principal covenant blessing Israel needs.

How, when, where?
Inevitably Christians speculate as to when, where and how. In answer to 'When?' all we know for sure is that it is after the fullness

of the nations have heard and responded. Maybe that is not so far away when we think of the access the gospel has to almost everywhere on the planet via the internet, radio and TV.

As to 'Where?' it is stating the obvious to say, wherever Jewish people live, which is almost everywhere in the world. However, it is difficult to avoid thinking that the return to the land has some significance. All eyes are on Israel, and not just Jewish eyes, but the whole world takes note of events in the Middle East. Everyone, well almost everyone, wants a peaceful resolution to the conflict. What better way to show the power of the gospel than for Arabs to turn to Christ, to provoke Jews to jealousy, and for all to be one in him?

In answer to 'How?' we can certainly say that it will be through hearing and believing the gospel. Scripture knows of no other way. To suggest, as some do, that Israel will believe when they see Jesus' return is clean contrary to a cardinal gospel principle that salvation is received by faith. It is often assumed that Israel's conversion will be sudden and dramatic but that may not be so. It could take place over a period of time, but it is difficult to imagine that being a very long time. One thing we know, the Lord's ways are not our ways, so some things about Israel's salvation will undoubtedly surprise us all, and glorify him.

Romans 11:30–32 – disobedience and mercy

Paul is still pressing the point home to his Gentile Christian readers that the Lord has not cast Israel away. He has one final perspective he wants them to adopt and it concerns disobedience and mercy. Immediately after revealing the future salvation of all Israel he underlines to his Gentile readers that, although they so often experience Jewish people to be their enemy, yet they are still beloved by God. Paul then develops this into a further reflection upon the mercy both Gentiles and Jews have received, and the interconnection.

All in need of mercy
Paul is asking any Gentile Christians inclined to boast to get off their high horse. He reminds them they are what they are because they, though a disobedient people, have received mercy. He then points

out that the same is happening and will happen for disobedient Israel: 'They also may obtain mercy.' It is as if Paul is asking: 'Will you begrudge them this? Bearing in mind what you have received by way of mercy, can you desire it be withheld from them?'

Jews and Gentiles need each other
But Paul also describes the intertwining again. In the purposes of God, the Gentiles received mercy through Israel's disobedience, and Israel receives mercy as a consequence of the mercy shown to the Gentiles. That this was deliberate in God's plan is indicated in verse 31; Israel was disobedient to the gospel precisely so that they should obtain mercy through God's mercy to the Gentiles. If that is God's plan then Gentile Christians should have no doubt of God's continuing purpose for Israel, and furthermore they should get on with presenting the gospel to them; their salvation depends on Gentile Christians!

To God be the glory
Paul's final reflections again have twin foci – the mercy of God and the mystery of the manner of his exercise of it. That is a good note to finish on. It is surely a great triumph of divine grace that a time will come when all Israel will believe. After centuries of some of the fiercest resistance to Yahweh's Son, at times uttering some of the most appalling blasphemies, God, who has seen and heard it all, finally shows how patient he has been all along by calling and receiving Israel back. Jesus' prayer will be answered abundantly, 'Father, forgive them, for they do not know what they do.'[29] While many Gentile Christians seem content to let them remain cast off, God is otherwise. He is ready to give a demonstration of his grace at which the entire world will marvel. God forgive our hardness and indifference, our 'I'm all right, Jack' attitude. However, I would not stress too strongly the uniqueness of Jewish hostility for there is no doubt that in these closing words of Paul he sees Gentiles and Jews as essentially on a level playing field; all are disobedient and equally in need of mercy.

And then there is the matter of how God has done what he has done. I can do no better than to quote fully Paul's glorious words and ask you to join me in saying a hearty 'Amen' to them.

Oh, the depth of the riches both of the wisdom and knowledge of God! How unsearchable are His judgments and His ways past finding out!

*'For who has known the mind of the L*ORD*?*
Or who has become His counselor?'
'Or who has first given to Him
And it shall be repaid to him?'

For of Him and through Him and to Him are all things, to whom be glory forever. Amen.

Subject Index

A
Aliyah, 33, 34
Anti-Semitism, 28, 43–44, 68, 86, 118, 121–122, 124, 143, 149,
    And anti-Zionism, 72–74, 208
    Christian response, 123–126
    In Christians, 74
    Justifications, 68ff
    Motivations, 71–75

B
Babylonian exile, 54
Boasting Gentiles 4, 7, 26–27, 117, 207, 232ff
Boasting Jews and Gentiles, 235
Boasting theology, 9

C
Christian, term, 163
Christian Palestinianism, 216
Christian Zionism, 34
Christians (Gentile) & Jewish customs, 79
Church/Ecclesia, 49, 145
    Fulfilment of promises, 9, 19, 49–51
    Jewishness, 26, 140, 158, 182–183
    Mission strategy, 11, 15–17, 31, 114, 127, 217–218
    Names for, 23, 145, 166, 168
    Olive tree, 21
Church Growth Movement, 191
Circumcision
    Apostleship of, 128
    Circumcision, the, 76–77, 81–82
    For Gentile Christians, 82
    Gospel of, 128, 130-131,
Council of Christians and Jews, 94
Covenant
    Abrahamic and interrelationship, 21, 51–52, 200
    Definition, 5
    Land today, 208–209
    Mosaic and New, 6, 19, 49, 57–58, 181
    New, 9, 19, 145, 181, 200–201, 224
    Promises to Abraham, 6, 93, 115, 119–121, 177, 199, 211, 228–229, 236, 237
    Unity and interrelationship, 25–26

D
Dialogue with Trypho, 190

E
Election, individual, 4, 40–41, 43–45, 163, 235
End-time prophecy, 33–34
Engrafting theology, 9–10, 26
Exclusion theology, 9

F
Fill up sins, 55–56, 58, 61
Fulfilment theology, 9–10, 25

H
Hebrew Christian Alliance, 30, 191
Hebrew roots, 79–81

Subject Index

Holocaust, viii, 59, 118, 119, 174, 194, 213, 241

I
Inter-testamental period, 206
Israel/Palestine conflict, 34–35, 64, 121
    influence on terminology, 161–162, 198

J
Jerusalem
    Destruction, 4, 54, 55, 56, 105, 203
    Times of the Gentiles, 203
Jealousy, provoking to, 133ff, 231
Jesus
    And Israel, 101ff
    As Israel, 115–116
    High priest, 178–179
    Mission to Jew and Gentile, 127–128
    Servant of the Lord, 127–128,
    Son, Saviour, Mediator, 176
Jewishness, 91, 159,
    Of church, 15, 182–183,
    Of early church, 165
    Of Jewish believers, 139, 158–160, 162, 186, 188, 190–193
Jews/Israel
    All Israel saved, 223ff, 232, 234–235
    Believers, church, see One New Man
    Believers, exhortations, 183–184
Believers, fellowship, 156–157, 184–185
Believers, Jewish culture, 192–193
Believers, Mosaic and Rabbinic practices, 165, 188–190, 194–196
Believers, pressures, 171–175
Believers, terms, 163
Chosen, 4, 107
Commission of Israel, 150, 155, 158
Covenant people, 5, 51–52, (also see Covenant)
Culture, 186–188,
Fullness, 114, 209, 229, 231–235, 237
God's wrath, 53ff

Grafted back, 24–27
Hardened, 65–66, 104–105, 230
Identity theft, 168
'Israel' in Romans 11, 228–229
Israel of God, 145, 163ff, 169–170
John's gospel and 'Jews', 69–70
Land of, names for, 161–162, 198–199
Natural branches, 16, 21–22, 25–27, 232
Opposition to the apostles, 85
Opposition to gospel, 58–59, 62, 64, 92–96
Opposition to Jesus, 83–85,
People of promise, 3, 6, 8, 12–13, 47, 108, 130, 133, 140, 142
Preserved, 119–121
Priority, 11ff
Privileges, 108–112
Promised land,
    And gospel, 208–209
    And Islam, 212, 216
    Divine right, 211–212
    Extent, 198–199
    In New Testament, 199–202, 208
    Names, 198
    Shadow/type, 177, 200
Remnant, 4, 51, 114, 160, 163, 170, 225, 229–230, 235
Responsible for unbelief, 41
Return to the land, 201ff
Solidarity, vii
State of Israel, viii, 27, 34, 72–74, 91, 105, 121, 197, 207, 209, 213, 215, 218
    Christian attitudes, 215–219
    Jewish attitudes, 213–215
Troubles, 53, 55, 56, 57, 66–67, 122
Unbelief, 4, 7, 8, 39ff, 54, 65, 101, 102, 105, 109, 138
Jews and Gentiles, salvation, 235, 239
Judaisers, 166
Judaism
    And gospel, 62–63, 86–92, 159, 177, 179, 181,
    And Jewish suffering, 57
    And Old Testament religion, 171, 178, 181

Subject Index

And return to land, 209–210
Effects, 24, 41 ,50–51, 62–63, 64, 66–67, 110–112
Teachings, 86–92, 102, 178, 181
Judeans, 54–55, 58, 60–61, 62–63, 68–70

K
Khazars, 8
Kingdom, 4, 24, 34, 46ff, 55, 116, 139, 173, 202, 236,
and covenant, 51

L
Law
Faith under, 42–43
Fulfilled, 86, 115–116 143
Insufficient, 179
Purpose, 42, 142
Righteous requirement, 23, 144
Love Israel, 32–33

M
Melchizedek, 178
Messianic congregations, 150–153, 191
And Gentiles, 78, 151–152, 154
Reasons for, 148–151,
Messianic fellowship, 156–157
Messianic Jews, 30, 152, 163
Messianic Jewish Alliance, 30, 157
Messianic Judaism, 82, 152–155, 157
Messianic movement, 77–78, 81, 138, 191
Messianic synagogues, see Messianic congregations
Middle-wall, 20, 142
Millennium, 198, 218
Missions to Jews, 94, 129–131, 152, 156, 191
Mystery, 207, 233, 236, 239

O
One New Man, 16, 140, 145–148, 156, 163, 218
In practice, 157–162, 185
Olive tree, 21ff, 28, 114, 206, 232

P
Paul & Israel, 112–114
Philo-Semitism, 157
Pre-millennialism, 236

R
Rabin, Yitzhak, 218
Replacement theology, 8–9

S
Southern Baptists, 95
Synagogue of Satan, 66

T
Transition period, Acts, 19–20
Two Covenant theory, 18, 95

Scripture Index

Genesis
12:1–3, 119
12:3, 6
14:13, 212
14:13–16, 212
15:16, 55
15:18, 198
17:9–11, 128
18:19, 202
21:25–31, 212
23:4, 16, 211
26:16–33, 212
32:27–28, 167
33:18–20, 212
34:10, 212

Exodus
20:5, 58, 134
33:7, 154

Leviticus
18:5, 42

Numbers
5:14, 134
6:1-21, 188
24:17–19, 180

Deuteronomy
18:18–19, 54
28, 54
29:20, 134
29:29, 120

30:6, 88
30:12–14, 42
32:16, 21, 134
33:29, 108

1 Samuel
7:5, 234

2 Chronicles
9:26, 199
15:15, 225
17:3–6, 155

Nehemiah
8:8, 12, 18, 225

Psalms
40:6-8, 180–181
51:5, 89
67:3–4, 29
98:3, 13
110:3, 139
110:4, 87, 90, 178
118:22, 60

Isaiah
1:9, 164
2:1–3, 224
11:13, 134
42:21, 115
49:3, 115
49:6, 116, 127
53:7–9, 60

Scripture Index

53:10, 90
56:1–8, 87
59:9–21, 116, 236
59:20 and 27:9, 206–207
59 – 60, 236–237
61:18, 201
65:9, 116
66:1-2, 87

Jeremiah
7:23, 5
31:31–34, 5,57,87,224
32:40, 201
50:7, 68

Ezekiel
37:26, 201

Daniel
9:4–19, 124

Amos
9:11–12, 205–206
9:15, 206

Zechariah
11:10–14, 57

Malachi
3:2, 84

Matthew
2:20, 162
6:23, 105
12:8, 86
15:14, 85
15:24, 127
16:18, 145
21:18–19, 50
21:23–46, 46
22:42–46, 89
23:13, 85
23:32, 55
23:39, 226
25:34, 48
26:26–28, 57
27:18, 60,84

Luke
2:32, 87
10:2, 131
11:53, 84
12:13–15, 216–217
13:34, 104
14:15, 47
18:8, 95
18:9–14, 87
19:28–48, 101
19:41–44, 4,54,68,102
21:20–24, 4,203,204
23:34, 239

John
2:19–22, 179
3:3, 48
4:22, 29
8:31, 163
9:16, 84
9:29, 84
10:26, 44
10:29–33, 84,89
11:7–8, 70
11:48–50, 48
16:12, 203
18:36, 48
19:4, 60
19:11, 61
19:30, 116,179

Acts
1:6, 156,202
1:7–8, 33
1:8, 11
2:23, 70
2:42, 152
3:25, 130
4:12, 18
6:14, 165
10:14, 188
10:25, 28
13:5, 12
13:27, 70
13:32–33, 12,130
13:39, 88

13:45, 134
13:46, 12
13:47, 29
14:19, 85
15, 79
15:1, 77,166
15:5, 146
15:15–17, 205-206
15:19–20, 147
15:28, 29, 188
16:3, 189
17:1–15, 59,148
17:2, 12
17:10, 12
18:18, 188
18:19, 12
21:20, 110,163,165
21:20–24, 189
21:28–31, 87
22:21–22, 87,137
28:11–31, 15
28:17, 12

Romans
1:16–17, 12,14
2:5–9, 14
2:25–29, 7,8
3:1–2, 109
4:3 88
4:13, 200
8:2, 146
8:4, 24,144
9 – 11, 4
9–10, 226–227
9:1–5, 47,59,106,109
9:6–7, 40,167,223,227
9:11, 40
9:15, 41
9:27–29,33, 224
9:29, 41
9:31–32, 42,93
9:31–10:3, 227
10:1, 97,219
10:3, 41,62
10:5–8, 42,227
10:8–10, 227

10:19, 134,224
10:21, 41,224
11, 3,21,228ff
11:1, 3,5,129
11:1–10, 228-230
11:5, 4,40,44,118,164
11:7, 7,116
11:7–10, 65
11:11, 133
11:11–15, 230-232
11:11,14, 134
11:13, 137
11:16–24, 232
11:17, 23,26
11:18–19, 9,26,138
11:21, 24, 22,27
11:23, 24
11:25–29, 233-238,233
11:26, 223
11:26–27, 117,206-207,226,229,236
11:28, 3,5,6,24,51,92
11:29, 8
11:30–32, 238
11:33, 223,235
11:33–36, 223
11:36, 4
14:1, 189
14:17, 48
14:21, 147
15:27, 30
16:17, 76
16:25–26, 233

1 Corinthians
1:23, 90
3:16, 50
9:20, 187
9:21, 189
10:32, 20
15:50, 48

2 Corinthians
2:6, 58
3:15, 65,230
11:13–15, 76
11:24, 85

Galatians
1:13–14, 62
2:1–10, 127-128
2:4, 76
2:11–13, 146,147
3:7, 29, 8
4:9–11, 151,166
4:17, 167
4:25, 67
4:26, 50
5:3–4, 79,166
5:10–12, 76,166,167
6:12, 76,166
6:13–14, 167
6:16, 164ff,169–170

Ephesians
1:12–13, 141
2:15, 16,140,219
2:19–22, 9,50,211
3:1-5, 207,211

Philippians
3:2, 76,77
3:3, 168

Colossians
2:4,8,16–23, 76,79,82
2:15, 116
2:16–3:3, 151
2:20–23, 77,150

1 Thessalonians
1:1, 148
2:14–16, 53

1 Timothy
1:4–7, 76
1:13, 63
4:1–5, 7, 76,211
6:3–5, 76

2 Timothy
2:14–16,23, 76
3:6–7, 76
4:3–4, 76

Titus
1:10–16, 76–77
3:9, 76,77

Hebrews
Hebrews, 171ff
1:1–2, 6
2:1, 172
3:1–6, 176
3:14, 184
4:11, 172,173
5:6, 178
7:3, 178
7:16, 24, 178
7:18–19, 178
7:20–22, 181
7:25, 179
8:2, 179
8:6, 58,181
8:13, 5,58,181,201
9:10, 179
9:11, 179
9:12, 179
9:15, 177
9:22, 178
9:28, 179
10:1, 9, 6,179
10:16–18, 181
10:23, 172
10:24–25, 185
10:26–27, 184
10:36, 184
11:10, 200
11:16, 176,200
12:1, 183
12:22–24, 237
13:9, 182
13:13, 154,182
13:20, 201

1 Peter
2:4–5, 9
2:9–10, 5,49

2 Peter
2, 76

1 John
2:18–19, 76
4:1–6, 76

Jude
Jude, 76

Revelation
1:1, 211
3:9, 66
12, 118ff
12:14, 121
12:17, 118

Endnotes

Introduction

[1] The term 'Holocaust' refers to the deliberate destruction of millions of Jewish people and their communal life by the Nazis during World War 2. It is not the term I prefer but I use it because it is the best known. My preference is for the term 'Shoah', which is used more widely now but it has not replaced 'Holocaust'. *Shoah* is a Hebrew word which means 'desolation', as for example in Isa. 47:11 referring to the fate of Babylon, whereas 'holocaust' is the Greek equivalent of the Hebrew word for a whole burnt offering, *olah*. The idea that the suffering and death of Jewish people might somehow atone for sin is not foreign to rabbinic Judaism but it is to the Bible and hence 'Holocaust' is a term I dislike.

[2] Most readers will be familiar with the term 'Messiah' as a title for God's promised deliverer. It is the English equivalent of *messias*, the transliteration into Greek of the Hebrew *Mashiach*, which means 'anointed'. As Israel's priests, kings and prophets were anointed so Messiah is the one anointed to fulfil all those roles. *Messias* occurs only twice in the Greek New Testament, the more usual term in the Greek being *christos*, meaning 'anointed', from which we have the English word 'Christ'. In this book I have used both Messiah and Christ as seemed appropriate in a particular context.

Introduction

1. Yahweh, the God of Israel

[1] Y H W H are the four Hebrew letters of the Divine name. The pronunciation Yahweh is indicated by the way the name was transliterated into Greek in early Christian literature. The pronunciation Jehovah is a much later one (12th century) which resulted from combining the consonants YHWH with the vowels of the Hebrew word *adonai* (my Lord), the latter being the word which the Jews had substituted for the Divine name when reading the text, as God's name was considered too sacred to pronounce. It could be argued that the spelling Yahveh better indicates the correct pronunciation but Yahweh is used as it is more familiar.
[2] Rom. 11:1 (AV, NIV)
[3] Rom. 11:28
[4] Luke 19:41–44, 21:20–24
[5] Rom. 11:20–21
[6] Rom. 11:5
[7] Rom. 11:30,33
[8] Rom. 11:36

2. His People

[1] Jer. 7:23
[2] 1 Pet. 2:9–10
[3] Rom. 11:1
[4] 1 Cor. 10:32
[5] Jer. 31:32,33; Heb. 8:13
[6] Rom. 11:28
[7] Gen. 12:13
[8] Heb. 1:1–2
[9] Rom. 11:7
[10] In his book *The Thirteenth Tribe*, Arthur Koestler, a secular Jewish author, argues that the conversion to Judaism in the mid-eighth century of the Khazar nation, a people of Turkish stock who lived in the region between the Black Sea and the Caspian Sea, meant that the majority of European Jewry became non-Semitic when those of Khazar descent intermarried with those of Semitic descent. His conclusion was that today's Jews should accept this reality, stop pretending to be different,

assimilate, and so end anti-Semitism. His argument is full of conjecture as there is scanty evidence of what happened to the Khazars after their empire was weakened by the Russians around 1000 AD, and destroyed by Genghis Khan in the mid-thirteenth century. Koestler assumes the survivors fled westwards in great numbers, remained faithful to Judaism, and massively swelled the numbers of the Jews of Eastern Europe. It is a big assumption, and its Achilles heel is the lack of Turkic loan words in Yiddish, the language of east European Jewry, which is essentially an East–Middle German dialect combined with Hebrew and Slavonic elements. Furthermore, one might say to Koestler, 'So what. Membership of the Jewish nation has always been granted to converts to Judaism, and as the Khazars were such then they were Jews.'

[11] Rom. 11:29
[12] Rom. 11:18–19
[13] Eph. 2:19–22; 1 Pet. 2:4,5 (some teach 1 Pet. is written to Jewish Christians only, but 2 Pet. 3:1 makes plain that he is writing the second epistle to the same audience as his first epistle, and his second epistle is clearly addressed to all Christians – see 2 Pet. 1:1).

3. For the Jew First

[1] Acts 1:8
[2] Rom. 1:16
[3] Acts 13:5
[4] Acts 17:10
[5] Acts 18:19
[6] Acts 28:17
[7] Acts 17:2 (my italics)
[8] Acts 13:46 (my italics)
[9] Acts 13:32–33
[10] Acts 17:30
[11] Eph. 2:12
[12] Ps. 98:3
[13] Rom. 2:5,9
[14] Acts 1:8
[15] Eph. 2:15
[16] Matt. 28:19

[17] Rom. 3:23
[18] Acts 4:12
[19] 1 Cor. 10:32

4. The Olive Tree

[1] Rom. 11:21,24
[2] Rom. 11:24
[3] Heb. 11:6
[4] 1 Sam. 25
[5] Rom. 11:17
[6] Rom. 11:24
[7] Rom. 8:4 (my italics)
[8] Rom. 11:23
[9] Rom. 11:28
[10] Rom. 11:17–18
[11] Rom. 11:19
[12] Rom. 11:24

5. Debtors

[1] Acts 10:25
[2] John 4:22
[3] Acts 13:47
[4] Ps. 67:3–4
[5] Rom. 15:27
[6] The UK's leading weekly Jewish newspaper
[7] Read any of her books, but especially *The Hiding Place*.
[8] Acts 1:7–8
[9] *Aliyah* is a term used by Jewish people to describe returning to live in the land of Israel.

6. Israel's Unbelief

[1] Rom. 8:39
[2] Rom. 9:6,7

Endnotes

3. 'Israel' means God's fighter or God's ruler. Prince with God conveys both concepts. In the context of Gen. 32:24–32 the name describes a man who trusts in God alone but who is made strong for God by that trust.
4. Rom. 9:11
5. Rom. 11:5
6. Rom. 9:15
7. Rom. 9:29
8. Rom. 10:21
9. Rom. 10:3
10. Rom. 9:31–32
11. Rom. 11:5

7. Kingdom: Then and Now

1. Matt. 21:43
2. Matt. 21:23
3. Rom. 9:1–5
4. Luke 14:15
5. Matt. 25:34
6. John 18:36
7. Rom. 14:17
8. John 3:3
9. 1 Cor. 15:50
10. Mark 11:17
11. John 11:48–50
12. Rom. 14:17–18
13. 1 Pet. 2:9
14. I am aware that some think 1 Peter was written to Jewish believers in Jesus. It is not possible to go into all the pros and cons of that argument here. It seems to me that it is briefly answered by considering 2 Pet. 3:1, which states the recipients of 1 Peter and 2 Peter are the same group. However, in addressing his readers in 2 Pet. 1:1 he uses no words which could be construed as referring specifically to Jews, such as 'pilgrims of the Dispersion' in 1 Pet. 1:1, but addresses them as those who have 'obtained like precious faith with us'. Both letters were written at least thirty years subsequent to Acts 2,

when many churches containing both Jews and Gentiles had been founded in the Gentile world, and as there is no evidence for separate Jewish churches among them then it is not possible to imagine he wrote only to Jews.

[15] 1 Cor. 3:16; Eph. 2:21
[16] Gal. 4:26
[17] Matt. 21:18–19

8. Wrath to the Uttermost

[1] Deut. 28:15,22,24,28,64,66
[2] Luke 19:44
[3] Deut. 18:18–19
[4] Jer. 31:31–34
[5] Zech. 11:10–14
[6] Matt. 26:26–28
[7] Heb. 8:13,6
[8] 2 Cor. 3:6
[9] Exod. 20:5
[10] Acts 17:1–15
[11] Rev. 2:9; 3:9
[12] Rom. 9:1–5
[13] Matt. 27:18
[14] John 19:4
[15] Isa. 53:7–9
[16] Ps. 118:22
[17] John 19:11
[18] Rom. 10:3
[19] Gal. 1:13,14
[20] H.L. Ellison, 'Judaism', in *New Bible Dictionary* (ed. J. D. Douglas; London: IVP, 1970), p. 670.
[21] 2 Cor. 3:15
[22] Rev. 3:9
[23] Matt. 11:28
[24] Rev. 6:1; Ps. 2
[25] Jer. 50:7
[26] Steve Motyer, *Anti-Semitism and the New Testament* (Cambridge: Grove Books, 2002).

Endnotes

[27] Luke 19:41–44
[28] John 11:7–8
[29] Acts 2:23
[30] Acts 13:27
[31] Esth. 3:8
[32] The term 'anti-Semitism' now has a wider usage, describing 'the hatred and persecution of Jews as a group; not the hatred of persons who happen to be Jews, but rather the hatred of persons because they are Jews' (Glock and Stark's definition, quoted by Graham Keith in *Hated Without a Cause: A Survey of Anti-Semitism*; Carlisle: Paternoster, 1997, p. 2). This hatred has a long pedigree, going back to Pharaoh in Exodus. Before the term 'anti-Semitism' existed, such hatred, if there was a term at all, was seen as anti-Jewishness or anti-Judaism. If I could set the clock back I would prefer that the general term was 'anti-Jewishness' and that 'anti-Semitism' be reserved for those whose opposition to Jewish people is based on believing they are racially inferior. I see such an understanding as especially evil and the cause of a completely different scale of destruction of Jewish people; hence I would prefer a distinct term for it. However, I cannot set the clock back and for the recipients of such hatred it no doubt makes little difference what term is used. So 'anti-Semitism' is the term in general usage today and it is the term I will use in this book. However, both terms need to be distinguished from 'anti-Judaism', which refers to opposition to the Jewish religion and does not imply opposition to the Jewish people. Of course, there are those Jewish people who see their religion as the product of their own native genius, so they see opposition to Judaism as opposition to Jews. But such thinking will land us in a ridiculous position. If we can never oppose people's ideas without being seen as opposed to them personally the world will be full of personal indignation and hurt feelings and we will all end up saying nothing which differs with anybody. For Christians, sin is the cause of false religion in the world and, knowing themselves to be sinners too, they are not prone to blame a people for its false religion, but sin, which affects us all.
[33] Kelvin MacKenzie, former editor of the *Sun* newspaper, quoted in the *Jewish Chronicle*, 7 December 2012, p.1

9. Talkers and Mutilators

1. Titus 1:10–11
2. Titus 1:10–16; 3:9; 1 Tim. 1:4–7; 4:1–5,7; 6:3–5; 2 Tim. 2:14–16; 2:23; 3:6,7; 4:3,4; Rom. 16:17; 2 Cor. 11:13–15; Gal. 2:4; 5:10–12; 6:12; Phil. 3:2; Col. 2:4,8,16–23; 2 Pet. 2; 1 John 2:18,19; 4:1–6; Jude
3. Titus 1:10–16; 3:9; 1 Tim. 1:4–7; Gal. 2:4; 5:10–12; 6:12; Phil. 3:2
4. 2 Cor. 11:13–15,22.
5. Titus 3:9
6. Col. 2:20–23
7. Acts 15:1
8. David Stern, *Restoring the Jewishness of the Gospel* (Jerusalem: Jewish New Testament Publications, 1988), pp.57–8.
9. Gal. 5:3,4
10. Col. 2:4–8, 16–23
11. Mark S. Kinzer, *Finding our Way through Nicaea: The Deity of Yeshua, Bilateral Ecclesiology, and Redemptive Encounter with the Living God* (Los Angeles: Hashivenu Forum, 2010).
12. Richard Nichol, *The Case for Conversion: Welcoming Non-Jews into Messianic Jewish Space,* Messianic Jewish Rabbinical Council http://www.ourrabbis.org/main/articles/on-conversion-main-menu-32 (accessed 31 January 2013).
13. Col. 2:20–21

10. Jewish Opposition to the Gospel

1. More information on witnessing to Jewish people, and responding to opposition can be found in my book, *Telling Jews about Jesus* (London: Grace Publications, 1994).
2. Mal. 3:2
3. Luke 11:53
4. Matt. 9:34
5. Matt. 12:2
6. John 10:29–33
7. Matt. 27:18
8. Matt. 21:23–27
9. John 9:16
10. John 9:29

Endnotes

11. Matt. 23:13
12. See Matt. 15:14
13. Acts 4:17
14. Acts 6:7
15. Acts 13:45
16. Acts 14:19
17. Acts 20:3, 23:12
18. Acts 24 – 26
19. 2 Cor. 11:24
20. Matt. 12:8
21. Mark 14:58
22. Acts 21:28–31
23. Acts 22:21–22
24. Isa. 56:1–8
25. Luke 2:32
26. Isaac of Troki, *Faith Strengthened* (New York: Ktav Publishing, 1970), p. 94.
27. Isa. 66:1–2; Ps. 110:4
28. Jer. 31:31–33
29. Luke 18:9–14
30. Acts 13:39
31. Rom. 4:3
32. Deut. 30:6
33. Chaim Pearl, *A Guide to Jewish Knowledge* (London: Jewish Chronicle Publications, 1975), p. 112.
34. Pearl, *Guide*, p. 112.
35. Ps. 51:5
36. John 10:31,33
37. Matt. 22:42–46
38. Michael Asheri, *Living Jewish: The Lore and Law of Being a Practicing Jew* (USA: Jewish Chronicle Publications, 1978), p. 297.
39. John 7:37–38
40. Louis Jacobs, *A Jewish Theology* (West Orange, NJ: Behrman, 1973), p. 293.
41. Ps. 110:4
42. Num. 6:22–27
43. 1 Cor. 1:23
44. David Berger, *Jews and Jewish Christianity* (Jersey City, NJ: Ktav Publishing, 1978), pp. 57–59.

45. Isa. 53:10
46. Rom. 11:28
47. Two Covenant teaching is a theologically sophisticated way of saying that Jews and Christians have separate and valid pathways to God.
48. Luke 18:8
49. Geoffrey Alderman, 'The End of Interfaith Relations', *The Jewish Chronicle*, 20 July 2012, final paragraph.
50. More information on the most frequent Jewish responses can be found in my book, *Telling Jews about Jesus*. For a full examination of almost every Jewish objection that has ever been heard, see the volumes by Michael Brown entitled *Answering Jewish Objections to Jesus* (Grand Rapids, MI: Baker Book House, Vol. 1 2000, Vol. 2 2000, Vol. 3 2003, Vol. 4 2006, Vol. 5 2010).
51. Rom. 10:1
52. Luke 6:26

11. The Compassion of Jesus for Israel

1. John 11:35
2. Luke 19:42–44
3. Mishnah, Sanhedrin XI, 1, 2
4. Mishnah, Makkoth III, 16
5. Luke 13:34
6. Matt. 6:23
7. Heb. 13:8

12. Paul's Heart's Desire and Prayer to God

1. Deut. 33:29
2. Rom. 9:5
3. Rom. 3:1–2
4. Acts 21:20
5. For the stories of nine of them see Richard Seigel and Carl Rheins, *The Jewish Almanac* (New York: Bantam Books, 1980), pp. 583–94, or put 'false Jewish Messiahs' into Google, or similar.
6. 1 Thess. 5:16
7. Luke 9:54

8 Luke 9:55–56
9 Gal. 4:19–20, my italics

13. Sin and Satan Defeated

1 Isa. 49:3
2 Isa. 42:21
3 Heb. 4:15
4 John 19:30
5 Col. 2:15
6 Isa. 49:6
7 Not all translations have the second half of Isa. 59:19 as 'When the enemy comes in like a flood, The Spirit of the Lord will lift up a standard against him.' This is the traditional English translation. The NIV has 'For he will come like a pent-up flood that the breath of the Lord drives along.' Both translations have their merits and make a similar point (see J. Alec Motyer, *The Prophecy of Isaiah*, Downers Grove, IL:, IVP, 1994, p. 492 for the detailed arguments) but the NIV translation requires a change to one vowel point, and fails to give the 'big picture' focus of the text, as it summarizes the whole thrust of Isa. 59.
8 Isa. 65:11,13
9 Isa. 65:9
10 Rom. 11:7
11 Isa. 59
12 Rom. 11:26
13 Rom. 11:5
14 Rev. 12:17
15 Rev. 12:6
16 Rev. 17:15
17 Gen. 12:1–3
18 People of Jewish descent have won approximately 20 per cent of the Nobel prizes awarded.
19 Mark Twain, 'Concerning the Jews', *Harper's Magazine* (1899).
20 Deut. 29:29
21 Rev. 12:14
22 Dan. 9:4–19

14. I am of Peter: the Apostleship to the Circumcision

1. Isa. 49:6
2. Matt. 15:24
3. Acts 1:1
4. Gal. 2:7–8. Some versions (the NIV is one) paraphrase v. 7 to read, 'I had been entrusted with the task of preaching the gospel to the Gentiles; just as Peter had been to the Jews.' This is inaccurate, it is literally: 'I have been entrusted with the gospel of the uncircumcision, as Peter of the circumcision.' Paul is referring to the gospel itself, not simply the preaching of it.
5. Gal. 2:9
6. Gen. 17:9–11
7. Gal. 2:8
8. John Calvin, *Calvin's Commentaries Romans – Galatians* (Wilmington, Delaware: Associated Publishers and Authors, no date), p. 1875.
9. Rom. 11:1
10. *Telling Jews about Jesus*
11. Gal. 1:6–7
12. Acts 3:25
13. Acts 13:32
14. Acts 17:29
15. Luke 10:2

15. Provoking to Jealousy

1. Rom. 11:11
2. John 8:32
3. Exod. 20:5
4. Deut. 32:16
5. Num. 5:14
6. Isa. 11:13
7. Deut. 29:20
8. 2 Cor. 11:2
9. John 2:17
10. Acts 13:45
11. Heb. 10:27
12. *Jewish Chronicle* (22 June 2001), p. 25.

[13] Acts 22:22
[14] Acts 23:16
[15] 1 Cor. 8:10; 10:19–21
[16] Rom. 11:18
[17] Ps. 110:3

16. One New Man from the Two

[1] Eph. 2:15
[2] Eph. 2:11
[3] Eph. 1:12–13, my italics
[4] Merrill F. Unger, *Archaeology and the New Testament* (Grand Rapids, MI: Zondervan, 1976), p. 102.
[5] Rom. 8:4
[6] Matt. 16:18
[7] Rom. 8:2
[8] Acts 15:5
[9] Gal. 2:11–13
[10] Acts 15:19–20
[11] Rom. 14:21
[12] Gal. 2:11–21
[13] Acts 17:1–4
[14] 1 Thess. 1:1
[15] Col. 2:20ff.
[16] A fuller discussion of this issue and a response to it can be found in Stan Telchin's book, *Messianic Judaism is not Christianity* (Grand Rapids, MI: Chosen, 2004), ch. 6, 'The Phenomenon: Gentiles in Synagogues'.
[17] Gal. 4:9–11
[18] All three quotations from 'Messianic Judaism – so what exactly is it?', *Messianic Jewish Life* 72 (July–September 1999).
[19] Chapter 2.5 in Rich Robinson, *The Messianic Movement: A Field Guide for Evangelical Christians* (San Francisco, CA: Purple Pomegranate Publications, 2005) details the development of this philosophy since 1999. This book is an excellent overview of the subject and contains plenty of valuable analysis.
[20] *Defining Messianic Judaism* is an article within the web site of the *Union of Messianic Jewish Congregations*: http://www.ucmjs.com/

21. A Jewish term (Hebrew: the way) referring to a way of life dictated by the law of Moses as interpreted and added to by the rabbis. Different Judaisms have produced their own *Halakha* – rules and regulations which govern every aspect of life in daily living, annual festivals and fasts, and observances related to the main markers of life from the cradle to the grave.
22. For example, see the web site of Union of Conservative Messianic Synagogues which has created over two hundred categories for regulating messianic Jewish life: http://www.ucmjs.com/mj_halacha.htm (accessed 31 January 2013).
23. 'The idea that Christians and Messianic Jews represent the two distinct parts of the unified congregation of Messiah. Messianic Jews are called to be Jews, remaining within our people, and partnering with our Christian brothers and sisters. Our communities are distinct, but our Messiah is the same. We share a bond, but there are differences in identity and way of life', Hashivenu Blog of Derek Lehmann (1 February 2010).
24. Cited in Gabriela M. Reason, 'Competing trends in Messianic Judaism: the debate over Evangelicalism', *Kesher, A Journal of Messianic Judaism* 17 (2004). Mark Kinzer is a leading academic and teacher within Messianic Judaism circles, being an adjunct professor at Fuller Theological Seminary and a teacher at the Messianic Jewish Theological Institute.
25. Heb. 13:13
26. Exod. 33:7
27. 2 Chr. 17:3–6
28. 1 Kgs 22:4; 2 Chr. 20:35–37; 2 Chr. 18:1; 21:1–6
29. Acts 1:6
30. David Baron, *Messianic Judaism or Judaising Christianity* (Chicago, IL: American Messianic Fellowship, 1911). This was reprinted from *The Scattered Nation*, the monthly magazine (October 1911) of the Hebrew Christian Testimony to Israel, Whitechapel, London.
31. Jer. 10:2
32. Matt. 2:20

17. The Israel of God

1. John 8:31

[2] Acts 10:45; 11:2
[3] Acts 21:20
[4] Isa. 1:9
[5] Rom. 11:5
[6] Acts 6:14
[7] Acts 21:20
[8] Acts 15:1; Gal. 5:7–12; 6:12–13
[9] Gal. 4:10; 5:3
[10] Gal. 4:12
[11] Gal. 4:17
[12] Gal. 5:7–12
[13] Gal. 6:13–14
[14] Rom. 9:6
[15] Gen. 32:27–28
[16] Phil. 3:3
[17] There is a view that translates the Greek according to the original word order, so that it reads: 'And as many as walk according to this rule, peace be upon them. And mercy be even upon the Israel of God.' This is legitimate, and it clearly distinguishes two groups, but it makes the second *kai* both awkward and superfluous. Those who adopt this understand 'Israel of God' to refer to all Jews, which they see as allowable because the translation separates the expression 'Israel of God' from those who walk according to the rule. It becomes a heart-cry from Paul for God's mercy for Israel. I like that, but it seems to me that such an understanding fails to pick up on the tension in the letter between the two groups of Jewish teachers, Paul and the others.
[18] For a more in-depth discussion of this issue see Steve Voorwinde, 'How Jewish is "Israel" in the New Testament?', *Reformed Theological Review* 67 (August 2008), pp. 80–84. His footnotes indicate those who have taken one view or the other. Among supporters of the view I have taken would be: Beza, Grotius, Estius, Bengel, Schott, de Wette, Ewald, Ellicott, and Bruce.

18. Pay Attention

[1] A Yiddish word used by Jewish people to describe gall, brazen nerve, presumption plus arrogance.
[2] Heb. 4:11

3. Heb. 6:12
4. Heb. 10:23
5. Heb. 12:1
6. Heb. 2:1
7. Heb. 3:12
8. Heb. 4:9–11
9. Heb. 10:32–34
10. Heb. 1:1–4
11. Heb. 2:9–18
12. Heb. 3:1–6
13. Deut. 28:1–14
14. Heb. 11:16
15. Heb. 4:10
16. Matt. 11:29
17. Heb. 9:15
18. Heb. 6:19–20
19. Heb. 9:22
20. Heb. 5:6, quoting Ps. 110:4
21. Heb. 7:3
22. Heb. 7:18–19
23. Heb. 7:16,24
24. Heb. 7:25
25. Heb. 8:2; 9:12
26. Heb. 8:1,2; 9:24; 7:26
27. Heb. 9:11; John 2:19–22
28. Heb. 9:6–7
29. Heb. 9:10,12–13
30. Heb. 10:1
31. Heb. 9:28
32. Heb. 9:12–14
33. John 19:30
34. Heb. 9:26
35. Num. 24:17–19
36. Ps. 40:6 describes the subject as having his ears opened but in Heb. 10:5 we have 'a body you have prepared for me'. The author of Hebrews has used the Septuagint, the Greek translation of the OT, which was in common use at the time, which has this particular wording. The Septuagint is not an accurate translation at this point but probably aims to paraphrase the idea contained in the opened ear concept – a life of obedience

to God. Hebrews sees Messiah as coming for this exact purpose and is content to use the wording of the Septuagint as expressive of the same idea, that Messiah comes into the world, in a body, to do God's will.

[37] Heb. 10:16–18
[38] Heb. 7:20–22
[39] Heb. 8:6–13
[40] Heb. 9:15
[41] Heb. 8:13
[42] Heb. 11:13–16
[43] Heb. 11:32–39
[44] Heb. 12:1–2
[45] Heb. 13:9
[46] Heb. 13:13
[47] See Chapter 19, 'Culturally Jewish'.
[48] Heb. 2:1
[49] Heb. 6:1
[50] Heb. 12:1
[51] Heb. 4:16
[52] Heb. 3:14
[53] Heb. 10:26–27
[54] Heb. 10:31; 12:29
[55] Heb. 10:36
[56] Heb. 6:10
[57] Heb. 10:24–25

19. Culturally Jewish

[1] 1 Cor. 9:20
[2] Acts 10:14
[3] Acts 15:28–29
[4] Acts 18:18
[5] Num. 6:1–21
[6] Num. 6:18
[7] Acts 16:3
[8] Acts 21:20–24
[9] Acts 21:24
[10] 1 Cor. 9:21
[11] Rom. 14:1

[12] From the profession of faith of the Church of Constantinople: from Assemani, Cod. Lit., I, p. 105, as cited in James Parkes, *The Conflict of the Church and the Synagogue* (New York: Athenaeum, 1974), pp. 397–8.
[13] D. McGavran, *Understanding Church Growth* (Grand Rapids, MI: Eerdmans, 1975), p. 198.
[14] Rosh Hashanah (Jewish New Year) to Yom Kippur (Day of Atonement) is a ten-day period, which Judaism decrees as a time for reflection, repentance and reconciliation.

20. The Return to the Land

[1] Gen. 15:18
[2] 2 Chr. 9:26
[3] Heb. 11:16
[4] Heb. 11:10
[5] Rom. 4:13, my italics
[6] Heb. 8:13
[7] Heb. 13:20
[8] Isa. 61:8; Jer. 32:40; Ezek. 37:26
[9] Gen. 18:19
[10] Acts 1:6
[11] John 16:12
[12] Luke 21:24
[13] Luke 21:22
[14] Amos 9:15
[15] Heb. 13:5
[16] Eph. 3:1–5
[17] Gen. 23:4,16
[18] Eph. 2:19–20
[19] Acts 11:27–28; Eph. 3:3; 1 Tim. 4:1; Rev. 1:1
[20] Gen. 34:10, in this instance things did not work out well, but Hamor's words show what was the then accepted norm of living together in the same land.
[21] Gen. 33:18–20
[22] Gen. 26:16–33, Isaac not only demonstrates a preparedness to compromise but the whole story illustrates God's provision for those who do.
[23] Gen. 21:25–31
[24] Gen. 14:13; 21:22–24; 26:28–30

25 Gen. 14:13–16
26 Eph. 2:14–15
27 Rom. 10:1

21. And so All Israel Shall Be Saved

1 Rom. 11:33
2 Rom. 9:6
3 Rom. 11:26
4 Rom. 11:33–36
5 Acts 16:11–15
6 Isa. 2:1–3
7 Rom. 9:27–29,33; 10:19–21
8 Jer. 31:31–4
9 2 Sam. 6:15
10 2 Chr. 7:3
11 2 Chr. 15:15
12 Neh. 8:8,12,18
13 Matt. 23:39
14 Rom. 9:6
15 Rom. 9:31 – 10:3
16 Rom. 10:5–8
17 Rom. 10:6
18 Rom. 10:8–10
19 'After the flesh' is unlikely to be a phrase referring to the physical descendants of Israel. It is a phrase that often has a depreciatory note in Paul and in context would be making the point that even mechanically done sacrifices still brought a person into communion, for good or ill, with the one to whom sacrifice is made, and hence 'after the flesh' points to those Israelites whose worship was carnal.
20 2 Cor. 3:15–16
21 The translation 'But through their fall' is unhelpful and inaccurate, it should be 'But through their trespass'. The word for 'fall' in the original is not the same word as is translated 'fall' in the first sentence.
22 If any reader is not familiar with the carrot-and-stick metaphor, it pictures a donkey (usually stubborn) being enticed by its rider to move forwards by tying a carrot to the end of a stick and holding it out in front of the donkey.

Endnotes

[23] Calvin on verse 15: 'How much more ought we to hope, he reasons, that the resurrection of a people, as it were, wholly dead, will bring life to the Gentiles?' On verse 26, 'When the Gentiles shall come in, the Jews also shall return from their defection to the obedience of faith.' *Calvin's Commentaries Romans – Galatians*, pp. 1479, 1480, 1484.
[24] Rom. 11:33
[25] 1 Cor. 1:29
[26] Isa. 59:15
[27] Isa. 59:20
[28] Heb. 12:22–24
[29] Luke 23:34

Paternoster is the theological imprint of Authentic Media, and publishes books across a wide range of disciplines including biblical studies, theology, mission, church leadership and pastoral issues.

You can sign up to the Paternoster newsletter to hear about new releases by scanning below:

Online:
authenticmedia.co.uk/paternoster

Follow us:

www.ingramcontent.com/pod-product-compliance
Lightning Source LLC
Chambersburg PA
CBHW050554170426
43201CB00011B/1690